THE LANGUAGE OF THACKERAY

THE LANGUAGE LIBRARY

EDITED BY ERIC PARTRIDGE

The Best English	G. H. Vallins
Better English (revised)	G. H. Vallins
Caxton and his World	N. F. Blake
Caxton's Own Prose	N. F. Blake
Chambers of Horrors	'Vigilans'
Changing English (revised)	Simeon Potter
Chaucer's English	Ralph W. V. Elliot
Dictionaries British and American (revised)	J. R. Hulbert
A Dictionary of Literary Terms	J. A. Cuddon
A Dictionary of Sailors' Slang	Wilfred Granville
Early English (revised)	John W. Clark
Early Modern English	Charles Barber
English Biblical Translation	A. C. Partridge
English Dialects	G. L. Brook
The English Language	Ernest Weekley
Etymology	A. S. C. Ross
Finno-Ugrian Languages and Peoples	Peter Hadju (trans. G. F. Cushing)
Good English: How to Write It	G. H. Vallins
A Grammar of Style	A. E. Darbyshire
A History of the English Language	G. L. Brook
An Informal History of the German Language	W. B. Lockwood
Introduction to the Scandinavian Languages	M. O'C. Walshe
Jane Austen's English	K. C. Phillipps
Joysprick: An Introduction to the Language of James Joyce	Anthony Burgess
Language and Structure in Tennyson's Poetry	F. E. L. Priestley
The Language and Style of Anthony Trollope	John W. Clark
Language in the Modern World (revised)	Simeon Potter
The Language of the Book of Common Prayer	Stella Brook
The Language of Dickens	G. L. Brook
The Language of Gerard Manley Hopkins	James Milroy
The Language of Modern Poetry	A. C. Partridge
The Language of Renaissance Poetry	A. C. Partridge
The Language of Science	T. H. Savory
The Language of Shakespeare	G. L. Brook
Languages of the British Isles Past and Present	W. B. Lockwood
Modern Linguistics (revised)	Simeon Potter
The Pattern of English (revised)	G. H. Vallins
The Pitcairnese Language	A. S. C. Ross
Scientific and Technical Translation	Isadore Pinchuck
Sense and Sense Development	R. A. Waldron
Spelling (revised)	G. H. Vallins (revised D. G. Scragg)
Swift's Polite Conversation	Eric Partridge
Tudor to Augustan English	A. C. Partridge
The Words We Use	J. A. Sheard

K.C.Phillipps

THE LANGUAGE OF THACKERAY

ANDRE DEUTSCH

First published 1978 by
André Deutsch Limited
105 Great Russell Street London WC1

Printed in Great Britain by
W & J Mackay Limited, Chatham

British Library Cataloguing in Publication Data

Phillipps, Kenneth Charles
    The language of Thackeray. – (The language
library).
    1. Thackeray, William – Language
    I. Title II. Series
    823'.8   PR5638

ISBN 0-233-96917-9

Distributed in the United States and Canada
by Westveiw Press, 1898 Flatiron Court,
Boulder, Colorado 80301, USA.

Contents

᎚᎚᎚᎚᎚᎚

For Patricia

Preface

🔹🔹🔹🔹🔹🔹

I WAS first led to the study of the language of the nineteenth century by a sentence in that very readable book, C. S. Lewis's *Studies in Words* (p. 311). Lewis writes:

> I am ashamed to remember for how many years, as a boy and a young man, I read nineteenth century fiction without noticing how often its language differed from ours.

One's motives, of course, may not be altogether disinterestedly philological or loftily elucidatory. G. L. Brook, in the Preface to his study of *The Language of Dickens*, has assessed his own very honestly:

> Two motives have combined to make me write a book on the language of Dickens. The first is that I believe that such a study can help in the understanding of both the history of the English language and the novels of Dickens. The second is that I enjoy reading Dickens.

These, *mutatis mutandis*, are my own reasons for having studied authors like Jane Austen and Thackeray over the past few years, and perhaps the second is the more powerful. Yet there is much in the language these great authors used which now calls for comment, and even elucidation. For this turning world, which even in the eleventh century seemed to the good Archbishop Wulfstan to be *on ofste* 'in haste', is now changing so rapidly, and these changes are reflected in language so faithfully and so immediately, that much that seemed plain English and common knowledge to our grandfathers is no longer clear.

I am deeply indebted to my wife, to whom this book is dedicated, and also to my colleague at Leicester, Dr J. R. Watson, both of whom have read the typescript and made valuable emendations. I should like to thank Dr W. Liebeschutz of the

7

Classics Department in Leicester, for assistance where expert knowledge of Latin was needed; the Headmaster and the Librarian of the Charterhouse for permission to quote from the manuscript of *The Newcomes* there; and the Research Board of Leicester University for two grants which greatly facilitated my work. Dr John Sutherland, Reader in English at University College, London, provided a good deal of useful information from his enviable knowledge of Thackeray's life and times, and was kind enough to show me the typescript of the Introduction to his forthcoming edition of *The Book of Snobs*, to be published by the University of Queensland Press. This casts some doubt on the assertion that I follow all previous lexicographers and other authorities in making, that the new development in meaning of the word *snob* (see pp. 86–8) was Thackeray's single-handed achievement.

Finally, I must record an enormous debt of gratitude to my old teacher and mentor, the late Professor Simeon Potter, who until recently was one of the joint editors of this series. It is very fortunate that this book was sufficiently ready for the press to have benefited, in many valuable ways, from his expert supervision.

Leicester K.C.P.
September 1976

Abbreviations

᧰᧰᧰᧰᧰᧰

I QUOTE *Vanity Fair* by page from the edition by Geoffrey and Kathleen Tillotson (Methuen, 1963); other novels are quoted from the Centenary Biographical Edition, edited with a biographical introduction by Thackeray's daughter, Anne, Lady Ritchie (Smith, Elder and Co., 1910–11). In this edition I refer chiefly to volume and chapter. The Letters are quoted from the four-volume edition, *The Letters and Private Papers of William Makepeace Thackeray*, ed. G. N. Ray, Oxford University Press, 1945–6, by volume and page.

YP	*Yellowplush Papers*	1837–8
MG	*The Tremendous Adventures of Major Ganagan*	1838
C	*Catherine*	1839–40
SGS	*A Shabby Genteel Story*	1840
CD	*Cox's Diary*	1840
IS	*The Irish Sketch Book*	1843
MW	*Men's Wives*	1843
BL	*The Luck of Barry Lyndon*	1844
DJ	*The Diary of Jeames de la Pluche*	1845–6
BS	*The Snobs of England* (later *The Book of Snobs*)	1846–7
VF	*Vanity Fair*	1847–8
P	*Pendennis* (2 vols.)	1848–50
E	*Henry Esmond* (3 vols.)	1852
EH	*The English Humourists of the Eighteenth Century*	1853
N	*The Newcomes* (2 vols.)	1853–5
V	*The Virginians* (2 vols.)	1857–9
LW	*Lovel the Widower*	1860
RP	*Roundabout Papers*	1860–3
FG	*The Four Georges*	1860
Ph	*The Adventures of Philip* (2 vols.)	1861–2

DD	Denis Duval	1864
CB	Christmas Books	various dates
L	Letters	

Other abbreviations

OE	Old English
ME	Middle English
OED	*A New English Dictionary on Historical Principles*, Oxford University Press, 1888–1933, with continuing *Supplements*, now commonly known as *The Oxford English Dictionary*.

Phonetic Symbols

THE following letters are used as phonetic symbols with their usual English values: p, b, t, d, k, g, f, v, s, z, h, w, l, r, m, n. Other symbols are used with the values indicated by the italicized letters in the key-words below.

Consonants

ʃ	s*h*ip	θ	*th*in
ʒ	plea*s*ure	ð	*th*en
tʃ	*ch*in	j	*y*es
dʒ	*j*u*dg*e	ç	German i*ch*
ŋ	si*ng*	ʍ	voiceless /w/

Vowels

i	s*i*t	ɑ:	f*a*ther
i:	s*ee*	ɔ	h*o*t
y:	French s*û*r	ɔ:	s*aw*
e	g*e*t	u	p*u*t
ɛ:	French f*ai*re	u:	s*oo*n
a	f*a*t	ʌ	b*u*t
ə	f*a*ther		
ə:	b*ir*d		

Diphthongs

ei	d*ay*	ɔi	b*oy*
ou	g*o*	iə	h*ere*
ai	f*ly*	ɛə	th*ere*
au	n*ow*	uə	g*ou*rd

Square brackets are used to enclose phonetic symbols. A colon after a phonetic symbol indicates length.

CHAPTER I

Style

𨖇𨖇𨖇𨖇𨖇𨖇

THE tradition in which Thackeray wrote was that of a literary gentleman. One feels that, like Dr Portman, the elderly vicar of Clavering, he would have approved of productions such as those of the youthful Pendennis, which 'had spirit, taste and fancy'; and of the kind of man who 'wrote, if not like a scholar, at any rate like a gentleman' (*P* I ch. 35). Still more, perhaps, the style of Pen's fellow-journalist, George Warrington, was the model: 'the strong thoughts and curt periods, the sense, the satire, and the scholarship' (*P* I ch. 31). It is by adopting and maintaining this gentlemanly tone that Thackeray is able, in Hannay's words (*Studies on Thackeray*, p. 13), to 'hit the right mean between a bookishness which is too stiff and a colloquialism which is too loose'.

The novelist seems to have had little doubt about the best preliminary training for acquiring these stylistic virtues. When *Jane Eyre* appeared, pseudonymously, in 1847, he appraised the style of writing in these terms:

> Who the author can be I can't guess – if a woman she knows her language better than most ladies do, or has had a 'classical' education. It is a fine book . . . the style very generous and upright so to speak. (*L* II p. 319)

David Masson, comparing *Pendennis* and *David Copperfield* (in G. Tillotson and D. Hawes, *Thackeray: The Critical Heritage*, p. 111), which were appearing in monthly numbers at about the same time, saw this classical training as working to Thackeray's advantage:

> There is a Horatian strictness, a racy strength, in Mr Thackeray's expressions, even in his more level and tame passages, which we miss in the corresponding passages of Mr Dickens's writings, and in which we seem to recognize the effect of those classical

studies through which an accurate and determinate, though somewhat bald, use of words becomes a fixed habit.

Thackeray, who received *David Copperfield* with enthusiasm, plumed himself more than once in letters to friends on having set Dickens a good example in this matter of what Masson calls 'Horatian strictness':

> It pleases the Other Author to see that Dickens who has long left off alluding to his the OA's works has been copying the OA, and greatly simplifying his style and foregoing the use of fine words. (*L* II p. 531; also p. 535)

There is, indeed, more to be said for classical learning in the acquisition of an English style than it is currently fashionable to admit. Most of Thackeray's distinguished predecessors in novel-writing, including his favourite, Fielding, had had such a grounding.

But a great writer does not merely inherit a tradition; he modifies it. One can observe the novelist doing so most interestingly in his first full-length novel *The Luck of Barry Lyndon*. In the early part of the novel, the anti-hero Lyndon owes much to his distinguished predecessor, Jonathan Wild, and is conceived with something of the ironic astringency of the *picaro*.[1] But Lyndon's 'luck' proves delusive; worldly success does not bring happiness – it merely enlarges his vices and issues in his eventual ruin. So the *vanitas vanitatum* theme emerges; and along with it there emerges a technique which we have come to consider as characteristically Thackerayan. Here, for example, the novelist is describing Hackton Castle, the Devon property which Barry Lyndon acquires through a worldly marriage to a wealthy widow, the Countess of Lyndon:

> From this main hall branched off on either side the long series

[1] It is curious that in his last, unfinished novel, *Denis Duval*, Thackeray was to come round again to this sort of tale. In a letter to his publisher Smith, written in January 1863, he declared that this novel should have 'no love-making: no observations about society: little dialogue, except where the characters are bullying each other: plenty of fighting: and a villain in the cupboard' (Ray, *Age*, p. 408). Dickens, a better novelist than critic, thought that *Duval* was in many respects Thackeray's best work. Most modern readers, while allowing the unfinished novel some merit and promise, would probably say, 'C'est magnifique, mais ce n'est pas Thackeray'. But the present vogue for *Barry Lyndon* perhaps heralds a new appreciation of the novelist's minor, and less typical works.

of state-rooms, poorly furnished with high-backed chairs and long queer Venice glasses, when first I came to the property; but afterwards rendered so splendid by me, with the gold damasks of Lyons and the magnificent Gobelin tapestries I won from Richelieu at play. There were thirty-six bedrooms *de maître*, of which I only kept three in their antique condition – the haunted room as it was called, where the murder was done in James II's time, the bed where William slept after landing at Torbay, and Queen Elizabeth's state-room. All the rest were re-decorated by Cornichon in the most elegant taste; not a little to the scandal of some of the steady old country dowagers; for I had pictures of Boucher and Vanloo to decorate the principal apartments, in which Cupids and Venuses were painted in a manner so natural, that I recollect the wizened old Countess of Frumpington pinning over the curtains of her bed, and sending her daughter, Lady Blanche Whalebone, to sleep with her waiting-woman, rather than allow her to lie in a chamber hung all over with looking-glasses, after the exact fashion of the Queen's closet at Versailles. (*BL* ch. 17)

Here the amassing of detail serves both to present grandeur and to undercut it with irony. It is an accumulation which has an ultimately unifying effect, and one that, as Barbara Hardy suggests, is fundamentally critical of the society that is described, and in many ways reductive and corrosive (*The Exposure of Luxury: Radical Themes in Thackeray*, p. 20). Proper names have a radical function here. The pictures may be splendid; but the fact that the rooms were decorated by an artist called *Cornichon* (French slang for 'greenhorn') modifies any rapture that one might have felt in contemplating them. The concern of these county ladies for their virtue is doubtless praiseworthy; but names like *Frumpington* and *Blanche Whalebone* imply that in any case they were, in Burns's telling phrase, 'aiblins nae temptation'. Detail also contributes to what we now call 'local colour': we are reminded that the Castle is in Devon by the reference to William III's landing at Torbay.

One sees the addition of such substantiating detail to the later novels in occasional manuscript emendations. Describing Barnes Newcome sowing his wild oats at Newcome, the Northern town whence the family originated, Thackeray first wrote, of the company Barnes kept:

When Barnes was a young man, and, in his occasional visits to Newcome, lived along with those dashing young blades Sam Jollyman (Jollyman Brothers and Bowcher), Bob Homer, Cross Country Bill, Al Rucker (for whom his father had to pay eighteen thousand pounds *on settling day*), and that wild lot. (*N* II ch. 17)

The three words *on settling day* have been emended to 'after the Ledger [sic] the year 'Toggery won it'. It is very interesting to see the author's mind at work here: the word *settling* probably suggested the word *ledger*, which in turn suggested to him the Doncaster races as a suitable place for a man of Northern provenance to waste his money. Such a play of mind between sound and sense is one of Thackeray's special gifts. His was the very antithesis of the 'wit single' which the Chief Justice attributes to old men like Falstaff (*2 Henry IV*, I ii 207). Incidentally, one of the meanings of the Victorian slang word *toggery* was the trappings or harness of a horse. Besides adding geographical and other verisimilitude, additional details could make a further satirical point. The Marquis of Farintosh declares he will remain loyal to Ethel and the other Newcomes despite the scandal brought upon the family by Barnes's behaviour. 'Lady Ann is different. She is a lady, she is. She is a good woman; and Kew is *a good fellow and I like him*' (*N* II ch. 21). This is the novelist's first draft; but he cannot resist altering it to 'a most respectable man, though he is only a peer of George III's creation'. Clearly the novelist here wants, among other things, to avoid making Farintosh as sympathetic a character as Lord Kew; but he also enjoys a remark so congenial to his reductive cast of mind.

There are times when he has to control his exuberance in the matter of detail; as when he tells us, for example, that despite the Sedleys' bankruptcy:

Edward Dale . . . was, in fact, very sweet upon Amelia, and offered for her in spite of all. He married Miss Louisa Cutts (daughter of Higham and Cutts, the eminent corn-factors), with a handsome fortune in 1820; and is now living in splendour, and with a numerous family, at his elegant villa, Muswell Hill. But we must not let the recollection of this good fellow cause us to diverge from the principal history. (*VF* p. 163)

The piling up of such detail in the case against society can also lead to the novelist's worst fault, his tendency to nag. Walter Bagehot complained that Thackeray had a compulsion to 'amass petty details to prove that tenth-rate people were ever striving to be ninth-rate people' (*Heritage*, p. 356). This, however, amounts to an underestimate of the power of the novels. The plangent conclusion of *Vanity Fair*, with its indictment against worldliness, is given weight by the massive accumulation of realistic detail that precedes it.

Dickens, manifestly, is another author who revels in detail. Both novelists are the reverse of the kind of writer who, in Jane Austen's phrase, deals 'more in notions than facts'.[1] But Thackeray himself, in a letter to David Masson, pointed out an important difference in this matter of detail:

> I think Mr Dickens has in many things quite a divine genius so to speak, and certain notes in his song are so delightful and admirable that I should never think of trying to imitate him, only hold my tongue and admire him. I quarrel with his Art in many respects: which I don't think represents Nature duly; for instance Micawber appears to me an exaggeration of a man, as his name is of a name. It is delightful and makes me laugh: but it is no more a real man than my friend Punch is: and in so far I protest against him . . . , holding that the Art of Novels *is* to represent Nature: to convey as strongly as possible the sentiment of reality – in a tragedy or a poem or a lofty drama you aim at producing different emotions; the figures moving, and their words sounding, heroically: but in a drawing-room drama a coat is a coat and a poker a poker; and must be nothing else according to my ethics, not an embroidered tunic, nor a great red-hot instrument like the Pantomime weapon. (*L* II p. 772)

With this remark of Thackeray's in mind, it is useful to compare a typical passage of description from each novelist. We might consider, for example, two rooms: the travellers' room at the White Horse Cellar, the coaching inn where Mr Pickwick sets off for Bath (*Pickwick Papers* ch. 35), and the front parlour of the

---

1 'Like my dear Dr Johnson . . . I have dealt more in Notions than facts.' *Jane Austen's Letters*, ed. R. W. Chapman, Oxford, 1932, p. 181; a jocular reference that is nevertheless capable of a wider application.

house of Mr and Mrs Bowls, formerly Miss Crawley's butler and lady's maid, in Half Moon Street (*VF* p. 401):

> The travellers' room at the White Horse Cellar is of course uncomfortable; it would be no travellers' room if it were not. It is the right-hand parlour, into which an aspiring kitchen fireplace appears to have walked, accompanied by a rebellious poker, tongs, and shovel. It is divided into boxes, for the solitary confinement of travellers, and is furnished with a clock, a looking-glass, and a live waiter – which latter article is kept in a small kennel for washing glasses, in a corner of the apartment.

> Becky . . . kissed the gentlewoman as soon as they got into the passage; and thence into Mrs Bowls's front parlour, with the red moreen curtains, and the round looking-glass, with the chained eagle above, gazing upon the back of the ticket in the window which announced 'Apartments to Let'.

The first passage is taken from G. L. Brook's *The Language of Dickens* (p. 36) to illustrate Dickens's favourite device of attributing human emotions and powers to inanimate objects. The poker here is more than the 'pantomime weapon' that Thackeray declared it had become in Dickens's hands; rebellious tendencies are predicated of it. Contrariwise, the only human being, the waiter, is entirely divested of life. There is a slight trace of this arbitrary animism in the *Vanity Fair* passage: the chained eagle over the mirror gazes on the back of the 'to-let' ticket.[1] But there is no doubt which of the two writers is here giving freer rein to his imagination. The travellers' room at the White Horse Cellar is part of 'the world which is not London, but which London has stimulated Dickens's fancy to create' (Lord David Cecil, *Early Victorian Novelists*, p. 33). Thackeray's London, however, is London. Yet the room is not merely 'photographed': details are selected to establish an air of shabby gentility. Moreen is a stout, coarse wool material; the chained eagle is ironically symbolic of the aspirations to gentility of these ex-domestics; and the mirror is used, as mirrors are elsewhere in *Vanity Fair* (for example,

1 It is exceptional to find in Thackeray such typically Dickensian personification as the following: 'The battered piano, which had injured its constitution wofully by sitting up so many nights, and spoke with a voice, as it were, at once hoarse and faint' (P I ch. 30). Dickens, however, would not have included the words 'as it were'.

p. 415), to suggest a kind of retroactive confinement, resulting in this instance from narrow means. This selection is part of the process of conveying 'as strongly as possible the sentiment of reality'.

We are now, of course, well acquainted with Thackeray's method. The play of irony upon multifarious and interconnecting details is familiar both from *Vanity Fair* and *The Newcomes,* and from reading the novelist who in our own day is the lineal descendant of the Showman of Vanity Fair (quite as much as C. P. Snow is of Trollope), namely Angus Wilson. It is difficult now to realize what a surprise and sensation *Vanity Fair* caused. Henry Kingsley, brother of Charles, was in his late teens when the novel began to appear in its yellow covers:

> Does any one remember the time when one began to hear such sentences as these flying from mouth to mouth – 'It is wonderfully clever.' 'It is so very strange.' 'One don't know whether to laugh or cry at it.' (*Heritage*, p. 330)

An American critic, writing in 1848, correctly put his finger on the precursor to *Vanity Fair*, and recommended it as preliminary reading:

> The charge began in the *Snobs of England*; it is now followed up in *Vanity Fair*. Any one, therefore, who reads the latter book should read the 'Snob Papers' in *Punch* by way of introduction to it. (*ibid.* p. 73)

Such a reader would also familiarize himself with the dense technique that Elizabeth Rigby, later Lady Eastlake, writing in the same year (*ibid.* p. 86) also clearly felt as innovatory:

> It is impossible to quote from his book with any justice to it. The whole growth of the narrative is so matted and interwoven together with tendril-like links and bindings, that there is no detaching a flower with sufficient length of stalk to exhibit it to advantage.

Henry Kingsley again (*ibid.* p. 335), who as a great Victorian traveller and adventurer would doubtless have appreciated the force of his own metaphor, referred to the Pumpernickel episodes in *Vanity Fair* as a 'wild jungle of fun'. One must not press this metaphor of the matted growth of the jungle too far. To do so would be to forget that Thackeray is a natural empiricist in method, or at least a pseudo-empiricist, suggesting to us general, if somewhat slanted, tendencies and working towards general conclusions from masses of observed detail. To quote Ray (*Age*, p. 427):

> Profoundly aware of the 'streamingness of experience,' he avoided wherever he could the delusive short-cut of abstraction. Like Newman, he knew that persuasiveness is most readily achieved by being 'simply personal and historical.' Faithful to the process by which we all arrive at lasting decisions in life, he devoted himself in his fiction to accumulating countless concrete details which taken together insensibly form his readers' impressions and opinions.

There was no doubt whence this strength in detail arose. What Kathleen Tillotson observes of *Vanity Fair* is true of all the novelist's best work; she says, 'It has . . . the buoyant inspiration in detail arising from the practised skill of the journalist' (*Novels of the Eighteen-Forties*, p. 225). Before *Vanity Fair* began to appear in 1847, the thirty-six-year-old Thackeray had worked for a dozen years as a journalist under various *noms de plume* and for various periodicals. As we shall see in a later chapter, one of the manifestations of this inspired journalism is the brilliant improvisation of proper names. Another, outside the scope of a book on the language of Thackeray, is the fondness for topical allusions. To take one brief example, Becky's maid, Fifine, absconds with many of her mistress's trinkets on Becky's downfall: she goes off 'in a cab, as we have known many more exalted persons of her nation do under similar circumstances'. The reference is to Louis-Philippe, who fled from Paris in March 1848, when Thackeray was writing this episode (*VF* p. 527; and the Tillotsons' footnote). An aspect of this topicality, however, that *is* related to the study of language is what we might call Thackeray's 'knowingness'. The word *knowing* had wider connotations in Victorian times than today. Jane Austen who, according to the *OED*, is the first to record the new nineteenth-century development of meaning, writes in *Sense and Sensibility* (ch. 19) of young men who 'drove about town in very *knowing* gigs', meaning (*OED knowing* ppl. a. 4) 'showing knowledge of "what is what" in fashion, dress and the like; stylish, smart'. In the same tradition Mrs General Baynes in *Philip*, 'had a *knowing* turban on' (*Ph* II ch. 5).

Thackeray who was recognized by his contemporaries as 'a natural swell', always had a keen eye for 'what was what' and a journalistic 'knowingness' in matters of fashionable and correct usage (G. A. Sala, *Things I Have Seen*, quoted in Ray, *Age*, p. 323). When Rawdon Crawley disposes of his portable property before Waterloo, the list of his belongings, though in execrable spelling, includes the names of foremost tradesmen of his day: 'Mv double-barril by Manton' (a well-known gunsmith of Davies Street, Berkeley Square); 'my regulation saddle-holsters and housings; my Laurie ditto' (Peter and John Laurie, Saddlers, Oxford Street), (*VF* p. 286, and the Tillotsons' footnotes). Thackeray is knowledgeable and correct, for example, about the kinds of vehicle used to convey people of various ranks in society. The impecunious landed aristocrat, Lord Bareacres, embarked for the continent with his 'chariot, *britska*, and *fourgon*, that anybody might pay for who liked' (*VF* p. 596). *Britska* or *britszka* is a Polish loan-word, from *bryczka* 'a light long travelling-wagon', diminutive of *bryka* 'a goods-wagon'; and it had come to mean 'an open carriage with a calash or folding top, and space for reclining'; a *fourgon* is for luggage, a French loan – this, according to the *OED*, is the first English quotation. Rawdon Crawley drives a *stanhope* (*VF* p. 186), a light, open one-seated vehicle, as made originally for the Honourable and Reverend Fitzroy Stanhope (1787–1864). Young James Crawley is embarrassed when, driving out with his wealthy aunt in her *barouche*, they encounter 'on the cliff in a *tax-cart*, drawn by a bang-up pony . . . , his friends the Tutbury Pet and the Rottingdean Fibber' (*VF* p. 331). The *barouche*, like the *britszka*, was for the rich, who were not concerned with the reduction in tax which was granted to the two-wheeled, somewhat contradictorily-named, *tax-cart* on the grounds that it was used mainly for agricultural or trade purposes.

On questions of transport generally, Thackeray is ready with the standard Victorian jibes; against the rudeness of hansom cab drivers or the slowness of parliamentary trains, for example:

The cabman, although a Hansom cabman, said 'Thank you' for the gratuity which was put into his hand. (*P* II ch. 36)

Ah, why was it the quick train? Suppose it had been the parliamentary train? – even that too would have come to an end. (*N* II ch. 3)

But, however slow the train might be, it was both speedier and more comfortable than the stage-coach. In the train, for example, there was no need to travel *bodkin* (*VF* p. 399), as it was put colloquially, that is, wedged as a third passenger between two others in a coach where there was really room for two only. Trains, indeed, were something that everybody, even Major Pendennis, had to come to terms with. Characteristically, Thackeray has him use rather old-fashioned phraseology about them: 'It's getting late, and I have made a *railroad* journey' (*P* II ch. 29). The *OED* quotes the *Civil Engineer and Architect's Journal* for 1838: 'Railway seems now we think the more usual term'; though the Dictionary reminds us that *railroad* was once 'equally (or more) common in Great Britain and is still usual in America'. Major Pendennis is the equivalent of the kind of gentleman who in our own day still uses *motor* as a verb.

Fashions in dress and items of adornment, however ephemeral, were subjects whose mention lent topicality to serials. The Chevalier Strong wears 'three little gold crosses in a *brochette* on the portly breast of his blue coat' (*P* I ch. 25). This is a pin or bar used to fasten medals, ornaments etc. to the uniform of the wearer. It is the first instance of the word's importation, in this sense, from French (*OED Supp.*, s.v. *brochette*). Blanche Amory praised 'the lovely *breloques* or gimcracks' which Foker wore on his watch-chain (*P* II ch. 2). The word seems to be another of the novelist's importations. A *paletot* was another French loan of the 1840s, the name of a loose outer garment, coat or cloak, for men or women. It was introduced at about the same time as that other loose-fitting garment, the *blouse*, one of the first illustrations for which in the *OED* is from Thackeray: 'Three Englishmen . . . dandy specimens of our countrymen: one wears a marine dress, another has a shooting jacket, a third has a *blouse*' (*Paris Sketch Book* ch. 1). *Blouse* has become permanently naturalized in the language, but not *paletot*. The latter seems not to have remained a smart garment for long – Sam Huxter in *Pendennis* is no fashion-plate: 'Huxter's fists plunged into the pockets of his *paletot*' (*P* II ch. 20). The novelist is the first, perhaps, to record in English the use of the word *imperial* for a small part of the beard left growing beneath the lower lip: 'From his continually pulling something on his chin, I am led to fancy that he believes he has what is called an *Imperial* growing there' (*BS* ch. 29). This sentence, first appearing in *Punch* in 1846, antedates the first *OED* example of 1856 and seems, incidentally, to call in question their explanation (*imperial* n. 8): 'so called because the Emperor Napoleon III wore his beard in this way'. Louis Napoleon did not become 'Emperor of the French' till 1852; although he was a figure in French politics before this date.

In general Thackeray, like Ian Fleming in our own day, liked to air his familiarity with the good things of fashionable life. Warrington, Pen's journalist friend in *Pendennis*, 'couldn't find a bit of tobacco fit to smoke till we came to Strasbourg, where I got some *caporal*' (*P* II ch. 31); this is the sole *OED* quotation to illustrate this word for a kind of superior tobacco. He seems to have been the first importer of the German word *Schimmel* for a roan horse (*VF* p. 648); of the French loan *Charlotte Russe* for a dish composed of custard enclosed in a kind of sponge cake (*N* I ch. 5); and of *gibus-hat* (*BS* ch. 18) for an opera or crush hat, from *Gibus*, the name of the Parisian who first made the article (see Eric Partridge, *Name into Word* s.v. *gibus*). For any journalist or novelist writing of high society, the London season which extended from Easter to mid-July was a matter of great moment. Barnes Newcome drawls out the fashionable phrase: 'the very *full* of the season' (*N* I ch. 6) (*OED full* n. 8). Occasions in the season like the Derby and Ascot were the great events for the sporting man; and words like *event* and *information* had special connotations for the gambler. A young buck in *The Book of Snobs* 'knows all the stables, and all the jockeys, and has all the "inform-ation"' (*BS* ch. 29). In *The Newcomes* Thackeray tells us, 'The London season was very nearly come to an end, and Lord Farintosh had danced I don't know how many times with Miss Newcome. . . . The young fellows were making an "event" out of Ethel's marriage, and sporting their money freely on it' (*N* II ch. 7).

Another manifestation of Thackeray's training as a journalist is the clever weaving into the narrative of literary allusions, often very slight echoes, but gratifying, doubtless, to the discerning and informed when located. It is right that sophisticated London

23

journalists like Warrington and Pen should be able to bandy quotations from Shakespeare:

> 'And under which king does Bezonian speak or die?' asked Warrington. 'Do we come out as Liberal Conservative, or as Government men, or on our own hook?' (*P* II ch. 31)

The reference is to *2 Henry IV*, V iii 119. And it is also right that Major Pendennis, though he is familiar with classical French drama (*P* II ch. 17), should be confused by a reference to the same Shakespeare play (V v 77):

> 'By Gad, sir,' cried the Major, in high good-humour, 'I intended you to marry Miss Laura here.'
> 'And, by Gad, Master Shallow, I owe you a thousand pound,' Warrington said.
> 'How d'ye mean a thousand? it was only a pony, sir,' replied the Major simply. (*P* II ch. 19)

The malevolence of Mrs Mackenzie ('the Campaigner'), Clive Newcome's mother-in-law, is suggested by a Shakespearean reference. She was 'attired in considerable splendour, and with the precious jewel on her head which I remembered at Boulogne' (*N* II ch. 40). The allusion is to *As You Like It* II i 14: 'which like the toad, ugly and venomous, wears yet a precious jewel in his head'. Describing how Becky and Rawdon contrived to 'live well on nothing a year', the novelist mentions the smaller tradesmen whom they ruined, echoing Iago's 'to suckle fools and chronicle small beer' (*Othello* II i 161): 'The bill for servants' porter at the Fortune of War public house is a curiosity in the chronicles of beer' (*VF* p. 360). A character in *The Newcomes*, Fred Bayham, whose speech is full of anachronisms such as 'It mislikes me' (*N* II ch. 26) and 'By cock and pye, it is not worth a bender' (*N* I ch. 11), is also prone to making Shakespearean allusions: 'the clouds which gathered o'er the sun of Newcome were in the bosom of the ocean buried, Bayham said' (*N* II ch. 27); the reference, of course, being to the beginning of *Richard III*. The habit of allusion also comes out in the novelist's letters: 'The stories have a sort of truth, a pennyworth say to an intolerable deal of fiction' (*L* II p. 214), which recalls Prince Hal's reading of Falstaff's bill (*1 Henry IV*, II iv 592): 'O monstrous! but one halfpennyworth of bread to this intolerable deal of sack'. Shakespeare can also be misquoted to amusing effect: 'Lady Kicklebury remarked that Shakspeare was very right in stating how much sharper than a thankless tooth it is to have a serpent child' (*CB* 'The Kickleburys on the Rhine', p. 234).

Later literature is also referred to, as when the tomboy daughter of Pitt Crawley is depicted with a reference to Pope's *Essay on Criticism* (l. 372): 'her pleasure was to ride the young colts, and to scour the plains like Camilla' (*VF* p. 90); or when George Warrington castigates a villain with words that recall the same poet's portrait of Sporus in the *Epistle to Arbuthnot*: 'This man goes about his life business with a natural propensity to darkness and evil – as a bug crawls, and stings, and stinks' (*N* II ch. 16). As his *English Humourists* testifies, Thackeray had a profound knowledge of eighteenth-century literature. When he writes in *The Newcomes* that 'a certain observer' conjectured that Clive Newcome must be in love, 'and taxed him with *the soft impeachment*' (*N* II ch. 3), the phrase echoes Mrs Malaprop (*The Rivals* V iii); when he says that 'Swift seems to me as good a name to point a moral or adorn a tale of ambition, as any hero's that ever lived' (*EH* p. 134), he is remembering that other great eighteenth-century writer, Johnson, in *The Vanity of Human Wishes* (l. 219). He takes up a remark of Swift's: 'the reputation of wit and great learning does the office of a blue riband or a coach and six' and embroiders on it by referring to a well-known song from Gay's *The Beggar's Opera*: 'and *he hears the sound of coaches and six*, takes the road like Macheath, and makes society stand and deliver' (*EH* p. 133). Some references to the literature of the previous century would be more familiar to the Victorians than to ourselves: 'Oh, George, how little you know about London and London ways. Whene'er you take your walks abroad how many poor you meet' (*V* II ch. 1); the second sentence here echoes the *Divine and Moral Songs for Children* of Isaac Watts (1720), which are hardly known now, except as they have been parodied by Lewis Carroll.

Allusions and echoes are not always to be taken too seriously. Keats's line from 'Ode on a Grecian Urn': 'Pipe to the spirit ditties of no tone' is clearly hinted at in the following bathetic context: 'At the end . . . is a broken-nosed damp Faun, with a marble panpipe, who pipes to the spirit ditties which I believe never had any tune' (*N* II ch. 9); and Thomas Hood's well-known lines from his poem 'The Bridge of Sighs', describing a suicide by drowning, are applied jokingly to the gourmet's attitude to wine: 'He takes up the bottle, fashioned so slenderly – takes it up tenderly, cants it with care' (*RP* 'On Two Children in Black'). Thackeray also echoes the Poet Laureate of his day, Tennyson: 'She cries sometimes over the cradle of the young heir. She is *aweary, aweary*' (*N* II ch. 14). The reference is to 'Mariana'.

The novelist could still hope that many of his readers would understand and appreciate references, whether in Latin or in English translation, to the great Roman authors. Not all Thackeray's readers would be in the lamentable state of ignorance of the classics of young James Crawley:

> No jokes, old boy; no trying it on on me. You want to trot me out, but it's no go. In vino veritas, old boy. Mars, Bacchus, Apollo virorum, hay? (*VF* p. 333)

As the Tillotsons explain in their note, this last inappropriate gibberish is a quotation, abbreviated and misapplied, from '*Propria quae maribus*', which begins the section on the gender of nouns in the old Eton Latin Grammar. By far the largest number of classical references are in fact to Horace. Elizabeth Nitchie has computed that of some 200 Latin quotations in Thackeray's writings, 140 are from Horace, and 104 of these are from the *Odes*. To take one example of many: 'Clive Newcome . . . went to fine dinners, and sat silent over them; rode fine horses, and black Care jumped up behind the moody horseman' (*N* II ch. 25); the reference is to the *Odes* (III i 40); 'Post equitem sedet atra Cura'.[1]

In addition, like most great English writers, Thackeray alludes to the King James Bible. He does so with varying success. At moments of flagging inspiration, which are more frequent in the later novels, he falls back on a surface pastiche of the Old Testament that strikes a false note:

> So Thomas Newcome, and Clive the son of Thomas, had wrath in their hearts against Barnes, their kinsman, and desired

[1] 'Horace and Thackeray', *Classical Journal* XIII (pp. 393–419). This particular quotation was a favourite of the novelist's: Elizabeth Nitchie computes that it occurs a score of times in his writings. She also points out how frequently his technique can be summed up in words from the poet's *Satires* (I i 69): 'Mutato nomine, de te/Fabula narratur': e.g. 'Be gentle with those who are less lucky, if not more deserving. Think, what right have you to be scornful, whose virtue is a deficiency of temptation' etc. (*VF* p. 552).

to be revenged upon him, and were eager after his undoing.
(*N* II ch. 26)

A slight biblical reminiscence is often more effective, as in the
subtle allusion to the ravens that fed the prophet Elijah by the
brook Cherith (1 Kings xvii 6) and that might have fed the im-
provident Jack Belsize in his time of need:

> As for Jack Belsize; how he lived; how he laughed; how he
> dressed himself so well, and looked so fat and handsome; how
> he got a shilling to pay for a cab or a cigar; *what ravens fed
> him*; was a wonder to all. (*N* I ch. 28)

The passage illustrates the novelist's mastery of tone; for Jack
Belsize, despite his faults, is a sympathetic character, who figures
in some of the more serious episodes in *The Newcomes*. Had Lady
Clara been allowed to marry him and not been persuaded to take
Barnes Newcome for his money she would have been a happy
woman. The biblical phrase hints at this serious theme in the
novel; and well illustrates a point made about such phrases by
Fernand Mossé in his authoritative *Esquisse d'une Histoire de la
Langue Anglaise* (p. 122):

> Un Anglais, de quelque condition qu'il soit, ne s'y trompe
> jamais: il suffit de quelques-uns de ces termes ou de ces formes
> pour donner à une phrase ou à un passage une résonance
> inimitable.

Often a slight allusion is the most effective. The comparison of the
impecunious Amelia giving up her son to his wealthy grandfather (*VF* p. 478) with Hannah yielding up her infant son Samuel
to Eli in the temple (I Samuel i 28) is a case in point.[1] Still more
subtle is the portentous use of *then*, so frequent in biblical
prophecies, concerning the same episode:

> 'There was an old gentleman with thick eyebrows and a broad
> hat, and large chain and seals . . . He looked at me very much.
> He shook very much . . .' Such was George's report on that
> night.
>   *Then* Amelia knew that the boy had seen his grandfather:
> and looked out feverishly for a proposal which she was sure

---

1 Thackeray carelessly refers to Georgy at one point as 'her Eli' (*VF* p. 541), a
mistake not corrected till 1898.

would follow, and which came, in fact, a few days afterwards. (*VF* p. 447)

One influence of his journalistic training which by later, more self-conscious traditions of novel-writing may seem deplorable, was Thackeray's readiness to appear at any point in the narrative as 'the Manager of the Performance', to quote the phrase he himself used in the Foreword to *Vanity Fair*. His approach was often the lively and versatile one of the successful magazine editor; sprightly, but apt to kill the allusion, as when he brings home the repetitiveness of all Miss Costigan's stage performances by referring the reader to a previous page, in the manner of a reference-book (*P* I ch. 6), or conveys Clive Newcome's good looks by giving instructions there and then to the illustrator of *The Newcomes*, Richard Doyle (*N* I ch. 6). These are much the same kind of 'little slaps at credulity' that Henry James found so discouraging in Trollope. Thackeray took the same 'suicidal satisfaction in reminding the reader that the story he was telling was only, after all, a make-believe' (*The Future of the Novel: Essays on the Art of Fiction* by Henry James, ed. Leon Edel, p. 247). In fact, one finds with Thackeray that the flaw (if such it must be called) was carried to greater lengths. Trollope, in the seventh chapter of his *Autobiography*, explaining that he always carried out his weekly stint of written pages, could hardly have destroyed more illusions about the vocation of the imaginative artist than does such a passage as this from *Philip*:

> Ah! how wonderful ways and means are! When I think how this very line, this very word, which I am writing represents money, I am lost in a respectful astonishment. A man takes his own case, as he says his own prayers, on behalf of himself and his family. I am paid, we will say, for the sake of illustration, at the rate of sixpence per line. With the words 'Ah, how wonderful,' to the words 'per line', I can buy a loaf, a piece of butter, a jug of milk, a modicum of tea, – actually enough to make breakfast for the family; and the servants of the house; and the charwoman, their servant, can shake up the tea-leaves with a fresh supply of water ... Wife, children, guests, servants, charwoman, we are all actually making a meal off Philip Firmin's bones as it were. (*Ph* II ch. 16)

We have already noted Thackeray's skill in playing on sounds of words; he was also exceptionally alive, as a book illustrator, to the appearance of words on the page, and aware how effective orthography could be as a means of caricature, or simply of maintaining interest. A letter to Jane Brookfield, the married woman with whom he fell in love, written in the form of her initials, J.O.B. (*L* II p. 516) suggests that, like Lewis Carroll with his 'Tale of a Tail', he would have made a very good 'concrete poet', though he would have guyed the pretensions of some 'concrete poets' unmercifully. In his letters he loved facetious spellings for their own sake, as when he asks to be invited to 'dinner or *T*' (*L* II p. 825), or mentions '*pugh*-openers' (*L* II p. 530), or states that Amelia Sedley, in *Vanity Fair*, 'has at present a quality above most people *whizz* love' (*L* II p. 309). He also enjoyed transliterating one language into the conventional spelling of another, as when he talks of dining 'with the lovely widow of Siromfridévy' (*L* II p. 518); or, contrariwise, makes the vulgar Mr Mugford in *Philip* refer to his villa as his *Russian Irby* (*Ph* II ch. 14). From sheer high spirits, or perhaps to indicate that he has a head cold, he sends the following missive to his clerical friend William Brookfield:

> Dearly beloved. If you are not engaged why not dine here? I've beal at Brightl ald very lear dul Peldellis. My parelts isl't yet cub.
>
> Your wellwisher WMT. (*L* II p. 522)

Such a lively wit soon found an outlet in the magazine *Punch, or The London Charivari* founded in 1841: Thackeray's first contributions appeared in 1842. He had something of the same kind of natural talent for burlesque that Jane Austen's juvenilia display. In congenial company he was an excellent mimic, and such exercises as 'Mr Punch's Prize Novelists' demonstrate his talent for parody. Parody, in fact, is the basis of some of his subtlest characterization. We might consider, to illustrate this point, the three prominent maiden ladies of *Vanity Fair*: Miss Pinkerton, Briggs, and Miss Crawley. Gordon Ray particularly admires the fact that 'no saying of any one of these three could possibly be assigned to either of the others' (*Uses*, p. 397). The reason for this is that the three may be presumed to have passed their formative years in the eighteenth century, and to owe their habits of speech to different literary progenitors.

Miss Pinkerton, for example, headmistress of a ladies' academy in Chiswick Mall, had been a friend of Dr Johnson and correspondent of the blue-stocking Mrs Chapone. Consequently her most everyday instructions are couched in Johnsonese: 'Have you completed all the necessary preparations incident to Miss Sedley's departure, Miss Jemima?' (*VF* p. 11). A letter or, as she would call it, 'a billet' from her was clearly a challenge for the novelist; particularly when, as is the case of both letters from her pen in *Vanity Fair*, they are also testimonials – to this day the last refuge of Johnsonese. Like the great lexicographer, Miss Pinkerton is prone to general statements regulated by antithesis and litotes: 'a young lady not unworthy'; 'those accomplishments . . . will not be found wanting in the amiable Miss Sedley'; 'her sweetness of temper has charmed her aged and her youthful companions' (*VF* p. 12). We note that Miss Pinkerton favours the adjective *amiable* (*VF* pp. 12, 97), which down to Regency times had not acquired the patronizing overtones it now conveys, and that she employs such elegant euphemisms as 'not personally well-favoured', 'a halt in her gait' and 'a trifling obliquity of vision' for 'ugly', 'a limp' and 'a slight squint' respectively. It is very Johnsonian also to weigh a polysyllabic noun with an equally ponderous Latinate adjective: 'my maternal cares have elicited a *responsive affection*'; 'if your own beloved young ladies had need of my *instructive superintendence*' (*VF* p. 97). Her only informality of speech or writing is the archaic '*tis* for *it's*, found also in *Henry Esmond* [*VF* pp. 23, 97).

The truth will out occasionally, however, even in the most verbose of testimonials. Thackeray is at his best when ironically exploiting the discrepancies of hypocrisy and pointing the contrast, as in this masterly postscript of Miss Pinkerton's, between the surface profession of a charitable and philosophical benevolence and the underlying assertion (in plainer English and in parenthesis) of vindictiveness and ill-will:

P.S. The Miss Sharp, whom you mention as governess to Sir Pitt Crawley, Bart., M.P., was a pupil of mine, and I have nothing to say in her disfavour. Though her appearance is disagreeable, we cannot control the operations of nature: and though her parents were disreputable (her father being a painter, several times bankrupt; and her mother, as I have since learned, with horror, a dancer at the Opera); yet her talents are considerable, and I cannot regret that I received her *out of charity*. My dread is, lest the principles of the mother – who was represented to me as a French Countess, forced to emigrate in the late revolutionary horrors; but who, as I have since found, was a person of *the very lowest order and morals* – should at any time prove to be hereditary in the unhappy young woman whom I took as *an outcast*. But her principles have *hitherto* been correct (I believe), and I am sure nothing will occur to injure them in the elegant and refined circle of the eminent Sir Pitt Crawley. (*VF* p. 97)

It will be seen that, like that other strong-willed lady Queen Victoria, Miss Pinkerton is much given to underlining her more forceful expressions, thus adding extra weight to the condemnation of poor Becky.

Another lady with roots deep in the eighteenth century is the weak-spirited Miss Briggs, companion to the wealthy and worldly Miss Crawley. If Miss Pinkerton owes much to Dr Johnson, Briggs derives from a more sentimental tradition. Thackeray writes: 'Miss Briggs, it will be seen by her language, was of a literary and sentimental turn, and had once published a volume of poems – "Trills of a Nightingale" – by subscription' (*VF* p. 130). Here is a specimen of her conversation:

What sort of person is this Miss Sharp, Firkin? I little thought, while enjoying my Christmas revels in the elegant home of my firm friends, the Reverend Lionel Delamere and his amiable lady, to find a stranger had taken my place in the affections of my dearest, my still dearest Matilda! (*VF* p. 129)

If nothing else, the repetition of 'my dearest, my still dearest Matilda' gives us Briggs' literary pedigree: like Sir Edward Denham in Jane Austen's *Sanditon* (*Minor Works*, ed. R. W. Chapman, Oxford, 1954, p. 404), her fancy 'had been early caught by all the impassioned, & most exceptionable parts of Richardsons'.

How provoking, then, to find one's well-turned phrases and finer flows of feeling brought to nothing by the astringency of Becky Sharp's staccato, simple sentences:

'She's not very ill any more. Console yourself, dear Miss Briggs. She has only overeaten herself – that is all. She is greatly better. She will soon be quite restored again. . . . Pray console yourself, and take a little more wine. .... When she's well I shall go.'

'Never, never,' Arabella exclaimed, madly inhaling her salts-bottle.

'Never be well or never go? Miss Briggs,' the other said, with the same provoking good-nature. (*VF* p. 128)

But when Briggs is needed to break the news to her Mistress that it is Miss Crawley's nephew Rawdon whom Becky has clandestinely married, Becky herself invokes the shade of Richardson and adopts a sentimental epistolary manner. The flattery in this letter is as implicit in the style as in the matter:

Claims even superior to those of my benefactress call me hence. I go to my duty – to my husband. Yes, I am married. My husband commands me to break the news as your delicate sympathy will know how to do it – to my dear, my beloved friend and benefactress. (*VF* p. 155)

Finally we should consider our third lady, Miss Crawley herself. Where shall we look, in the previous century, for her predecessor? A spoilt, rich, self-willed old sinner, full of romantic ideas culled from the 'cargo of novels' that Briggs regularly fetches from the library, her Radical notions, which prove so shallow in practice, are owing to her previous association with 'Mr Fox'; and one can best see her in the tradition of a character drawn by one of that Whig entourage: she is Lydia Languish, in Sheridan's *The Rivals*, grown old. Her accents are staccato, imperious and uncharitable, as Lydia's are. She is importunate, 'instant in season and out of season', her speech distinguished by 'the vigour and frequency of her sarcasms' (*VF* p. 317):

Not let Miss Sharp dine at table! ... My dear creature, do you suppose I can talk about the nursery with Lady Fuddleston, or discuss justices' business with that goose, old Sir Giles Wapshot? I insist upon Miss Sharp appearing. Let Lady Crawley remain upstairs, if there is no room. But little Miss Sharp! Why, she's the only person fit to talk to in the country! (*VF* p. 104)

For an ironist, dealing freely, and indeed perhaps compulsively, with the discrepancy between the actual and the ideal, between profession and practice, it is often a question of choosing the right wrong word; and here, too, Thackeray is a master. Sometimes, to make a point of character or convey an impression, he will even expatiate on the inappropriateness of a word. Thus the difference between the normal meaning of the word *hint* and old Osborne's use of the word to describe his dealings with his associates is a matter for explicit sarcasm:

> When the elder Osborne gave what he called a 'hint', there was no possibility for the most obtuse to mistake his meaning. He called kicking a footman downstairs, a hint to the latter to leave his service. With his usual frankness and delicacy he told Miss Haggistoun that he would give her a check for five thousand pounds on the day his son was married to her ward; and called that proposal a hint, and considered it a very dexterous piece of diplomacy. (*VF* p. 197)

Similarly, the eclectic profusion in the furniture of wealthy but vulgar Victorians, such as Lady Clavering in *Pendennis*, is condemned by the repetition of the ironically inappropriate word *chaste*:

> Pen and his uncle declined the refection, but they admired the dining-room with fitting compliments, and pronounced it 'very chaste', that being the proper phrase. There were, indeed, highbacked Dutch chairs of the seventeenth century; there was a sculptured carved buffet of the sixteenth . . . [etc. etc.], there were old family portraits from Wardour Street, and tapestry from France, bits of armour, double-handed swords and battleaxes made of *carton-pierre*, looking-glasses, statuettes of saints . . . , nothing, in a word, could be chaster. . . . But what could equal the chaste splendour of the drawing rooms . . . etc. (*P* I ch. 37)

Flux for *flow*, with its medical overtones of excess and morbidity, has a secondary appropriateness to describe the pompous outpourings of the sanctimonious Pitt Crawley: 'though he had a fine *flux* of words . . . yet he failed somehow' (*VF* p. 84). The descriptions of the elderly Miss Briggs bathing at Brighton as a *nymph* (*VF* p. 241) and of Becky going through a church service 'with the gravest *resignation*' (*VF* p. 362) are good examples of this clever choice of the unsuitable word.

33

Becky's sycophancy, her obsequious and gushing ways when she is ingratiating herself, are often indicated by an emotionally-charged word in prosaic circumstances, as when she pleases the Sedleys' housekeeper 'by evincing the deepest *sympathy* in the raspberry-jam preserving' (*VF* p. 32). It is a favourite device to contrast her pretensions to fine feelings with something more prosaic: carpet-rods, for example, or a brandy-bottle:

> Then she gave him ever so gentle a pressure with her little hand, and drew it back quite frightened, and looked just for one instant in his face, and then down at the *carpet-rods*. (*VF* p. 33)

> She put her hand to her heart with a passionate gesture of despair, burying her face for a moment on the bed.
> The *brandy-bottle* inside clinked up against the plate which held the cold sausage. Both were moved, no doubt, by the exhibition of so much grief. (*VF* p. 632)

So, too, in the incongruous mixture of the affectionate and the humdrum in the following:

> After a scene in which one person was in earnest and the other a perfect performer – after the tenderest caresses, the most pathetic tears, the *smelling-bottle*, and some of the very best feelings of the heart, had been called into requisition – Rebecca and Amelia parted. (*VF* p. 66)

When a verb is in question, such incongruity can lead to a syllepsis, or to what most people would call, less than correctly, a zeugma:

> Her mamma ordered her dresses, her books, her bonnets, and her ideas for her. (*VF* p. 321)

> Miss Briggs . . . buried her crushed affections and her poor old red nose in her pocket-handkerchief. (*VF* p. 127)

At other times, an effect of anticlimax is obtained by other belittling means, and helped along by a fine sense of cadence:

> . . . deep in talk about roads, rivers, conveyances, sumpter-horses and artillery-train; . . . the provincial Militia Colonel has bits of bread laid at intervals on the table before him, and stations marked out, on which he has his finger . . . till a negro-

servant, changing the courses, brushes off the Potomac with a napkin, and sweeps up the Ohio in a spoon. (*V* I ch. 9)

George Saintsbury (in *A Consideration of Thackeray*, p. 148) particularly delighted in the cadence of the following sentence from *The Book of Snobs*: 'The most good-natured of women pardoned the error, and the butler removed the bird' (*BS* ch. 1).

This brings us to one of the novelist's peculiar excellences, his fine ear in prose composition. We shall frequently have occasion to note his accurate rendering of the varied nuances of speech: 'All those curious phonetic dialogues of his – Joyce-like in their way,' writes V. S. Pritchett in *In My Good Books* (London, 1943, p. 126), 'indicate something like the modern ear's curiosity.' But along with this he retains something that is perhaps more characteristic of our earlier literature and may well bear witness to his classical training at Charterhouse: a long-breathed impetus in sentence structure, a quiet mastery of the ebb and flow of sentence and paragraph. The long sentence was a necessary vehicle for the massed detail that constitutes so much of his method. The accumulation of particularities in delineating character, for example, can lead to a final assessment in which rhythm and syntax play important roles; as in this account of Colonel Newcome's step-mother, Sophia Alethea Newcome, of Clapham:

> His wife never cared about being called Lady Newcome. To manage the great house of Hobson Brothers and Newcome; to attend to the interests of the enslaved negro; to awaken the benighted Hottentot to a sense of truth; to convert Jews, Turks, Infidels, and Papists; to arouse the indifferent and often blasphemous mariner; to guide the washerwoman in the right way; to head all the public charities of her sect, and do a thousand secret kindnesses that none knew of; to answer myriads of letters, pension endless ministers, and supply their teeming wives with continuous baby-linen; to hear preachers daily bawling for hours, and listen untired on her knees after a long day's labour, while florid rhapsodists belaboured cushions above her with wearisome benedictions; all these things had this woman to do, and for near fourscore years she fought her fight womanfully: imperious but deserving to rule, hard but doing her duty, severe but charitable, and untiring in generosity as in labour: unforgiving in one instance – in that of her

husband's eldest son, Thomas Newcome; the little boy who had played on the hay, and whom at first she had loved very sternly and fondly. (*N* I ch. 2)

We note in this well-managed sentence the overall coherence and rhythmic impetus despite a wealth of detail. The unwearying philanthropy, meeting a demand as continuous as the baby-linen, is given its due; but there is a suggestion, in the references to the blasphemous mariner and the washerwoman, of that favourite butt of Thackeray's wit, the alarmist language of the tract; and a further hint, in the indiscriminate proselytizing, of what Dickens had just taught the Victorians to call Jellybyism. So the pros and cons are antithetically deployed: *wearisome* against *benediction*, *severe* against *charitable*, with a final debit to the account (for Thackeray had found his mother's evangelicalism irksome, as his daughters were to do after his death), that such charity does not always have its beginnings in an entirely happy home life.

Perhaps no other English novelist was so consistently skilful in calling just the right tune for a sentence, a paragraph, or even, as we shall see, a whole chapter: in suggesting the crescendo of an auction-sale, for example:

> Mr Hammerdown is sitting on the great mahogany dining-tables, in the dining-room below, waving the ivory hammer, and employing all the artifices of eloquence, enthusiasm, entreaty, reason, despair; shouting to his people, satirizing Mr Davids for his sluggishness; inspiriting Mrs Moss into action; imploring, commanding, bellowing, until down comes the hammer like fate, and we pass to the next lot. (*VF* p. 160)

Without wishing to 'number the streaks of the tulip', in Dr Johnson's phrase, we might note here the repetition (with variation) of words like *dining-tables* and *dining-room*, *Hammerdown* and *hammer*, the echoing gradation of sounds in '*el*oquence, *en*thusiasm, *en*treaty, *rea*son', all suggesting a succession of bids; together with the circuitously reductive effect of the sale of the item, as the initial surname is answered by the final '*down* comes the *hammer*'. An auction sale, Thackeray tells us, is just the place where 'Satire and Sentiment can visit arm in arm together' (*VF* p. 158); and the orchestration of the prose serves him well in contributing to the description of something so congenial to his cast of mind which, in the words of Saintsbury (*op. cit.* p. 269) was always accustomed to 'feel in earnest while thinking in jest'.

A similar achievement of rhythm occurs in the following passage, describing the entry to a great house, with the lengthy staircase and the mounting excitement matched by the syntax, as one approaches the distinguished host in the upper room:

> The familiar house of which the lights used to shine so cheerfully at seven o'clock, of which the hall-doors opened so readily, of which the obsequious servants, as you passed up the comfortable stair, sounded your name from landing to landing, until it reached the apartment where jolly old Dives welcomed his friends!

Arrived at the top of the staircase, the grandeur of the establishment is further suggested in the orchestration of the prose, with doubled cadences:

> What a number of them [sc. friends] he had; and what a noble way of entertaining them! How witty people used to be there, who were morose when they got out of the door; and how courteous and friendly men who slandered and hated each other everywhere else! He was pompous, but with such a cook what would not one swallow? he was rather dull, perhaps, but would not such wine make any conversation pleasant? (*VF* p. 159)

Amid much that defies analysis we may note here the variety within the repeated clauses; how the slight grammatical disquiet of the separation of the relative pronoun from its antecedent in the first part of the second sentence ('How witty *people* used to be there, *who* were morose . . . ') is almost liturgically answered by the closing of this gap in the second part ('How courteous and friendly *men who* slandered . . . '), all by way of counterpointing rhythmically the soothing effect of wealth, good food and good wine in removing sources of discord.

George Saintsbury particularly admired the hundred pages or so of *Vanity Fair* between the arrival of the younger Sir Pitt Crawley in Curzon Street, and the sudden catastrophe where Becky is discovered with Lord Steyne by Rawdon on his release from jail (chs. 43–54). 'Not merely is it all good,' he wrote (*op. cit.* p. 174) 'but there is in it that steady crescendo of expectation and satisfaction which only occurs at supreme moments of life and literature. The catastrophe itself is beyond praise – it is one of the greatest things in English: but it is perfectly led up to.' The fifty-first chapter, one might add, in which events are screwed towards the climax in a *tour de force* of sustained and indeed mounting excitement, is also one of the great passages in the book. It describes Becky's triumphant night of charades at Gaunt House. Nearly all the items redound *ad majorem gloriam Rebeccae*, and the evening is wound up to a higher pitch, with page after page of uproarious climax. The narrative gallops forward at great speed – one discovers a new appropriateness in expressions like *fast living* as one reads. About half the sentences in the culminating narrative begin with the pronoun *she*, as Becky's triumphs are catalogued:

> *She* passed by Lady Stunningham with a look of scorn. *She* patronized Lady Gaunt and her astonished and mortified sister-in-law – *she* écraséd all rival charmers. . . . The greatest triumph of all was at supper time. *She* was placed at the grand exclusive table with his Royal Highness. . . . *She* was served on gold plate. *She* might have had pearls melted into her champagne if she liked – another Cleopatra. (*VF* p. 499)

This is hubris, of course; and nemesis follows a few lines later. The pace and the noise quieten down, carriages are called for, and Mrs Rawdon rides away in hers. As Thackeray puts it, onomatopoetically, 'Mrs Rawdon Crawley's carriage . . . rattled into the illuminated court-yard, and drove up to the covered way.' (One is reminded of 'Maud', which Tennyson was to write a few years later: 'Low on the sand and loud on the stone/The last wheel echoes away'.) Meanwhile Rawdon walks home at the invitation of Wenham who, in the dense orchestration of the earlier part of this chapter, has already sounded a disquieting note. Now Wenham acts as a decoy, and Rawdon is taken up for debt. The whole chapter is a tone poem, ending on this note of quiet ominousness, presaging the stormy climax of the book.

Few English writers understood better how to choose sentences of the right length for special effect; as in this description of fashionable London, with staccato short sentences contributing to an overall effect summed up at the end:

Horses, under the charge of men in red jackets, are pacing up and down St James's Street. Cabmen on the stand are regaling with beer. Gentlemen with grooms behind them pass towards the Park. Great dowager barouches roll along, emblazoned with coronets, and driven by coachmen in silvery wigs. Wistful provincials gaze in at the clubs. Foreigners chatter and show their teeth, and look at the ladies in the carriages. . . . It is five o'clock, the noon in Pall Mall. (*N* I ch. 6)

Contrast with this rather desultory use of short sentences, the speed achieved in the following use of co-ordinate clauses joined with *and* to form a climax and an anticlimax:

Thus the Newcomes entertained the Farintoshes, and the Farintoshes entertained the Newcomes. And the Dowager Countess of Kew went from assembly to assembly every evening, and to jewellers and upholsterers, and dressmakers every morning . . . ; and Lady Kew made a will, leaving all she could leave to her beloved granddaughter, Ethel . . . ; and Lord Kew wrote an affectionate letter to his cousin, congratulating her and wishing her happiness with all his heart; and I was glancing over the *Times* newspaper at breakfast one morning, when I laid it down with an exclamation which caused my wife to start with surprise.
'What is it?' cries Laura, and I read as follows: DEATH OF THE COUNTESS DOWAGER OF KEW. – We regret [etc. etc.]. (*N* II ch. 16).

This is a technique analogous to the speeding up of a reel of film, temporarily, to suggest frenzied activity; followed by a cacophony from the background music when the blow falls.

Thackeray is sparing of descriptive passages, preferring to delineate a scene, as the Tillotsons observe in the Introduction to their edition of *Vanity Fair* (p. v), 'by means of a few strokes only'. *Henry Esmond* has one or two scenes that might be called 'painterly', particularly descriptions of the Hall at Castlewood: 'its grey familiar towers, a pinnacle or two shining in the sun, the buttress and terrace walls casting great blue shades on the grass' (*E* I ch. 9). But landscape is generally landscape with figures, and then it can be very spirited. The Christmas celebrations at Queen's Crawley make a country Christmas card worthy of comparison with Dickens's more urban Yuletide scenes (*VF* chs. 44, 45). Occasionally there is an effective widening of the lens. The following passage describes the aftermath of a funeral, not a wedding; but this account of travel to wider horizons through a peopled landscape on a hot day reminds one of the mood so successfully conveyed by Philip Larkin in the title poem of his volume *The Whitsun Weddings*:

> Then the tenantry mounted on horseback again, or stayed and refreshed themselves at the Crawley Arms. Then, after a lunch in the servant's hall at Queen's Crawley, the gentry's carriages wheeled off to their different destinations: then the undertaker's men, taking the ropes, palls, velvets, ostrich feathers, and other mortuary properties, clambered up on the roof of the hearse, and rode off to Southampton. Their faces relapsed into a natural expression as the horses, clearing the lodge gates, got into a brisker trot on the open road; and squads of them might have been seen, speckling with black the public-house entrances, with pewter pots flashing in the sunshine. (*VF* p. 408)

What emerges here and elsewhere from such narrative is a rich underlying stratum of poetic imagination. Thackeray considered that his verse was 'small beer'; but the strain of poetry which deepens the inspiration of many passages of prose was recognized in the novelist's own day by James Hannay (*Studies on Thackeray*, p. 85), and has never been better defined than in Hannay's words:

> Inside his fine sagacious common-sense understanding there was, so to speak, a pool of poetry, – like the *impluvium* in the hall of a Roman house, which gave an air of coolness and freshness and nature to the solid marble columns and tessellated floor.

CHAPTER 2

Regency English in the Victorian Period

🐍🐍🐍🐍🐍🐍

THE student of the prose of nineteenth-century novelists will frequently discover that his findings tend to corroborate general statements in Professor Ian Gordon's authoritative book *The Movement of English Prose*. One sentence, especially (p. 141), is proved right again and again:

> The normal manner of Richardson and Fielding was to provide the basic prose for most of the novel-writing of the eighteenth and nineteenth century, and Fanny Burney, Jane Austen, and Thackeray (to name no others) remain heavily in their debt.[1]

I propose, in this chapter, to examine a small part of this inheritance, considering briefly Thackeray's linguistic legacy from the English of the Regency period.

Major Pendennis, a Regency dandy grown old, may serve as an embodiment of the tradition, and his conversation indicates this. He is brought in to nip in the bud any *mésalliance* which could result from his nephew's infatuation for the Irish actress, Miss Costigan. He combats this infatuation, not with threats, but with diplomacy; as previously in similar circumstances when, he says, 'I implored, I entreated gentle *measures*'. Then, his advice had not been taken, and 'what was the *fact*? . . . The young people had been married for three months before Lord Ferrybridge knew anything about it.' In this case he appeals to Pen's ambition: 'I don't care to own to you that I had other and much higher *views* for you' (*P* I ch. 8). He hopes it is 'no unworthy *object* . . . which Pen has formed' (*P* I ch. 6). He insists that matrimonial speculators should not think that his nephew is '*a fortune*' (*P* I ch. 10). Pen becomes a favourite of his uncle while a student; the Major

---

1 See P. N. Furbank's Introduction to his edition of *Martin Chuzzlewit*, Penguin Books, 1968, pp. 26–7, for a discussion of the Regency element in the style of Dickens.

compliments him on his acquiring the art of flattery; 'it was exceedingly *well* for a beginner'; and suggests further ways for him to ingratiate himself – with M.P.'s, for instance: 'Ask Mr Foker for a *frank* – they like it' (*P* I ch. 17) (M.P.'s had the privilege of free postage). Considering Pen's future career, he wonders whether a Duke of his acquaintance would '*bring* him *in* for one of his boroughs' (*P* I ch. 20). Over a later love-affair of his nephew's, however, he is less sympathetic, accusing him of '*allying*' himself with a low-born kitchen-girl (*P* II ch. 19), and advising him not to '*sit down* for life upon a miserable fifteen hundred a year', but to use his 'good *parts*' to better himself. He has heard that Pen was '*famous* as an orator' (*P* II ch. 21); with his '*person* and expectations' he should make a good marriage (*P* I ch. 37), though there will be competition: the bankers, for instance, of the Major's acquaintance are '*wild after* grand marriages' (*N* I ch. 24).

This is Austenian language,[1] and reflects turn-of-the-century usage, as Jane Austen's novels do. As *Henry Esmond* supremely testifies, Thackeray has a sure touch with obsolescent and archaic language. One word can often give just the desired effect in evoking a period. Reviewing *The Diary and Letters of Madame D'Arblay* (Fanny Burney) in *The Morning Chronicle*, he describes how, when one of her novels first appeared, 'Six lovely princesses wept over . . . *Camilla*, read it hastily in their apartments at Windsor, or "*comfortably*" together at Weymouth' (William Thackeray, *Contributions to the Morning Chronicle*, ed. Gordon Ray, Illinois, 1955, p. 184). With Major Pendennis, the novelist goes to the further expedient of attempting to reproduce something of the Major's old-fashioned pronunciation: 'by *Gad*' or 'by *Ged*'; 'the course for us to *pursoo*' (*P* II ch. 16); 'a *doosid* deal' (*P* II ch. 19);[2] while Pen is made to mimic the Major's pronunciation of his frequent word *devilish* as *dayvlish* (*P* II ch. 25). In the tradition of Sir John Middleton of *Sense and Sensibility*, the Major has

---

1 See K. C. Phillipps, *Jane Austen's English*, London, 1970, s.v. the index for each of the italicized words, with the exception of *well* (*OED well* adj. 8c), *a fortune* (*OED fortune* 7), and *sit down* (*OED sit* 21).

2 This vowel, [uː] for [ju], was clearly felt in Victorian times to be a Regency eccentricity. Harriet Martineau, in her *Autobiography*, records a conversation with Wordsworth on the popularity of his poem *The Happy Warrior*: 'Ay,' said Wordsworth, 'that was not on account of the poetic conditions being best fulfilled in that poem; but because it is' (solemnly) 'a chain of extremely *valooable* thoughts.' (Quoted by Mary Moorman, *William Wordsworth: The Later Years*, Oxford, 1965, p. 44.)

phrases like *monstrous pretty*; but again, the novelist brings us nearer to the actual pronunciation of the Regency period, standing out as old-fashioned by early Victorian times: '*mons'ous* fine girls' (*P* I ch. 37), '*mons'ous* affecting' (*P* II ch. 2).

Thackeray's narrative relies heavily on traditional vocabulary for certain themes, such as courtship: Rawdon Crawley, for instance, '*distinguished*' Becky Sharp a great number of times at the beginning of their acquaintance (*VF* p. 106); a similar state of affairs occurs when a suitor's attentions to a young lady become 'a little *particular*' (*Ph* I ch. 14); young men boast '*an attachment*, an ardently cherished *attachment*' (*P* I ch. 3); and young ladies respond to their advances, particularly if they represent 'a most eligible family *connexion*' (*VF* p. 173); but they are warned, 'Be cautious . . . be wary how you *engage*' (*VF* p. 172). They 'sell themselves for . . . an *establishment* every day' (*N* I ch. 28), though '*interested* marriages' have wretched consequences (*N* II ch. 21).

The social set-up was in many ways similar to what it had been when Jane Austen was writing: Laura Bell, for instance, makes her 'first *appearance*' at a ball in Baymouth, i.e. Sidmouth (*P* I ch. 25); Blanche Amory, though 'promised' for a dance, will say that she has a previous '*engagement*' with Pen and will waltz with him. On the same social occasion, Pen '*quizzed* unmercifully all the men in the room' (*P* I ch. 26), and on another, Ethel Newcome showed her presence of mind by looking *unconscious*, or 'unembarrassed' (*N* II ch. 4). It was still idiom to be '*secure of* a friend' (*N* II ch. 36). Good natural ability could still be described as 'good natural *genius*' (*SGS* ch. 2). 'Signs of *intelligence*' could mean signs of mutual understanding (*VF* p. 442). A secret could still be *surprised*, that is, come upon unexpectedly (*P* II ch. 30). *Character* still frequently had its more public sense of 'reputation': Becky Sharp, after her downfall, 'tried to make a *character* for herself, and conquer scandal' (*VF* p. 621). A young man, if good-looking, could still be a *beauty* (*P* I ch. 1).[1] *Expensive* was still used of people and could mean 'extravagant'[2]: Pen had been thrown into '*expensive* society', his mother thinks, by his Uncle's encouragement (*P* I ch. 21). *Interest* could mean 'influence': 'He must have

1 'He is a *beauty* of my mother's.' *Jane Austen's Letters* (ed. Chapman), p. 58.
2 'X was *expensive*, and became poor.' Line from 'The Picture Alphabet' of c. 1834, quoted in *The Oxford Nursery Rhyme Book*, ed. Iona and Peter Opie, Oxford, 1953, p. 107.

good *interest*, though. He must have got the Colonel the place' (*VF* p. 533). *Liberal* could still be used in the sense of 'magnanimously gentlemanlike', though by the time of the writing of *Vanity Fair* (1847–8) the political overtones which the word was acquiring would have given extra point to the irony of the following dialogue between George Osborne and Dobbin:

> 'A governess is all very well, but I'd rather have a lady for my sister-in-law. I'm a *liberal* man; but I've a proper pride, and know my own station; let her know hers . . .'
> 'I suppose you know best,' Dobbin said, though rather dubiously.
> 'You always were a Tory, and your family's one of the oldest in England. But – '. (*VF* p. 62)

To notice in the sense of 'to pass remarks about' and *to remark* in the sense of 'to notice' are both instances of Regency usage still surviving to Victorian times, though hardly to the present:

> As we travelled homeward in the omnibus, Fred Bayham *noticed* the circumstances to me. (*N* II ch. 26)

> A royal princess had *remarked* him. (*VF* p. 224)

So also with *varieties* in the sense of 'variations': 'No small *varieties* of London life were presented to the young man' (*P* I ch. 36); and *to form* in the sense of 'to train': 'Her manners are excellent, now I have *formed* her' (*VF* p. 146); and *hopeless* used, as it rarely is nowadays, in contexts which imply no value-judgment but literally mean 'without hope': 'It was evident that the youth, though *hopeless*, was still jealous and in love with his charming cousin' (*N* II ch. 10). (With this last we can compare the way the surgeon, after Louisa Musgrove's accident, is 'not *hopeless*'; Jane Austen, *Persuasion*, ch. 12.) Nor can we any longer use, as Jane Austen could, the verb *carry* with a personal object, at least not in the sense of 'to drive' or 'to convey': 'At the houses to which he has been *carried*, you have taken care not to show him a woman that is not a fright' (*V* I ch. 17).

The verb *to admire* is freely used in *Esmond*, as we shall see, in the neutral eighteenth-century sense of 'to wonder or marvel at', without the normal modern suggestion of esteem and approbation. Such usage is now, as the *OED* says, archaic (*admire* v. 2), and was doubtless beginning to be so in Thackeray's day; though he could usefully revive overtones of the old meaning for ironic purposes:

> I, for my part, have known a five pound-note to . . . knock up a half century's attachment between two brethren; and can't but *admire*, as I think what a fine and durable thing Love is among worldly people. (*VF* p. 95)

The formal language of advertisements in early Victorian times tended to be rather old-fashioned, and to contain elements more common in the Regency period: as with *inmates* in a sense innocent of the modern suggestion of being 'institutionalized' in some way;[1] and *burst*, a favourite noun of Jane Austen's which has since tended to acquire bathetic overtones:

> Mrs Sedley . . . had not spirit enough to bustle about for 'a few select *inmates* to join a cheerful musical family' such as one reads of in *The Times*. (*VF* p. 374)

> The theatre . . . was no better filled than country theatres usually are in spite of the 'universal *burst* of attraction and galvanic thrills of delight' advertised . . . in the play-bills. (*P* I ch. 4)

Even *se'nnight* for 'week', which was seemingly old-fashioned in Jane Austen's day, occurs once, in a police report, in *Philip* (*Ph* II ch. 20).

Among the smaller details of social life one may note that Mrs Elton's *rout-cakes* (Jane Austen, *Emma* ch. 34), small rich cakes suitable for routs or receptions, are still being consumed, twenty-four at a time, by Jos Sedley in *Vanity Fair* (p. 31). A chef comes and *dresses* a dinner (*P* I ch. 36), much as a leg of Hartfield pork is *dressed* for Mr Woodhouse (*Emma* ch. 21). Blanche Amory begs Laura Bell to 'take the *second*' (under-part) in a song (*P* I ch. 25), as Frank Churchill had done for Emma (*Emma* ch. 26). Though

---

1 See John W. Clark, *The Language and Style of Anthony Trollope* p. 75). A similar fate has overtaken the word *asylum*, so that Thackeray's 'In vain he tried to find her an *asylum* among the respectable ladies of his regiment' (*MG* ch. 1), is apt to be taken wrongly. By the end of the century the association of the word *asylum* with lunacy was so strong that, to quote James Pope-Hennessy's biography of Queen Mary 'some old goose declared she would not enter the "Asylum" [the Royal Cambridge Asylum] unless it was named a "Home".' *Queen Mary*, London, 1959, p. 70.

guineas ceased to be coined in 1813, *seven shillings*, a third of this amount, was still a casual unit of exchange in conversation, as it had been when *Sense and Sensibility* was written (ch. 49):

> Mar had actially refused him twice, and had had to wait three months to get *seven shillings* which he had borrered of 'er. (*P* II ch. 23)

Major Pendennis's valet Morgan had 'a *receipt* for boot-varnish' (*P* II ch. 29), with which we can compare Mrs Norris's '*receipt* for a famous cream cheese' (*Mansfield Park* ch. 10). *Receipt* in this sense of 'recipe', though by two centuries the older of the two words in this sense, is now old-fashioned, but perhaps not quite obsolete. *Work* still occurs with the special sense of 'needlework', as it had done at the turn of the century (*Sense and Sensibility* ch. 23): 'Play your whist, or read your novel, or talk scandal over your *work*, ye worthy dowagers' (*N* II ch. 11).[1] Amelia Sedley, like Jane Fairfax (*Emma* ch. 19), *crosses* her letters (*VF* p. 114), that is, economizes on paper and postage by turning a written page through ninety degrees and writing across it. Admiral Croft's referring to a young man by the (partly naval) term *younker* (*Persuasion* ch. 18) is echoed, in a civilian context, by old Osborne to his grandson: 'It's not respectful, sir, of you *younkers* to be imitating of your relations' (*VF* p. 590). Memories of the renowned landscape gardener, Lancelot (Capability) Brown (1716–83), are evoked by Captain Strong in *Pendennis*, when he sees *capabilities* in Clavering Park (*P* I ch. 22), as Henry Crawford does on his first inspection of Sotherton (*Mansfield Park* ch. 9); and there are various idioms such as 'in an *under* voice' (*P* I ch. 38), *in the way* with no idea of obstruction, as 'Strong was luckily *in the way* when wanted' (*P* I ch. 26), and collocations like 'Mr

---

1 The substitution for *work* in this sense is now either *needlework*; or, more self-consciously, *art needlework*, or somewhat contemptuously, *fancy work*. I offer this last term as a tentative example of what, in counterblast to Professor Ross's 'U'-usage, one might call 'W'-usage, where W stands for Working, as distinct from 'U', Upper-class, usage. The contempt of the artisan for what seems to him or her a profitless occupation is apparent. Other candidates for this sort of usage might be *books* in the sense of 'magazines' ('do you take in any weekly *books*?'); *mate* for 'friend' (though as an appellative *mate* is classless, if somewhat contemptuous); and *mam* and *mammy* for lower-middle class (and upward) *mum* and *mummy*. *Mammy*, though now déclassé, is much older-established in the language than *mummy*, and by no means so exclusively negro as one might be led to believe from the BBC. Thackeray regularly begins letters to his mother, 'My dearest *Mammy*'.

Bolders . . . would *take* Gaberlunzie Castle . . . *on his way* south' (*Ph* I ch. 19).

On the other hand, whereas Catherine Morland and Isabella Thorpe 'adjourned to eat *ice* at a pastrycook's' (*Northanger Abbey* ch. 15), just as a hundred years before them Lady Mary Wortley Montagu had written, in a letter of 1716: 'The company are entertained with *ice* in several forms, winter and summer',[1] with Thackeray the modern idiom has arrived: George Osborne 'ate *ices* at a pastry-cook's shop in Charing Cross' (*VF* p. 120). A *muffin*, which in Jane Austen's time, and in Richardson's before her, was evidently a large single cake to be cut up and handed round, still remained so in some contexts of Thackeray; but in others the more individual small cakes are clearly meant: 'Be so good as to hand the *muffin*' (*LW* ch. 6); 'That's it: strawberries and *muffins* for tea' (*LW* ch. 3). A period reference to the word *closet* in *The Virginians* (ch. 28) has apologetic inverted commas round the word, which had still been respectable enough for quite elevated contexts in Jane Austen: 'Some of our great-grandmothers used to have cordials in their "closets" ' (*V* I ch. 38). As J. Copley puts it (*Shift of Meaning* p. 39): 'The Victorian use of the *water-closet* has spoilt the word for other uses.'

Only one reference to Jane Austen occurs in Thackeray's writings, so far as I have observed; in which she is associated with the phrase 'a dish of tea' in a way that suggests that this phrase too is obsolescent by mid-Victorian times:

> A dear little old Hampshire town . . . so like a novel of Miss Austen's that I wonder was she born and bred there? No, we should have known, and the good old ladies would have pronounced her to be a little idle thing, occupied with her silly books and neglecting her housekeeping. There were other towns in England, no doubt, where dwelt the widows and wives of other navy captains; where they tattled . . . , took their *dish of tea* at six, played at quadrille. (*RP* 'On a Peal of Bells')

There is a good deal of evidence to show that the phrase *a dish of tea* (see *JAE*, p. 98) was going out of fashion even at the beginning of the century. One other instance of the phrase occurs in *Pendennis*,

---

1 *OED* quotations, s.v. *ice* 5a. The editors add the interesting note: 'In French the plural *glaces* in this sense was admitted by the Academy in 1762; but as late as 1825 it was asserted to be incorrect to say *une glace*.'

in what clearly represents the echoed dialogue of servants: 'If Mrs Smith's maid should by chance be taking *a dish of tea* with yours' (*P* I ch. 36).

What happened to *a dish of tea* was also happening to several other words and phrases in Victorian times: '*quite the gentleman*, *partial to* (in the sense of 'fond of'), *party* (in the sense of 'person'), *in the matrimonial* (or some other) *line, female* in the sense of 'lady' and *lady* in the sense of 'wife', and the adjective *genteel* could all be used at the beginning of the century without irony or depreciation, even by a natural ironist like Jane Austen. In Victorian times these did not so much change their meaning, as become lowered in status. We might take the word *genteel* as a sort of paradigm. The *OED* has this to say in the preliminary note to this adjective:

> A few years before the middle of the nineteenth century the word was much ridiculed as being characteristic of those who are possessed with a dread of being taken for 'common people', or who attach exaggerated importance to supposed marks of social superiority. In serious laudatory use it may now be a vulgarism; in educated language it has always a sarcastic or at least playful colouring.

This playful colouring, however, was not present at the beginning of the century; and the *OED* well illustrates the change by juxtaposing a quotation from *Emma* to the effect that the Cole family are 'of low origin, in trade, and only moderately *genteel*' (*Emma* ch. 25),[1] and this quotation from Thackeray's *Sketches and Travels in London*:

> I was not *genteel* enough for her circle – I assume that to be the reason ... And why? Because my coat was a trifle threadbare; ... Gentility is the death and destruction of social happiness amongst the middle classes in England. ('On a Lady in an Opera-box')

The following examples of phrases which underwent this demotion occur in either the speech, or the echoed speech or thoughts (*erlebte Rede*) of more or less vulgar characters:

---

1 It may be objected that this passage, too, is ironic. But it is possible with Jane Austen as with Chaucer, to trace irony where none exists, where both these authors are writing 'with full devout corage', as C. S. Lewis appositely quotes of Chaucer. See *The Allegory of Love*, Oxford, 1936, p. 163.

She liked Mr Ridley to come, for he always treated her father so respectful, and was *quite the gentleman*. (*Ph* I ch. 6)

She was notoriously *partial* to her cousin. (*P* II ch. 2)

Her own heart had been lacerated by many previous disappointments *in the matrimonial line*. (*P* I ch. 8)

It is particularly interesting to follow the fortunes of the word *party* in the sense of 'the individual person concerned or in question', a sense that was already being extended from the legal use in Middle English and which, as the *OED* observes (*party* n. 14) was 'formerly common, and in serious use', but is now 'shoppy, vulgar or jocular'. It was evidently quite respectable usage in Jane Austen (*JAE* p. 29) and seems also to be acceptable in serious contexts in Thackeray's earlier novels. Thus Pen's friend Warrington, a sympathetic character of impeccable social origins, uses the word slightly condescendingly, perhaps, of the humble Fanny Bolton, but certainly with no sense of its being comic at this serious point in *Pendennis*:

> Warrington looked very grave when he heard this story. Putting the moral delinquency out of the question, he was extremely glad for Arthur's sake that the latter had escaped from a danger which might have made his whole life wretched: 'which certainly,' said Warrington, 'would have occasioned the wretchedness and ruin of the other *party*.' (*P* II ch. 16)

Fifteen years later, by the time of *Philip* (1861–2) the substandard element has arrived:

> My lord, who had just heard from Twysden all about that young woman – that *party* at Paris, Mr Ridley, . . . my lord turns upon the pore young fellar. (*Ph* II ch. 2)[1]

---

1 We might well compare the script of *Iolanthe* (1882) by W. S. Gilbert:

> Though the views of the House have diverged
> On every conceivable motion,
> All questions of Party are merged
> In a frenzy of love and devotion;
> If you ask us distinctly to say
> What Party we claim to belong to,
> We reply without doubt or delay,
> 'The *party* we're singing this song to.'

The noun *female* also lost status in the nineteenth century. In Jane Austen's day quite acceptable as a synonym for 'lady', it is now (*OED female* B 2b) 'commonly avoided by good writers, except with contemptuous implications' in such social contexts. When did this down-grading take place? I cannot find in Thackeray's writings any instance comparable in vituperative impact to the last *OED* quote under *female* from the *Pall Mall Gazette* of 1889: 'They are no ladies. The only word good enough for them is the word of opprobrium – *females*!' But there is a passage in *Vanity Fair* which suggests that the more respectable use was growing less current. Always adept at presenting prosaic characters in an amusing way, the novelist shows us Sir Pitt Crawley evincing his disapproval of Becky's character, and of her association with Lord Steyne:

> Pitt Crawley declared her behaviour was monstrously in-decorous, reprobated in strong terms the habit of play-acting ... as highly unbecoming a British *female*; and after the charades were over, took his brother Rawdon severely to task for appearing himself, and allowing his wife to join in such improper exhibitions. (*VF* p. 508)

Part of the deliberately-contrived staleness of this harangue is due to the old-fashioned use of *female*, which was beginning to have an insecure status. *Lady* in the sense of 'wife', respectable in Jane Austen, is now, according to Henry Bradley,[1] 'only jocular'. The ironic use is beginning to be apparent in *Vanity Fair*:

> Miss Crawley's gracious reply greatly encouraged our young friends, Rawdon and his *lady*, who hoped for the best from their aunt's evidently pacified humour. (*VF* p. 318)

Another word that was taking the downward path was *flame* in the sense (*OED flame* 6b) of 'the object of one's love'. This was formerly poetic usage, but is now jocular; so much so that Prior's well-known line: 'Euphelia serves to grace my measure, but Chloe

---

1 In the Appendix to R. W. Chapman's edition of *Sense and Sensibility*, Oxford, 1926, p. 405. Mr Harold Macmillan's references to 'President Kennedy and his *lady wife*' were much ridiculed by the satirists of the early sixties. On the tendency for certain eighteenth-century phrases to become vulgar in Victorian times, see Joan Platt, 'The Development of English Colloquial Idiom during the Eighteenth Century,' in *Review of English Studies* II (1926), pp. 70–81, 189–96.

is my real *flame*' can hardly be read today with a straight face.[1] The demotion was probably a nineteenth-century process. There is an amusing, and rather subtle instance in *Vanity Fair*. Miss Crawley tells her nephew Rawdon of Becky Sharp's friend Amelia, whom Miss Crawley has 'taken up': 'Of course, on this Rebecca instantly stated, that Amelia was engaged to be married – to a Lieutenant Osborne – a very *old flame*' (*VF* p. 135). Becky's first motive here, of course, is to forestall any claims Amelia might have on Rawdon's attention. But in addition, the rather passé phrase *old flame* is intended to show that Rebecca now patronizes Amelia, and wishes to suggest that despite Miss Crawley's approval, Amelia has qualities which Rawdon and herself would doubtless agree in calling *slow*. A final example of a word which can hardly be used seriously any more, though it was serious enough in earlier English, is *treasure* when used in the sense of 'an extremely valuable person' (*JAE* p. 105). With Thackeray the ironic down-grading has begun. Arthur congratulates his uncle, the Major, on having such a wealthy valet in Morgan, 'on having such a *treasure* in his service', as he sarcastically puts it (*P* II ch. 24).

One may often sense that older language is being used for a satirical purpose. When Thackeray wishes to say that George IV was notoriously the dupe of gamblers, he does so in Regency language: 'He was a *famous pigeon* for the play-men' (*FG* p. 110); similarly *lounge* is used of the Prince Regent in the sense of 'an idle stroll or saunter', different from the predominant modern meaning of 'an idle recumbent position': 'When George, Prince of Wales, was twenty ... "the Prince's *lounge*" was a peculiar manner of walking which the young bucks imitated' (*RP* 'De Juventute'). The use of *revolve* and *powers* in the following was possible down to Jane Austen, and may even perhaps be found in archaizing contexts today; but the novelist intends such obsolescent usage to contrast in its highflown register with something more colloquial, or to represent a mock-heroic discrepancy between aspiration and reality:

At the end of his speech she said, 'Law, Bell, I'm sure you

---

1 *Esmond*, incidentally, is set in Prior's life-time, and the jargon of fashionable love is contrived to be comparable:

He was an Amadis and deserved a Gloriana; and oh! *flames* and darts! what was his joy at hearing that his mistress was now with her Majesty. (*E* II ch. 9) are too young to think of such things;' but intimated that she too would *revolve* them in her own virgin bosom. (*P* I ch. 8)

F.B. has mended some of his ways. I am trying a course of industry, sir. *Powers*, perhaps naturally great, have been neglected over the wine cup and the die. (*N* II ch. 6)

Similarly when Ethel Newcome, after her engagement with Lord Farintosh is terminated, takes with something less than spontaneity to good works, she repeats parrot-fashion in a letter the rather stale Austenian phrases (printed in italics) by which the local clergyman is habitually descrided:

Little Barnes comes on bravely with his Latin; and Mr Whitestock, *a most excellent and valuable person* in this place . . . speaks highly of him. (*N* II ch. 30)

Or we can contrast Pen's description of the Fotheringay as 'a stunner' with the more measured language of the previous generation with which Dr Portman, the elderly vicar of Clavering, shows that he too is aware of her charms: 'I must say, Major, she is endowed with very considerable *personal* attractions' (*P* I ch. 9). Or again, when Captain Costigan takes down 'his venerable and murderous duelling-pistols, with flint locks, that had done the business of many a *pretty fellow* in Dublin' (*P* I ch. 12), we may take it that the collocation *pretty fellow* is as antiquated as the weapons. More subtly, the note of priggishness and condescension in Pen's affair with the humble Fanny Bolton is struck from the start at their Vauxhall meeting by the hero's considering the affair in his mind in terms of rather threadbare, not to say Richardsonian, language:

I will not play with this little girl's heart . . . and forget my own or her honour. She seems to have a great deal of dangerous and rather contagious sensibility, and I am very glad the fireworks are over, and that I can take her back to her mother. (*P* II ch. 8)

One departure from Regency usage which perhaps reflects a changing outlook is the word *country*, significantly emended to *county* in editions of *Vanity Fair* later than the 1853 edition which the Tillotsons use for their text:

And they told her how much the Hall was changed for the better . . . and how Pitt was taking his station in the *country*, as became a Crawley in fact. (*VF* p. 435)

Country for *county* is usual in Jane Austen, though *county* also occurs; and it is perhaps not far-fetched to see in this change a widening of horizons brought about by the new railways and wider travelling.

Phrasal verbs which occurred at the beginning of the nineteenth century (*JAE*, pp. 71–2) but which are now unfamiliar, still flourished: such as *put up* for *put away*, *turn off* and *turn away*, both meaning 'to dismiss, to sack' (an employee), and *come across*, meaning 'to cross one's mind, occur to one':

She . . . tried to obey, She *put up* the two or three trinkets. (*VF* p. 171)

I heard something of that quarrel . . . but Mirobolant was not *turned off* for that? (*P* I ch. 36)

I have *turned away* one artist: the poor creature was utterly incompetent. (*N* I ch. 15)

The thought *came across* him in their conversations. (*N* II ch. 25)

A noteworthy trio are *take down*,[1] meaning 'to humiliate or abate the arrogance of' (a person); *take up*, meaning 'to adopt as a protégé' and *take off*, meaning 'to portray or draw the likeness of (someone or something)'. In the last two quotations below Thackeray appreciates and exploits the rather precarious colloquial basis for the metaphorical overtones of such phrasal verbs:

She made a tremendous assault upon Harry Foker, who sat next to her, and to whom she gave all the talk, though I *took* her *down*. (*P* II ch. 2)

'What could Lady Rockminster have meant by taking her up?' After the first season, indeed, Lady Rockminster, who had *taken up* Lady Clavering, *put* her *down*. (*P* II ch. 21)

Then Clive proposed to the Rev Charles Honeyman to *take* his

---

1 Compare and contrast this with Mrs Bennet's remark to Mr Bennet, about Mr Darcy: 'I wish you had been there, my dear, to have given him one of your *set-downs*' (*Pride and Prejudice* ch. 3).

head *off*; and made an excellent likeness in chalk of his uncle. (*N* II ch. 6)

It is still possible for food to *go off*, but hardly a love-affair (in abstract contexts *fall through* is now preferred); and *put on* now means 'exploited', not 'encouraged':

But my mother did not like her, and the affair *went off*. (*P* II ch. 21)

She was always dangling and ogling after him, I recollect now; and I've no doubt she was *put on* by her old sharper of a father. (*VF* p. 220)

A passage of dialogue like the following, also, is still of the earlier period in its idiom:

'How *cut up* your pretty little friend will be; hey Becky?' 'I daresay she'll *recover it*;' Becky said. (*VF* p. 166)

There is one word whose development at the beginning of the nineteenth century is of special interest, as it reflects the religious movements of the time. This is *serious*, meaning 'earnest about the things of religion' (*OED serious* 2). The first *OED* quotation in this sense is dated 1796 ('I could wish . . . that the custom of drinking toasts was banished from the tables of the *serious* because it leads to excess'). This semantic development is specially interesting because, up to a point, we can trace its rapid spread, and, if not its demise, at least the delivery of a *coup de grâce* by an influential hand. The only Jane Austen novel where the religious overtones of the word are apparent is *Persuasion*. Mr Elliot, in that novel, we learn, 'had been, at least, careless on all *serious* matters . . . How could it ever be ascertained that his mind was truly cleansed?' (ch. 17). In Thackeray, as in at least the early novels of Dickens, *serious* could be applied directly to persons, when the meaning is often 'of the evangelical persuasion'. Thus, in the brief glimpse that we are given, at the beginning of *The Newcomes*, of the upbringing of Colonel Newcome, we learn that the Colonel's stepmother had a 'mansion at Clapham . . . long the resort of the most favoured amongst the religious world'. There, even the servants qualified for the adjective: 'The lodge-keeper was *serious*, and a clerk at a neighbouring chapel.' When young Tom deserved a flogging, she 'summoned the *serious* butler' to administer it (*N* I ch. 2). When Becky Sharp encountered such *seriousness* among the nobility, she soon contrived to exploit it, ingratiating herself with Lady Southdown by submitting to her for both quack remedies and religious instruction: 'She hoped that a past life spent in worldliness and error might not in-capacitate her for *more serious* thought in the future' (the italics here are Thackeray's). Later, among her cronies, Becky mimicked Lady Southdown by preaching 'a great sermon in the true *serious* manner . . . and for the first time in her life the Dowager Countess of Southdown was made amusing' (*VF* pp. 405–6).

In Thackeray's last complete novel, *Philip*, this meaning hardly occurs. The word was losing ground to a synonym; and at the instance of no less a personality than Dr Arnold. In the preface to the sixth (1858) edition of that Victorian best-seller *Tom Brown's Schooldays* the author, Thomas Hughes, writes: 'Boyish-ness in the highest sense is not incompatible with seriousness, or earnestness, if you like the word better.' A footnote directs us to the source of this emendation: 'To [Arnold] and his admirers we owe the substitution of the word *earnest* for its predecessor *serious*.' The tendency clearly was for the less specialized, more secular meanings of *serious* to re-assert themselves, to the exclusion of this special meaning, after some of the novelty of the evangelical movement had worn off. Looking for a change of heart in the worldly Blanche Amory, Pen asks himself: 'Has she become *serious* and religious? Does she tend schools and visit the poor?' (*P* II ch. 25). The extra two words after *serious* mark the tendency of this word to re-assume its secular meaning.

Serious is one of several words and phrases which were given special evangelical overtones. A cluster of them occurs in the second chapter of *The Newcomes*, in the masterly account of the Hermitage in Clapham, 'a serious paradise', as the novelist calls it. The density of texture of this chapter in what Ray (*Age* p. 23) calls 'in some respects the richest, not only of Thackeray's books, but of all Victorian fictions' is partly due to the author's know-ledge and deployment of the special language of Evangelicalism and Nonconformity. Thus the widower, Thomas Newcome senior, having fallen in love with the wealthy Quaker heiress and owner of the Hermitage Miss Hobson, becomes, even before his second marriage, 'an awakened man': *awakened* being used in the theological sense (*OED awaken* 5) of 'roused to a sense of sin'.

The novelist is sardonic about this word elsewhere: Amelia Sedley, on going to bed for the first time after joining George's regiment, is given three tracts by the pious Mrs Kirk, 'bent upon *awakening* her before she slept' (*VF* p. 259). The weekly worship of the house at Clapham is described: 'On a Sunday (which good old Saxon word was scarcely known at the Hermitage) the household marched away in separate couples or groups ... each to *sit under* his or her favourite minister.' The word preferred to the native *Sunday* is of course *Sabbath* which, from the Hebrew root *shabath* 'to rest', suggests the restrictions associated with that day in the household. In England, the *OED* informs us, *Sabbath* as a synonym for *Sunday* did not become common till the seventeenth century; though the transference of the word for the Jewish rest day ('The seventh day is the Sabbath of the Lord thy God', Exodus xx 10) to the day of the Resurrection ('The first day of the week cometh Mary Magdalene early', John xx 1) is much earlier. To *sit under* here has the special sense (*OED sit* 28) of 'to listen to, attend the church of' (a particular preacher). When Mrs Newcome reconsiders a meeting she has just attended 'where a delightful Hebrew convert had spoken, oh! so *graciously*!' we are to take *graciously* to mean 'by means of divine grace' (*OED graciously* 3), though the Dictionary last illustrates this meaning of the adverb from *Measure for Measure*. It is also in its special Nonconformist usage, in this same second chapter of *The Newcomes*, that the word *meeting* occurs (*OED meeting* 3b) for 'an assembly gathered for the purposes of religious worship'. This the *OED* describes as now rare, except with reference to Quakers; and it also draws our attention to the frequent omission of the article when this noun follows a preposition. All this, needless to say, Thackeray has observed:

> Mr Newcome, with his little boy ... met Miss Hobson as she was coming *out of meeting* one Sunday ... the next Sunday [Newcome] was *at meeting*. (*N* I ch. 2)

Young Tom, later Colonel Newcome, cannot maintain such high standards of conduct, and is sent to India: 'It was not possible that such a *castaway* as this should continue in a house where her two little cherubs were growing up in innocence and grace' (*N* I ch. 2). *Castaway* echoes St Paul in his First Epistle to Corinthians ix 27.

One cannot categorically say, of course, that older meanings of words and expressions, whether religious or secular, are even now entirely obsolete; one finds a tendency to be consciously formal and accordingly somewhat old-fashioned in later writers. Henry James and Ivy Compton-Burnett are especially fond of recalling earlier significances in vocabulary. In *The Portrait of a Lady*, for instance, one comes upon expressions like 'his being *by character* and in fact a mover of men' (ch. 13); 'He neither blushed . . . nor looked *conscious*' (ch. 44); and James speaks of the *inmates* of Gardencourt, the Touchetts' country house (ch. 19); and of biased motives as *interested views* (ch. 10). It is only rarely, in fact, that one comes, in Thackeray, upon a word that is so archaic as to be incomprehensible, and therefore to qualify as obsolete. But such, perhaps, are *outcry* for 'auction' (see p. 130), and *notable* used of women in the sense of 'capable in household management, contriving': 'She instructed her daughters how to bear poverty cheerfully, and invented a thousand *notable* methods to conceal or evade it' (*VF* p. 385) – it seems, by the way, that in this sense the word was pronounced with a short [o]. Perhaps also the 'somewhat facetious' use of *to discuss* in the sense of 'to consume (food or drink)' (*OED discuss* 8) is confusing to today's reader: 'Mr Chaplain was back again bawling for another bottle. This *discussed*, they joined the ladies' (*V* I ch. 15).

Other out-of-mode, or at least old-fashioned, usage includes *absent* in the sense of 'absent-minded', *mother-in-law* in the sense of 'step-mother' and *milliner* (originally 'purveyor of goods from Milan') in the sense of 'one who sells women's finery', but not necessarily headgear (usage found also in Trollope: Clark, p. 77):

'I am too *absent*,' Arthur said with a laugh, 'to drive a cab in London.' (*P* II ch. 23)

You silly, blind creature – if anything happens to Lady Crawley, Miss Sharp will be your *mother-in-law*. (*VF* p. 135)

The most brilliant costume. . . . A score of years hence that, too, that *milliner's* wonder, will have passed into the domain of the absurd. (*VF* p. 461)

One curious and quite common use is that of the verb *to dodge* meaning not, as now, 'to avoid' but 'to dog, to follow stealthily, perhaps with shifts to avoid discovery' (*OED dodge* v. 4):

Mr Foker began to *dodge* Miss Amory through London. (*P* II ch. 2)

Why are you following me about? . . . I don't choose to be *dodged* about in this way. (*P* II ch. 24)

He took two pistols out of his pocket . . . and said, from the other end of the table where he stood *dodging* me, as it were, – 'Advance a step and I send this bullet into your brains!' (*BL* ch. 5)

Some of the ideas of avoidance now inseparable from the verb *to dodge* are assigned, in Thackeray's language, to the verb *to shirk*:

I made for the door, but Macshane held me and said, 'Major, you are not going to *shirk* him, sure?' (*C* ch. 5)

Sam Newcome, who was *shirking* from his sister and his mamma. (*N* II ch. 16)

He and his comrades had been obliged to *shirk* on board at night, to escape from their wives. (*P* II ch. 22)

There are interesting idiosyncrasies in the use of the expression *don't care*. As the *OED* explains (*care* v. 4), in negative constructions *not to care* passes from the sense of 'not to trouble oneself' to those of 'not to mind, not to pay any deference or attention, to pay no respect, be indifferent'. One sees the transition by comparing the first two and the last three instances here:

I was tired and *did not care* to go further. (*BL* ch. 6)

There had been little love between her and the child. He *did not care* to show much grief. (*VF* p. 548)

I took all his money and clothes – I *don't care* to conceal it. (*BL* ch. 5)

'*I don't care* about owning it,' Waterloo Sedley would say to his friends, 'I am a dressy man.' (*VF* p. 570)

And they will be down on me. But *I don't care* to prevent it: I'm used to it. (*P* II ch. 24)

As John W. Clark puts it (see p. 76), a naive reader of our time would seriously misunderstand novelists like Trollope and Thackeray in one particular: our age, over-preoccupied with the subject of sex, has given explicit sexual meaning to certain phrases which in earlier periods did not carry these suggestions. Such a phrase is *to make love*. Even when Barry Lyndon says 'I had *made a very deep love* to her during my stay under her roof' (*BL* ch. 5), this would not be taken by Victorian readers as including sexual intercourse. So, too, when Becky disillusions Amelia about her dead husband George: 'He used to sneer about you to me, time after time; and *made love* to me the week after he married you' (*VF* p. 658); and similarly, as the circumstances indicate, in this passage from *Lovel the Widower*: 'There was Dick . . . actually *making love* to her over the prostrate body of the Captain' (*LW* ch. 5). *Passionate*, too, is a word now liable to be confined to amorous contexts, and not to refer to the emotion of anger: '*Passionate* little Lady Fanny, if she had not good cards, flung hers into Lady Mary's face' (*FG* p. 38).

Sexual innuendoes do occur, however; in fact, Thackeray became expert at circumventing the inhibitions of his time in such matters. We shall see in discussing *Esmond* that a broken-off sentence is a favourite device. Instances are to be found in other novels also:

> His father's evident liking for Miss Sharp had not escaped him. He knew the old gentleman's character well; and a more unscrupulous old – whyou – he did not conclude the sentence, (*VF* p. 133)

Favourite imagery to touch on forbidden subjects is apt to be either reptilian or fishy:

> Faugh! there is more than one woman we see in society smiling about from house to house, pleasant and sentimental and *formosa superne* enough; but I fancy a fish's tail is flapping under her fine flounces and a forked fin at the end of it! (*N* I ch. 36)

> 'I am innocent, Rawdon,' she said, 'before God, I am innocent.' She clung hold of his coat, of his hands; her own were all covered with *serpents*, and rings, and baubles. (*VF* p. 515; also pp. 432, 617)

Nevertheless, as Thackeray was to lament more than once (see pp. 172–4), the freedom of the eighteenth-century novelist in such matters was denied to the writer of early Victorian times.

CHAPTER 3

Slang

𝕊𝕊𝕊𝕊𝕊𝕊

IN the first half of the nineteenth century the lowly and disreputable associations of the word *slang* were more to the fore than
they are now, and it occurred more often in contexts where social
and even moral condemnation was implied. Thus the lubricious
clergyman, Hunt, one of the villains in *Philip*, 'garnished his
conversation with slippery double-entendre and dirty old-world
slang' (*Ph* I ch. 10). Given the contrast between Regency and
Victorian England, *old-world* could here imply 'salacious' and
'indecent' – it is the kind of contrast that is fully canvassed in *The
Four Georges*. Used attributively, the word could have similar
connotations: Hunt is referred to elsewhere in the same chapter
as 'the *slang* parson'.[1] The sense of abusive and quite probably
obscene language derives partly from the verb *to slang*, meaning
'to hurl abuse' (*OED slang* v. 3, 'to rail in abusive or vulgar
language'); nor must we ignore the possible etymological connection with the verb *to sling*, meaning 'to throw with a loose
movement of the arm'. In the twenty-third chapter of *The Book
of Snobs*, entitled 'English Snobs on the Continent', the 'English
Raff Snob' speaks French 'with *slang* familiarity', and is heard also
'startling the midnight echoes of quiet Continental towns' with
'shrieks of English *slang*'.

Even in exclusively male company, on formal occasions, slang
expressions are apt to be introduced apologetically:

---

[1] With a weaker, but nevertheless still pejorative, use of the word, Queen Victoria
wrote on the subject of dress to the Prince of Wales in 1857:

> We do not wish to control your own tastes and fancies, which, on the contrary,
> we wish you to indulge and develop, but we do expect that you will never wear
> anything extravagant or *slang*, not because we don't like it, but because it would
> prove a want of self-respect and be an offence against decency, leading – as it
> has often done in others – to an indifference to what is morally wrong.

(Quoted by Sir Philip Magnus, *King Edward the Seventh*, London, 1964, p. 41.)

Mr Van John, whose health was drunk as representative of the
British Turf . . . said that he had never known anything about
the turf or about play, until their old schoolfellow, his dear
friend – his *swell* friend, if he might be permitted the expression
– Mr Ringwood, taught him the use of cards. (*Ph* II ch. 21)

Colonel Newcome, of the older generation, is amused as well as
puzzled by the slang of the younger men:

'Am I to understand, Colonel Newcome,' says Mr Frederick
Bayham, 'that you are related to the eminent banker, Sir Brian
Newcome, who gives such uncommonly swell parties in Park
Lane?'
'What is a *swell party*?' asks the Colonel, laughing. (*N* I ch. 12)

It was expected of ladies, especially, that they should not only
eschew the most vulgar language, but be ignorant of it. Mrs
Pendennis and Laura, for example, do not fully appreciate Pen's
praises of 'the Fotheringay' taking the part of Mrs Haller:

'And Mrs Haller?' said Mrs Pendennis.
'She's a *stunner*, ma'am,' Pen said, laughing, and using the
words of his revered friend, Mr Foker.
'A what, Arthur?' asked the lady.
'What is a stunner, Arthur?' cried Laura, in the same voice.
(*P* I ch. 5)

It is clear that a lady's speech, like a lady's virtue, must be guarded.
Given the increased refinement of early Victorian times, it is
sometimes the younger generation of ladies, with superior
education, who are called upon to assert standards, as with
Blanche Amory and her vulgar mother, Lady Clavering:

'Yes, Lady Rockminster has took us up,' said Lady Clavering.
'Taken us up, Mamma,' cried Blanche, in a shrill voice.
. . . 'I always think a dinner's the best the second day,' said
Lady Clavering, thinking to mend her first speech. 'On the 14th
we'll be quite a *snug little party*;' at which second blunder, Miss
Blanche clasped her hands in despair, and said, 'O, Mamma,
vous êtes incorrigible.' (*P* I ch. 37)

There is evidence, too, that men found slang in women unacceptable. Even Foker, the friend of Arthur Pendennis and, as we shall
see, a promoter and even an inventor of substandard expressions,

draws the line at slangy 'chaff' from his lady friends: 'The way in which that Pinckney talks slang is quite disgusting. I hate chaff in a woman' (*P* II ch. 2).

Pendennis appeared from 1848 to 1850, and seems to reflect the early Victorian attitude to unrefined language from women fairly faithfully. But there is some evidence[1] that, as the century proceeded, slang from the lips of ladies was becoming less unacceptable. In an amusing *Roundabout Paper* entitled 'On a Peal of Bells', Thackeray 'up-dates' a passage from Fanny Burney's *Evelina*, first re-printing the passage (vol. III letter xv), and then contrasting it with the way the story might be told by a heroine of the time of the *Papers* (1860–3):

> 'And here, whilst I was looking for the books, I was followed by Lord Orville. He shut the door after he came in, and approaching me with a look of anxiety, said, 'Is this true, Miss Anville – are you going?'
>
> 'I believe so, my lord,' said I, still looking for the books. 'So suddenly, so unexpectedly: must I lose you?'
>
> 'No great loss, my lord,' said I, endeavouring to speak cheerfully.
>
> 'Is it possible,' said he gravely, 'Miss Anville can doubt my sincerity?'
>
> 'I can't imagine,' cried I, 'what Mrs Selwyn has done with those books.'
>
> 'Would to heaven,' continued he, 'I might flatter myself you would allow me to prove it!'
>
> 'I must run upstairs,' cried I, greatly confused, 'and ask what she has done with them.'
>
> 'You are going then,' cried he, taking my hand, 'and you give me not the smallest hope of any return! Will you not, my too lovely friend, will you not teach me, with fortitude like your own, to support your absence?'

Thackeray's version runs:

> Whilst I was looking for the books, Lord Orville came in. He looked uncommonly down in the mouth, as he said: 'Is this

---

1 For the use of colloquialisms by ladies of Trollope's novels, see Clark, pp. 49–52. A character like Lily Dale in *The Small House at Allington* makes use of slang expressions with the evident approval of her creator, if not of the ladies with whom she associates.

true, Miss Anville; are you going to cut?'
'To absquatulate, Lord Orville,' said I, still pretending that I
was looking for the books.
'You're very quick about it,' said he.
'Guess it's no great loss,' I remarked, as cheerfully as I could.
'You don't think I'm chaffing?' said Orville, with much
emotion.
'What has Mrs Selwyn done with the books?' I went on.
'What going?' said he, 'and going for good? I wish I was such
a good-plucked one as you, Miss Anville.'

Even in early Victorian times, however, fashionable ladies always
had their own kind of informal speech, the kind that Thackeray
sometimes refers to as *jargon*. It was the sort of sophisticated talk
they shared with the denizens of Mayfair: 'that darling London
jargon, so dear and indispensable to London people, so little
understood by persons out of the world' (*P* II ch. 25). In this
there seems to have been a reduced element of slang, but a
larger number of affected French phrases. In the novels of Jane
Austen, the town-bred Mary Crawford (in *Mansfield Park*) and
Mrs Elton (in *Emma*) had both been prone to the affectation of
foreign phrases in conversation. Here, continuing this tradition, is
'Mrs Rawdon Crawley' at the celebrated ball given in Brussels on
the eve of Waterloo (but, for our purposes, she effectively
represents the over-sophisticated metropolitan lady of the 1840s):

> Mrs Rawdon ran and greeted affectionately her dearest Amelia,
> and began forthwith to patronize her. She found fault with her
> friend's dress, and her hair-dresser, and wondered how she
> could be so *chaussée*, and vowed that she must send her *corsetière*
> the next morning. ... It is a fact, that in a fortnight ... this
> young woman had got up the genteel *jargon* so well, that a
> native could not speak it better; and it was only from her
> French being so good, that you could know she was not a
> born woman of fashion. (*VF* p. 277)

Ethel Newcome, in *The Newcomes*, against her better nature,
adopts similar *jargon*:

> Ethel had been crying when I went into the room ... but she
> looked up ... began to laugh and rattle, would talk about
> nothing but Lady Hautbois' great breakfast the day before,

and the most insufferable Mayfair *jargon*; and then declared it was time to go home to dress for Mrs Booth's *déjeuner*. (*N* II ch. 12)

The distinction between this kind of *jargon* and male *slang* is nicely shown when the 'fast' young James Crawley, with his sporting tastes, is introduced into the sophisticated society of old Miss Crawley, and finds himself tongue-tied 'in a house full of old women, jabbering French . . . to him. "Regularly up a tree, by jingo!" exclaimed the modest boy . . . whereas, put him at Iffley Lock, and he would *out-slang* the boldest barge-man' (*VF* p. 331). A disparaging word for the more desultory form of this *jargon* seems to have been *slipslop*: ultimately emanating, doubtless, from Mrs Slipslop in Fielding's *Joseph Andrews*: 'that easy, fashionable *slipslop* which has so much effect upon certain folks of small breeding.' This was Becky Sharp's style of speech at Boulogne, after her downfall, which she used to impress her fellow-exiles with her former London acquaintance (*VF* p. 619). So, too, Mrs Frederick Bullock entertained Amelia 'with fashionable fiddle faddle and feeble Court *slipslop*' (*VF* p. 594).

But, although occasional instances of substandard language are found in the speech of ladies, there is no doubt that in the nineteenth century the most outspoken slang, like the broadest dialect, is a male prerogative. Eric Partridge has demonstrated, for example, the connection between English slang and games and sports of all kinds; and Thackeray's novels, which in this respect owe much to the masculine tradition in the English novel of Fielding and Smollett, amply bear this out: as when, for example, a schoolboy is described in *Pendennis* as 'a butt or *cockshy*', from the barbarous sport of throwing missiles at cocks (*P* I ch. 3); or when young Lord Kew, in *The Newcomes*, observes that 'Lady Kew still *pulls stroke-oar* in our boat' (*N* I ch. 30), meaning that she has a controlling influence in the family; or when those who follow the fortunes of prizefighters are referred to by the Regency colloquialism 'the fancy': 'Mr William Ramm, known to *the fancy* as the Tutbury Pet' (*BS* ch. 14). It was particularly Thackeray's skilful deployment of manly slang that David Masson praised in a review of *Pendennis* in the *North British Review* of May 1851 (*Heritage*, p. 112):

In the ease, and, at the same time, thorough polish and propriety with which Mr Thackeray can use slang words, we seem especially to detect the University man. *Snob, swell, buck, gent, fellow, fogey* – these, and many more such expressive appellatives, not yet sanctioned by the Dictionary, Mr Thackeray employs more frequently, we believe, than any other living author, and yet always with unexceptionable taste. In so doing, he is conscious, no doubt, of the same kind of security that permits Oxford and Cambridge men, and even, as we can testify, Oxford and Cambridge clergymen, to season their conversation with similar words – namely, the evident air of educated manliness with which they can be introduced, and which, however rough the guise, no one can mistake.

Masson goes on to admire the 'unconscious ease' with which Thackeray deals with all ranks of society without either 'seeming a tufthunter' or showing any of the 'affectation of Radicalism'. Certainly, so far as easy and uninhibited employment of different speech-levels are concerned, his novels compare very favourably with nearly all the many (mostly ill-informed) articles on slang in Victorian periodicals. Most of these list 'fast' words and phrases with an air of dare-devil naughtiness, and then go on to condemn them, with Pecksniffian horror, as slovenly and barbarous. (There was always, of course, the consideration that by first discussing and then deploring slang words, the 'penny-a-liner' might produce twice as much copy!) Thackeray, in contrast, simply observes the fact of slang; he acknowledges that *vox populi*, or popular usage, is the real arbiter of the matter:

A youth . . . now appeared before him in one of those costumes to which the public consent, which I take to be as influential as Johnson's Dictionary, has accorded the title of 'swell'. (*P* I ch. 3)

Indeed, he welcomes new colloquialisms into the language:

The honest habitués . . . have many harmless arts . . . and innocent '*dodges*' (if we may be permitted to use an excellent phrase that has become vernacular since the appearance of the last dictionaries). (*P* I ch. 29)

This is not to say, however, that he would agree with the levelling assertion of Fred Vincy in *Middlemarch* (ch. 11): 'All choice of words is slang . . . Correct English is the slang of prigs who write history and essays. And the strongest slang of all is the slang of poets.' Thackeray was too fond of running up and down the gamut of registers, too well aware of the comic effect that contrasted speech-levels can produce, ever to agree with this. Thus he sometimes underlines the comedy by embedding vulgar expressions in grandiloquent contexts:

> Nor could George Robert, Earl of Gravesend and Rosherville, ever forget that on one evening when he condescended to play at billiards with his nephew, that young gentleman poked his Lordship in the side with his cue, and said 'Well, old cock, I've seen many a bad stroke in my life, but I never saw such a bad one as that there.' (*P* II ch. 1)

> The attack was so sharp that Matilda – as his reverence expressed it – was very nearly 'off the hooks'. (*VF* p. 130)

> Cinqbars was filled with a longing to go and see his old friend Brandon, and determined, to use his own elegant words, 'to knock the old buck up.' (*SGS* ch. 7)

Again, when Harry Foker asks Pen the question 'Is your Mamma acquainted with your absence?' in the fifth chapter of *Pendennis*, we are to take it as a sesquipedalian rendering of the current catchphrase, duly recorded in the third: ' "His mother knows he's out, sir," Mr Foker remarked; "don't she, Pendennis?" '

If men sometimes objected to women's use of slang, there were a great many more retaliatory remarks from the ladies. An early objector to slang in nineteenth-century fiction had been Marianne Dashwood, who was annoyed by Sir John Middleton's expression 'to set your cap at a man': 'I abhor every commonplace phrase by which wit is intended; and "setting one's cap at a man" or "making a conquest" are the most odious of all. Their tendency is gross and illiberal' (*Sense and Sensibility*, ch. 9). No doubt Marianne would also have objected, as Thackeray intends that his readers, in a milder way, should, when subjects as sacred to the Victorians as courtship and marriage are spoken of in 'illiberal' slang by rumbustious, insensitive characters like Harry Foker and Mr Frederick Bullock:

> 'When you're of a proper age, you'll marry Lady Ann.'
> 'Well, sir, if Ann's agreeable, *I say ditto*. She's not a bad-looking girl.' (*P* II ch. 1)

Frederick insisted that the half of the old gentleman's property should be settled upon his Maria, and indeed for a long time, refused '*to come to the scratch*' (it was Mr Frederick's own expression) on any other terms. (*VF* p. 412)

The counting-house cliché of Foker here, and Bullock's inappropriate sporting metaphor (whether from cricket or boxing – see *OED scratch* n. 5) are quoted against them, and also against the mercenary basis of many marriages of the day.

An example of this disregard of finer feelings that occurs in many Victorian novels is the habit that young men had throughout the century (and indeed earlier – see *OED filly* 2) of referring to young ladies as if they were horseflesh. Rawdon Crawley's first reaction to Becky is 'By Jove, she's a neat little *filly*' (*VF* p. 101). Ethel Newcome, too, is sometimes discussed in terms of horse racing: 'For the last three months Miss Newcome has been . . . the winning horse. . . . You think it is wicked in me to . . . say that your heart's darling is . . . being paced up and down the Mayfair market to be taken away by the best bidder' (*N* II ch. 3).

A great opponent of such insensitivity in male slang is Laura Pendennis, née Bell. She appears not only in *Pendennis*, but also participates in the narrative and the action of both *The Newcomes* and *Philip*. In the course of the three novels she is transformed from a rather naive and spiritless girl into what for the modern reader (though Thackeray may not have intended this) represents the worst type of tyrannical Victorian wife and mother. She ranges from mild, if rather arch, jesting on the subject:

'Sir,' said she, 'when you were so wild – so *spoony*, I think is your elegant word – about Blanche, and used to put letters into a hollow tree for her. . . . ' (*Ph* I ch. 18)

to a deeper probing of the whole question, accusing those who use slang of cowardice as well as coarseness: the 'most sacred subject of all' she mentions here is marriage for love, as against marriage for wealth to – of all things – a rich half-caste, the 'tawny Woolcomb':

Oh for shame, Pen, no levity on this – no sneers and laughter on this the most sacred subject of all. . . . You are . . . cynical . . ., and you carry your lantern dark, It is not right to '*put your oar in*' as you say in your jargon (and even your slang is a sort of cowardice, sir, for you are afraid to speak the feelings of your heart): – it is not right to meddle and speak the truth, not right to rescue a poor soul who is drowning – of course not. . . . That is the language of the world, baby darling. (*Ph* I ch. 13)

That the more extreme colloquialisms have a brief life we can also illustrate from Thackeray, as one expression appears hard at the heels of another in the quest for novelty. Helen Pendennis, as we have seen, has to inquire the meaning of the word *stunner*; but meanwhile, her son's generation has moved on. *Stunner* is inadequate, after all, to describe the charms of the Fotheringay:

'I say, Pen, isn't she a stunner?' asked Mr Foker. . . . 'She is a *crusher*, ain't she now?' (*P* I ch. 4)

Indeed, it requires some effort to keep up with Foker. Though no scholar, he is, as he says himself, 'rather downy', that is, wide-awake, 'knowing'. It is he who introduces Pen to the new university meaning of the originally slang word *coach*: 'to prepare, or one who prepares, a person for examinations by intensive teaching'. The first *OED* example of the noun (*coach* n. 3) is from 1848 (Clough's *Bothie*)[1]. The verb (*coach* v. 3), first illustrated in the *OED* from *Pendennis*, occurs in fact a little earlier, in *Vanity Fair*. Clearly the word was in the air, and Thackeray was recording, faithfully as usual, and not inventing. But perhaps the synonym *drag* (implying a heavier kind of wheeled vehicle, in the first place – *OED* *drag* n. 1d) used metaphorically in the same sense, is a tribute to Foker's inventiveness, and his creator's:

The superb Cuff himself . . . helped him on with his Latin verses; '*coached*' him in play-hours. (*VF* p. 51)

'He was blowed if he didn't think Pen was such a flat as not to know what *coaching* meant.'
'I'm come down with a *coach* from Oxbridge. A tutor, don't you see, old boy? He's coaching me, and some other men, for the little-go. Me and Spavin have the *drag* between us.' (*P* I ch. 3)

---

1 The word had occurred in 1841 in a letter from Oxford by Thomas Hughes' brother, George: 'Men reading for honours now generally employ a "coach". If you will condescend to be my coach, I will try to answer to the whip to the best of my power'. Thomas Hughes, *Memoir of a Brother*, London, 1873, p. 62.

Even so, it is characteristic both of Foker, and of the nature of slang, that next day, when Pen meets him again, he has moved on to a further variant:

> 'She sent me down here with a *grinder*. She wants me to cultivate my neglected genius.' (*P* I ch. 5)

Grinder, though now, and possibly then, less acceptable than *coach*, appears to be the earlier term in this sense (*OED grinder* 5). *Coach* has for most people ceased to be slang entirely, although I am reliably informed that it is still unacceptable in Oxford, *private tutor* being the official term.

As a further instance of the way slang words rapidly change in meaning, usage and currency, we might consider the word *ticket*. From the original meaning of a short written notice or label, it had come, among other uses, to be a regular late eighteenth-century word for a visiting-card. A character in Fanny Burney's *Cecilia* (1782) says, 'Why, a *ticket* is only a visiting card, with a name upon it; but we call them all tickets now' (ch. 3). The word has this meaning in Jane Austen and, very occasionally, in Thackeray. Major Pendennis, however, trying to keep abreast of the young, attempts the latest colloquialism:

> 'We shall only have to leave our *pasteboards*, Arthur.' He used the word '*pasteboards*', having heard it from some of the ingenious youth of the nobility about town, and as a modern phrase suited to Pen's tender years. (*P* I ch. 36)

Old and new variants occur in this passage from *Philip*:

> Has it ever happened to you to leave a *card* at that house – that house which was once *the* house – almost your own? . . . And now your friendship has dwindled to a little bit of *pasteboard*, shed once a year, and poor dear Mrs Jones (it is with J you have quarrelled) still calls on the ladies of your family and slips her husband's *ticket* upon the hall table. (*Ph* I ch. 13)

Meanwhile, *ticket* itself appears in a more abstract context. Mr Woodhouse's phrase, used of Frank Churchill, 'That young man is *not quite the thing*' (*Emma* ch. 29), has before mid century acquired a significant variant. Embarrassment, and the need to dispel embarrassment by an atmosphere of increasing intimacy that colloquial language induces, is a frequent source of slang. Thus the mixture of vagueness and discomposure which is felt in attempting to define what makes for ineligibility in the best society results in the early Victorian embroidery of 'not the thing' into 'not the ticket':

> 'And so about Aunt Maria, she's very handsome and she's very finely dressed, only somehow she's not – she's *not the ticket*, you see.'
> 'Oh, she's not the ticket?' says the Colonel much amused.
> 'Well, what I mean is – but never mind,' says the boy, 'I can't tell you what I mean.' (*N* I ch. 7)

The speaker here is Clive Newcome, as a schoolboy. As we shall see, Thackeray makes effective use of schoolboy slang. But children are sometimes in a state of blissful ignorance regarding grown-up slang: young Georgy Osborne is confused by the dialogue of Becky Sharp's unscrupulous friends at Ostend:

> 'What can they mean?' asked Georgy, who did not like these gentlemen. 'I heard the Major say to Mrs Crawley yesterday, "No, no, Becky, you shan't keep the old buck to yourself. We must have the bones in, or dammy, I'll split." What could the Major mean, Mamma?' (*VF* p. 657)

The childhood of Becky Sharp, however, has been less sheltered. She has 'the dismal precocity of poverty' (*VF* p. 21), and by the time she takes her first post as governess at Queen's Crawley she is able to explain in a letter to her friend Amelia any colloquialisms that may occur:

> This gentleman and the guard seemed to know Sir Pitt very well, and laughed at him a great deal. They both agreed in calling him an *old screw*; which means a very stingy avaricious person. (*VF* p. 75)

Schoolboy slang is employed most tellingly in *The Newcomes*. Charterhouse, or Grey Friars as it becomes in the novels, was the school which Thackeray himself attended. Consequently, he makes Arthur Pendennis, Colonel and Clive Newcome, and Philip Firmin into Carthusians. The founder of Charterhouse had provided both a school for boys and a hostel for elderly and destitute pensioners. Colonel Newcome, after the ruin of his fortunes, becomes one of the latter – one of the *codds*, as the boys call them: *Codd Colonel*, in fact [N II ch. 42). *Tibbing out* was another Carthusian expression, with the meaning 'going out of bounds': '*Tibbing out*, and receiving the penalty therefor' (N I ch. 2). A few pages before the end of the novel, the Colonel, whose mind is wandering, recalls the custom of *tibbing out*, and of answering 'Adsum' to one's name at roll-call. All this is by way of preparation for one of the most famous in the long roll-call of Victorian death-bed scenes:

> And just as the last bell struck, a peculiar sweet smile shone over his face, and he lifted up his head a little, and quickly said 'Adsum!' . . . and lo, he, whose heart was as that of a little child, had answered to his name, and stood in the presence of The Master (N II ch. 42)

Thackeray observes the language of the young closely. As a youth Clive Newcome, for example, frequently uses the expression *that's all*, by way of adding extra emphasis to his statements. It is an idiom peculiar to schoolboys and minors, and Clive does not use it when he becomes a man:

> Wasn't Reynolds a clipper? *that's all*! and wasn't Rubens a brick? (N I ch. 12)

> 'Mr Smee, you are looking at my picture of "Boadishia",' says Gandish. Wouldn't he have caught it for his quantities at Grey Friars, *that's all*? (N I ch. 17)

And neither, presumably, would young Georgy Osborne, had we been permitted to see him grow up a man in his father's footsteps:

> When I'm in the army, won't I hate the French? – *that's all*. (VF p. 653)

A similar interrogative collocation, from children, can sometimes be followed by an enclitic *though*:

> Oh, grandma! don't he *though*? And wasn't there a row at the 'Star and Garter'; and didn't Pa pay uncle Clarence's bill there, *though*? (LW ch. 3)

Comparable status should be assigned to Clive Newcome's *no end of*, meaning 'a great many': '*No end of* handsome shops; *no end of* famous people' (N I ch. 22); to his verb *to prig* meaning 'to steal', originally thieves' cant: 'I used to *prig* things out of the dishes . . . but I'm past that now' (*N* I ch. 7); to Georgy Osborne's *prime*, meaning 'first-rate': 'And I say, Dob, how *prime* it would be to have you for my uncle' (*VF* p. 589); to the expressions *a oner* and *twice of* in the following: 'You should see her eat; she is such *a oner* at eating . . . she had *twice of soup* . . . and then *twice of fish*' (*Ph* II ch. 16); and to the following idiom: 'He tried to look knowing over the Latin grammar when little Rawdon showed him what part of that work he was "in".' (*VF* p. 504).

In addition, grown-ups used, and still use, childish words by a 'playful or familiar meiosis', as the *OED* puts it (*toddle* v. 2b), as slang in grown-up situations. Bertie Wooster's *to toddle* for 'to walk', for example, had already occurred in Thackeray: 'Foker said . . . that it was time to "*toddle*" ' (*P* I ch. 4). Comparable with this is 'poor Rawdon's' name for the watch he disposes of before Waterloo: *a ticker* (*VF* p. 286). With *toddle* for 'to walk' we can also compare Foker's *to tool*, meaning 'to drive'. 'I thought I'd just *tool* over, and go to the play' (*P* I ch. 3). It shows the way Thackeray was associated in the public mind with the successful exploitation of substandard language, that when A. J. Munby happened to catch sight of the novelist in London in 1862, the year before he died, the slang word *tool* immediately suggested itself to him (though he seems to use it in the sense of 'walking' – see *OED Supp.* s.v. *tool*):

> Near S. Martin's Lane, I met W. M. Thackeray; '*tooling*' along quietly, alone, with hands in pockets and absent air; evidently on his way to the Garrick. *Munby, Man of Two Worlds*, (ed. D. Hudson, London, 1972, p. 116)

Thackeray was a Cambridge man himself, though he left before taking a degree; but he resorts to both Oxford and Cambridge for the purpose of educating the young men in his novels. Henry Esmond studies at Thackeray's old college, Trinity; but young James Crawley is an Oxonian, going, in his own words, to 'the other shop' (*VF* p. 331). As for Pen, he is educated at *Oxbridge* on the *Camisis* river (*P* I ch. 20), though he later has a friend who is a *Camford* man (*P* II ch. 14). I suspect that *Oxbridge*, the only one of these blends or portmanteau words to be perpetuated, may be Thackeray's coinage. It is possible, too, that he favoured *skip*, a word specifically associated (*OED skip* n. 3) with Trinity College,

Dublin, for a college attendant, because it happened to be a blend of Oxford *scout* and Cambridge *gyp*. At all events, when Pen first entered St Boniface's College at Oxbridge, 'Davis, the *skip* or attendant, led the way' (*P* I ch. 17). The slang expression 'to *sport* a door', earlier 'to *sport oak* or *timber*' (*OED sport* v. 11), meaning 'to shut a door from the inside, as a sign that one is engaged or does not wish to be intruded on', is originally University usage: 'He had courage enough to resist them . . . and go home to Strong, and "*sport*" the outer door of the chambers' (*P* II ch. 22). By the time of *Philip* the characteristic mid-Victorian use of *wine* for an undergraduate wine-party had arrived: 'They met at a *wine* in my rooms in Corpus' (*Ph* I ch. 7). A University slang word of fairly frequent occurrence is *tuft*, meaning an under-graduate at Oxford or Cambridge who wears a tuft or gold tassel in his cap, signifying that he is a peer or the eldest son of a peer: 'The same man we remember at Oxbridge, when he was truckling to the *tufts*' (*P* II ch. 23). Hence the word *tufthunter* (*N* II ch. 7), for a toady or sycophant.

From freemasonry comes the slang expression *tiled*, from the figurative use of the man who tiles a house, the *tiler*, as the keeper of the uninitiated from intruding into the secrecy of the Lodge. *Tiled*, accordingly, means 'bound to secrecy': 'I . . . was going to say that I didn't know one word about all these matters . . . when the Major . . . said . . . "Come, come, Snob, my boy, we are all *tiled*, you know" ' (*BS* ch. 25).

Thackeray is particularly good at portraying young bucks, ne'er-do-wells, sharpers, and men-about-town. He might well have remained such a man himself, if he had not lost most of his money at the age of twenty-two, through the failure of Indian investments. Such men are often trendsetters in slang and, as we shall see, are often awarded slang surnames. Theirs is a world where, in the parlance of the time, 'the rooks' are always preying on 'the pigeons', 'the sharps' on 'the flats' or 'the spooneys'. This last word for a simpleton is very common: Dobbin, in *Vanity Fair*, qualifies for the epithet: 'This history has been written to very little purpose if the reader has not perceived that the Major was a *spooney*' (*VF* p. 641). It is often not profitable to speculate on the etymology of slang words, but George Eliot offers a suggestion for the origin of this one that is tempting, if only for its implications about the nature of slang in general. Writing of 'horsey' men generally, she comments: 'To get all the advantage of being with men of this sort, you must know how to draw your inferences, and not be a *spoon* who takes things literally' (*Middle-march* ch. 23). So, in the hands of an expert like Foker, slang can add both metaphor and subtlety, embroidering and refining on simple meaning in a way that it is not altogether far-fetched to compare with the blank verse of the dramatic poet. Here he takes up the embarrassing point that the Costigans are not an eligible family connection for the Pendennis family, from a hint of the Major's:

> 'I think you seem tolerably wideawake, too, Mr Foker,' Pendennis said, laughing.
> 'Pretty well, thank you, sir – how are you?' Foker replied imperturbably. 'I'm not clever, p'raps, but I *am* rather downy; and partial friends say I know what's o'clock tolerably well. Can I tell you the time of day in any way?'
> 'Upon my word,' the Major answered, quite delighted, 'I think you may be of very great service to me. You are a young man of the world, and with such one likes to deal. And as such I need not inform you that our family is by no means delighted at this absurd intrigue in which Arthur is engaged.'
> 'I should rather think not,' said Mr Foker. 'Connection not eligible. Too much beer drunk on the premises. No Irish need apply. That I take to be your meaning.' (*P* I ch. 10)

Men of Foker's type are not usually teetotallers. After many a *drain* or drink (*N* II ch. 9), they might *beat up the quarters* of their friends (*N* I ch. 8) or 'visit them unceremoniously' as the OED defines the phrase (*beat* v. 28), and *buzz* a few *bottles* (*VF* p. 332), that is, finish them to the last drop; doubtless smoking a few *weeds* (*BS* ch. 41), cigars or cheroots, the while. Soon their gait would become unsteady; they would begin to lurch or *pitch*: 'When I begin to talk too much,' says a character in *Pendennis*, '. . . when I begin to *pitch*, I authorize you . . . to put away the brandy-bottle' (*P* II ch. 22).[1] A danger was that a man in this condition would have too much to say; and there would be those ready to *trot him out*, to draw him out in conversation so as to make him appear

---

1 Here I follow the OED (*pitch* v. 19d), where this quotation occurs: but just conceivably *pitch* may here be an intransitive instance of the meaning of OED 17d signifying 'to tell (a yarn or tale)'.

ridiculous or compromise him. So, despite his protests, young James Crawley is outwitted by his more sober cousin Pitt Crawley, and loses his wealthy aunt's favour: 'No trying it on on me. You want to *trot* me *out*, but it's no go. In vino veritas, old boy' (*VF* p. 333). The outcome, doubtless, was frequently that the drinker would finish by being 'pretty considerably *sewn up*' (*SGS* ch. 1), or 'devilish *cut*' (*P* II ch. 12), both phrases meaning 'extremely drunk'; perhaps to be 'taken up *glorious*'[1] and put to bed if, like Barry Lyndon, he was lucky enough to have servants (*BL* ch. 18). Some, of course, were hardened drinkers with strong heads; or having *hot coppers*, that is, a mouth and throat parched through excessive drinking: 'Nothing like that beer . . . when the *coppers* are *hot*. Many a day I've drunk a dozen of Bass at Calcutta' (*P* II ch. 5). In *The Book of Snobs* there is a vivid picture of a plethoric colonel 'inhausting his smoking tea, which went . . . hissing over the "hot coppers" of that respectable veteran' (*BS* ch. 22). A general word for drink is *tap*, and it could be applied both literally and figuratively. Young James Crawley describes his aunt's wine as 'precious good *tap*' (*VF* p. 333). Philip Firmin decides at one point in his career: 'My *tap* in life is to be small beer henceforth' (*Ph* II ch. 12). The novelist assessed his own aptitude for verse in similar terms: 'I have a sixpenny talent, small beer, but . . . the right *tap*' (quoted by F. Locker-Lampson, *My Confidences*, London, 1896, p. 292).

A great deal more was eaten and drunk at the tables of the wealthy than is nowadays. Foker explains to Blanche Amory: 'I don't care about much wine afterwards – I take my *whack* at dinner – I mean my share you know' (*P* I ch. 38). There was enough to satisfy the most hearty appetite, or 'a deuce of a *twist*', to give the slang equivalent of a good appetite (*P* I ch. 34). Major Pendennis, however, is characterized by a more refined Epicureanism; more than once he proclaims his predilection for '*snug* little dinners' (*P* I ch. 20). It is the usage of the elderly: the Major 'vowed that he liked *snug dinners* of all things in the world' (*P* I ch. 37). The colloquial use of *mahogany*, meaning a dining-table, epitomizes the purse-proud attitude of many early Victorians in such matters: 'I'll lay my life I . . . can lay a better dinner on my

1 *OED glorious* 6 'ecstatically happy from drink'. The *OED* quotes Burns' 'Tam o' Shanter': 'Kings may be blest, but Tam was *glorious* / O'er a' the ills of life victorious'.

mahogany, than ever they see on theirs' (*VF* p. 414), boasts old Osborne.

Money is a theme peculiarly liable to produce slang expressions. Two alternatives for money are *stumpy* and *rowdy*: 'But has he got the *rowdy*?' (*P* II ch. 37) was a frequent question. More specific terms are *a pony* and *a plum*, meaning, respectively, 'twenty-five pounds' and 'one hundred thousand pounds':

'I'll give you twenty pound.'
'You said a *pony*,' interposed Clavering. (*P* II ch. 22)

I . . . heartily wish that someone would leave me a trifle . . . I should sink into my grave worth a *plum* at least. (*SGS* ch. 1)

When Thackeray writes, 'Grigg offered ninety for the mare yesterday . . ., and like a fool I wouldn't let her go *under the two O's*' (*VF* p. 286), or 'I'll give you half if you can get anybody *to do us a little fifty*' (*P* II ch. 23), one feels he is illustrating the way money matters were discussed in his day. There were slang expressions, too, for raising money on bills of exchange, promissory notes and accommodation bills: 'How-dy-do, Barney?' one of his man-about-town friends greets Barnes Newcome, 'How are the Three per Cents, you little beggar? I wish you'd *do me a bit of stiff*' (*N* I ch. 6), that is, 'offer me credit' (in some form). The phrase *flying a kite*, meaning specifically raising money on bills of exchange, negotiable instruments not representing any actual transaction but used for raising money on credit, is summed up in the Victorian saying that with boys the wind raised the kites, but with men the kites raised the wind: 'Strong's his man of business, draws the Governor's bills, and indosses 'em . . .: and I suppose Altamont's in it too. . . . That *kite-flying*, you know . . . always takes two or three of 'em' (*P* II ch. 24).

The assertion of the finer distinctions of social rank, too, sometimes called for slang expressions; often, as with money, to obviate embarrassment. *Tap*, as we have seen, is a word whose meaning can be extended figuratively from quality of drink to quality in general. So also with the word *chop*; but here the reference was not originally, as perhaps it was understood to be, to different cuts of meat. *Chop* is an Eastern loan-word, Hindi *chhāp*, meaning 'impression, print, stamp or brand'. The word is used a good deal, predictably, in *The Book of Snobs*: 'They are a sort of *second-chop* dandies; they cannot imitate that . . . admirable vacuous folly which distinguishes the noble and high-born chiefs of the race' (*BS* ch. 40). 'We are better than all the world . . . it's an axiom. . . . We are *the first-chop* of the world' (*BS* ch. 22). Given such an attitude, it was clearly important to be a *top-sawyer*, an obvious extension of meaning from the man who works the upper handle of the pit-saw (as opposed to the one underneath who gets the sawdust in his eyes). Colonel Newcome, it was reported in the town of Newcome, 'had called for a bottle of sherry and a bottle of claret, like a gentleman; . . . had paid the post-boys, and travelled with a servant, like a *top-sawyer*' (*N* I ch. 15), that is, a superior person. But when Morgan 'Pendennis', the Major's valet, counters a want of respect on the part of another valet by claiming, 'We go here to the best houses, *the tiptops*, I tell you' (*P* II ch. 22), his expression indicates that he is a mere camp-follower. The assertion of standards in society would necessitate many a rebuff, given and taken; many a *sticker* (*P* I ch. 25) or *topper* (*N* I ch. 6).

Hats, boots and gloves were sure indications of status. Clive Newcome has a low opinion of a schoolfellow's father 'who came to see his son lately in *highlows*, and a shocking *bad hat*, and actually flung coppers amongst the boys for a scramble' (*N* I ch. 6). One would be hard put to it to say how far the word *hat* here is to be understood figuratively; but one can compare a remark accredited to the Duke of Wellington, as he viewed the new Members of Parliament after the 1832 Reform Bill: 'I never saw so many shocking *bad hats* in my life' (see Philip Guedalla, *The Duke*, London, 1931, p. 409). *Highlows* were so called because they were 'a covering for the foot and ankle, too high to be called a shoe, and too low for a boot.' Fanny Bolton cannot but compare Pen's 'neat shining boot, so, so unlike Sam's *highlow*' (*P* II ch. 20).[1] When Altamont is ordered by a policeman to move on and not stare in at the windows of Belgravia, he retorts: 'Who's to prevent

[1] 'Highlows and no straps' (*BS* ch. 15) were signs of the lower orders in early Victorian times. At University, Pen is beaten in mathematics by 'very vulgar young men, who did not even use straps to their trousers so as to cover the abominably thick and coarse shoes and stockings which they wore' (*P* I ch. 18). Berlin gloves – gloves made of Berlin wool but, *pace* the *OED*, sometimes of cotton – were also indications of vulgarity. Kid, of course, was the wear. At a journalist's party, Pen dines with men 'in creaking shoes and Berlin gloves' (*P* I ch. 34).

me from staring, looking at my friends, if I like? Not you, old *highlows*' (*P* I ch. 38).

A horse and its equipage was also a sign of status: 'He rolls in his coach, he does, and I walk in my highlows;' laments Philip Firmin (*Ph* I ch. 7). Georgy Osborne's snobbish tutor, the Rev. Mr Veal, says, 'Master Osborne, I give you full permission to go and see your *carriage* friends' (*VF* p. 549). A *'bang-up* pony' (*VF* p. 331) was very well; but the ultimate distinction was one's own carriage with one's arms blazoned on it. So at least it seemed to an aspiring young dandy like Bob Jones in *The Newcomes*: 'Might not he quarter a countess's coat on his brougham along with the Jones's arms, or more *slap-up* still, have the two shields painted on the panels with the coronet over?' (*N* I ch. 31). *Bang-up* and *slap-up* were clearly terms of approval among men who, in T. S. Eliot's phrase, knew 'a horse, a dog, a wench'; but, applied in strained grammatical contexts, the vulgarity of such phrases becomes apparent:[1]

'She sings well, don't she, Fo?'
'*Slap up*,' said Fo. (*P* II ch. 1)

Thackeray is always aware of tradition, even in the comparatively evanescent language of slang. Words like *cut* for 'drunk' and phrases like *to beat up quarters* have at least some earlier history in the language. In a *Roundabout Papers* essay 'De Juventute', he writes of looking up in the British Museum a copy of 'Tom and Jerry', that is, Pierce Egan's *Real Life in London*, or possibly Moncrieff's *Tom and Jerry, or Life in London* which drew heavily on that popular book. Both volumes are chiefly valued nowadays as repositories of Regency slang. 'Tom and Jerry' had been the delight of his youth, but he finds it, as a fifty-year-old, more curious than amusing; while at the same time lamenting that 'there is an enjoyment of life in these young bucks of 1823 which contrasts strangely with our feelings of 1860.' But perhaps it was the novelist and not the young bucks who had changed. If Corinthian Tom and Jerry Hawthorn could end up knocking down a *Charley* or nightwatchman, young men in *Pendennis* were also liable to begin 'the operation which is entitled "*squaring*" at

---

1 We can compare the attributive use of an adverbial phrase in Edmund Sparkler's habitual remark in *Little Dorrit*, 'A doosed fine gal . . . with *no biggodd nonsense* about her'. See *Brook*, p. 145.

Policeman X' (*P* I ch. 38); and in *A Shabby Genteel Story* a character boasts of having *milled* a policeman (*SGS* ch. 8), of having beaten or thrashed him. When Barnes Newcome castigates someone he dislikes as 'an adventurer . . . a blackleg, a regular *Greek*' (*N* I ch. 36), he uses a word for a cheat that the young Thackeray would almost certainly have read in the pages of 'Tom and Jerry'. When the novelist writes of an elderly man who in his youth had had dealings with 'packed cards and *cogged* dice' (*N* I ch. 28), he would be aware that this word was already a 'ruffians' term' in Tudor times; though perhaps, like many archaizing writers, he mistakenly thought it meant a loaded dice (see *OED* s.v. *cog* v.[3] I Preliminary note) and not, as the earliest users seem to have understood the term, a die or dice fraudulently directed in fall.

The life of the young buck had not changed in essentials for centuries. A young buck might still be a rascal, the sort of man who could be defined in the rather old-fashioned slang of the Major as a *tiger*:[1]

> A man may have a very good coat-of-arms, and be a *tiger*, my boy . . . that man is a tiger, mark my word – a low man. . . . There is an unmistakable look of slang and bad habits about this Mr Bloundell. He frequents low gambling-houses and billiard-hells, sir. (*P* I ch. 19)

The Major's use of out-moded colloquialisms is one of the many linguistic touches that contribute to the authenticity of that brilliant portrait. To take a small but significant example, when he says, 'Times are changed now, – there's a *run upon* literature' (*P* I ch. 36), he is using the older form of the phrase for 'an extensive or well-sustained demand' (*OED run* n. 15b); superseded, from the time of Sir Walter Scott, the *OED* quotations suggest, by *run on*. It is characteristic that he hesitates to admit to the franchise of his usage words which had already ceased to be slang for most speakers: 'The Major wished that Pen, too, should take particular notice of this child; incited Arthur . . . to give him a dinner . . . and to *tip* him, as the phrase is, at the end of the day's pleasures' (*P* II ch. 6). Perhaps Thackeray was remembering that his favourite novelist, Fielding, a hundred years before, had hesitated

---

1 More commonly, the word meant a smartly-liveried boy acting as a groom or footmar (*P* I ch. 17; *N* I ch. 25).

over the verb: 'He advised his friend . . . to begin with *tipping* (as it is called) the great man's servant.'[1] It would not be consonant with the Major's age or dignity for him to understand immediately the turf expressions of his manservant Morgan:

> 'Having some information, and made acquaintance with the fam'ly through your kindness, I *put on the pot*, sir.'
> 'You did what?'
> 'I laid my money on, sir.' (*P* II ch. 24)

When Pen has failed his examination at Oxbridge, or been *plucked*,[2] his uncle has only vague and erroneous notions of what this means: 'The Major had heard of *plucking*, but in a very vague cursory way, and concluded that it was some ceremony performed corporally upon rebellious university youth' (*P* I ch. 20).

The world continued to be full of trickery, though the colloquial equivalents for 'to cheat' might vary. In *Barry Lyndon*, appropriately, eighteenth-century words like *bit* and *bubbled* are favoured; the latter word having memories of delusive financial speculations such as the South Sea Bubble: 'I was infernally *bit* and *bubbled* in almost every one of my transactions' (*BL* ch. 17). To *humbug* occurs as a verb, meaning 'to trick' or 'to delude': 'He *humbugged* the Governor that I was the greatest screw in the army' (*BS* ch. 29). It was more serious to be *hocussed*, or stupefied by drugs for criminal purposes: 'Mr Frederick Pigeon avers . . . that he was *hocussed* at supper and lost eight hundred pounds to Major Loder' (*VF* p. 625). There was a good deal of fraudulent dealing in horses, and the slang verb for this was *to chant*: 'You may as well say that horses are sold in heaven, which, as you know, are . . . *chanted* on to the market' (*Ph* II ch. 1). The noun *martingale*, normally a piece of harness, could be used figuratively of a doubtful system of gambling: 'They try their infallible *martingale*' (*VF* p. 625). Even a boxing match might be a contest lost by collusion between the pugilists – a *cross*, to use the slang expression (*VF* p. 531). The verb also occurs, albeit unrecorded in the *OED* till the 1972 *Supplement*: 'Didn't he shoot Captain

---

1 See *OED tip* v. 2. This quotation is from *Amelia*.
2 *Ploughed* is a later variant. The *OED* first illustrates (*plough* v. 8) from that important source of Victorian slang 'Cuthbert Bede', *The Adventures of Mr Verdant Green* (1853), and also quotes Charles Reade's novel *Hard Cash* of 1862: ' "Ploughed" ' is the new Oxfordish for "plucked".'

Marker? . . . Didn't he *cross* the fight between Bill Soames and the Cheshire Trump?' (*VF* p. 103). The adjective *shy* could be used colloquially with the meaning of 'shady' disreputable'; 'Clothes hanging out to dry on the gooseberry bushes. . . . Rather a *shy* place for a sucking county member' (*P* I ch. 25).

To combat such fraud, it was best to be 'an old *file*', a shrewd and cunning person, like Mr Chopper, old Osborne's chief clerk, who was one of the first to get wind of Sedley's approaching bankruptcy (*VF* p. 124). Better to be such a one than a *gaby*, or simpleton: 'Who but a *gaby* ever spoke ill of a woman to her sweetheart?' (*V* I ch. 17); or than the sort of man whom the younger generation voted 'stoopid, a fellow of no ideas, and a *fogey*, in a word' (*P* II ch. 29). A variant of *old fogies* for those who were behind the times was *old foozles* (RP 'Chalk-mark'), a slang word first quoted in the *OED* from Thackeray. The word *quack*, too, besides having the long-established meaning of an impostor in medicine, could also mean a charlatan in general, one who professed to knowledge he did not possess: 'That Wenham is as dull a *quack* as ever quacked; and you see the carriage in which he drove to dinner' (*P* I ch. 35).

One sees continuity, too, in at least one slang variant for a young lady: 'a pretty bit of *muslin*' (*P* II ch. 12), first quoted in the *OED* from *Tom and Jerry*. It recalls, in idea at least, Justice Shallow's assessment of Jane Nightwork as a *bona-roba* (2 *Henry IV*, III ii, 220); and looks forward, presumably, to the 'pretty bit of skirt' of the early twentieth century. A lady could also be a *stunner*, as we have seen; or *stunning* (*N* I ch. 33); or a *clipper* (*N* I ch. 34) or *clipping* (*P* I ch. 38); the sort of woman whom one could be, in another authentic-sounding phrase, 'right slick up over head and ears in love with' (*SGS* ch. 3). Even a joke could be very old – old enough in some instances to be known as a *Joe Miller* (RP 'Notes of a Week's Holiday'), from *Joe Miller's Jests, or The Wit's Vade Mecum*, published in 1739, the year after the said comedian's death.

The process whereby a lively, even a witty expression becomes hackneyed and meaningless and eventually obsolete, is sometimes temporarily arrested when the original meaning is reverted to; as when Lord Steyne describes Becky, playing the role of Clytemnestra murdering Agamemnon in a charade as 'quite *killing* in the part' (*VF* p. 494); or when an American (the use of *grit* meaning 'firmness of character' or 'pluck' is originally American) compliments both Philip Firmin and his father: 'If you were a chip of the old block you would be just what he called '*the grit*' (*Ph* II ch. 12). If the slang word *swell*, meaning a richly or extravagantly dressed person, grows stale from over-use, recourse can be had to one of the earlier meanings of the word: 'the rising or heaving of the sea', and the superlative *heavy swell* can occur with figurative as with literal import: 'Who was that uncommonly *heavy swell*?' (*P* II ch. 36). *Cut up* in the sense (*OED cut* v. 59) 'to admit of being cut up or divided, to turn out as to fortune after death' is also especially related by Miss Crawley's cynical doctors to the literal incisions of surgery:

'Of course the old girl will fling him over,' said the physician . . . 'She'll cut up well, I suppose.'
'Cut up,' says Clump with a grin, 'I wouldn't have her *cut up* for two hundred a year.' (*VF* p. 185)

The abusive epithet *pump*, meaning 'a duffer' or 'a muff', was particularly appropriate when used, as in a digression in *The Virginians*, of speechifying teetotallers:

I say, in the face of all the *pumps* which ever spouted, that there is a moment in a bout of good wine at which, if a man could but remain, wit, wisdom, courage . . . were his (*V* I ch. 31)

This extended slang meaning of the noun *pump*, incidentally, which has no place in the *OED*, is defined at length in *Punch* for December 1847, with particularly interesting exemplification:

Pump – A term of profound contempt. A Fast Man divides the human family into only two branches – the 'Pumps' and the 'Bricks'. . . . Any one whose habits are opposed to those of a Fast Man, is necessarily a 'Pump'. If a person will not smoke, or sing, or drink, when asked . . . he is everlastingly condemned as a 'Pump'. We have no doubt that Prince Albert is frequently anathematized by the Fast Man as a Pump, because he does not contract debts, or build toy-palaces, or wear white kid inexpressibles, and commit similar breaches of good taste, which earned for his blessed Majesty, George IV, the imperishable title of 'The greatest Gent in Europe'.

It can happen that a slang word appears in what is now an uncommon or even an obsolete sense. The predominant modern meaning of *blackleg*, for example, as an abusive epithet for a man willing to work when his fellow-workers are on strike, is first illustrated from 1865 in the *OED*. But as a term for a turf swindler the word dates from the late eighteenth century, and by the mid-Victorian period it is common with the meaning of a swindler in other forms of gambling. Mrs O'Dowd told Becky that her husband was 'no betther than a *blackleg*' (*VF* p. 353), when young officers lost large sums to Rawdon at cards. Another word which comes from the turf but has changed its meaning is *cocktail*, meaning originally 'having a docked tail', as was the case with hunters and stage-coach horses, predominantly not thorough-breds; hence applied, by Thackeray in the first instance, according to the *OED* (*cocktail* 1b), to a person assuming the position of a gentleman, but deficient in gentlemanly breeding. Clive Newcome evinces his detestation of his cousin: 'such a selfish, insolent coxcomb as that, such a *cocktail* as Barnes Newcome' (*N* I ch. 30). Meanwhile the American and quite separate development of a mixed alcoholic drink (*OED cocktail* 3) was appearing across the Atlantic, being first dated in the *OED* from 1809 (Washington Irving); but Thackeray does not have this usage.

As well as differences of meaning, differences in the construction and currency of slang expressions often occur in Victorian English. We should hardly now use *lick*, meaning 'to beat' or 'to overthrow', intransitively; nor on the other hand, the verb *to split*, meaning 'to tell tales, inform' transitively, as here:

> They fought thirteen rounds, and Dobbin *licked*. (*VF* p. 50)

> What did I say? . . . Did I *split* anything? (*P* II ch. 5)

The slang verb *to lark* in the sense of 'to play tricks' is normally intransitive today, as in the Road Safety slogan 'Stop children *larking* near vehicles *parking*'. With Thackeray this verb is sometimes transitive:

> A staid English maid . . . whom Georgy used to '*lark*' dreadfully with accounts of German robbers and ghosts. (*VF* p. 641)

There are other differences. The expression *a screw loose* tends now not to be used of circumstances, but of eccentric or mad people. In Thackeray, as in Trollope (Clark, *Trollope*, p. 50n.), the phrase rather indicates something amiss in the nature of things: 'I am sure there is some *screw loose*,' Clive Newcome remarks, 'and the Colonel and the people in Park Lane are at variance, because he goes there very little now' (*N* I ch. 24). *Not half* generally appears in present-day colloquial English as a form of litotes. Thus 'I don't half relish' in the first quotation below would not mean 'I do not relish by halves, I relish a good deal'; the meaning intended is 'I do not relish it so much as half, not very much at all':

> And let me tell you *I don't half relish* having my conduct called base. (*P* II ch. 15)

In this older sense the expression goes back to the sixteenth century (*OED half* adv. 3) and is not anachronistic, therefore, in *Esmond*:

> We must have no more talk ... for he *does not half* like you, cousin, and is as jealous as the black man in your favourite play. (*E* III ch. 4)

Nevertheless, the modern implication of understatement was developing in the nineteenth century, and this quotation from *A Shabby Genteel Story* nicely illustrates the transitional stage. One would have difficulty in glossing 'I don't half like him' here:

> 'Law, Bell,' said Miss Rosalind, 'what a chap that Brandon is! *I don't half like him*, I do declare!' Than which there can be no greater compliment from a woman to a man.
> 'No more do I neither,' says Bell. 'The man stares so, and says such things!' (*SGS* ch. 2)

It is usual now to confine the word *tick* to the stereotyped phrase *on tick*, meaning 'on credit'. The noun occurred separately in Victorian English meaning 'a credit account':

> They put up at a hotel in Covent Garden, where Bloundell had a *tick*, as he called it. (*P* I ch. 19)

But Thackeray also has the noun with the different meaning of 'a debit account, a debt':

> There are some of my college *ticks* ain't paid now. ... Tailors' ticks, tavern ticks, livery-stable ticks. (*P* II ch. 19)

Hence also the word occurs as equivalent to the state of being in debt. Pen's friend Warrington tells him, 'Impecuniosity will do you good. ... I don't know anything more wholesome for a man ... than a state of *tick*. It is ... a tonic' (*P* I ch. 31).

The colloquial shortening of words has long been a tendency of slang, though the words abbreviated have varied at different periods of the language. It is eighteenth-century usage, for example, to abbreviate *positive* to *poz*, and the last *OED* instance is from *Catherine*, set in that period: 'I will have a regiment to myself, that's *poz*' (*C* ch. 11). In the novels set in the nineteenth century, *pineapple* is shortened to *pine* (*VF* p. 42), 'a bottle of champagne' to 'a bottle of *sham*' (*P* I ch. 4) and a verb *to polk* is formed, meaning 'to dance the polka' (*P* II ch. 22).

Slang words have a way of coming into vogue, being heard on everyone's lips, and then growing less common either through becoming obsolete or through being elevated to acceptance within the standard language. In the mid eighteenth century the word *humbug* had appeared in just this way, and the use of it had soon become a vogue word. The *OED* quotes the periodical *The Student, or the Oxford and Cambridge Monthly Miscellany* for January 1751:

> There is a word very much in vogue with the people of taste and fashion, which though it has not even the 'penumbra' of a meaning, yet makes up the sum total of the wit, sense and judgment of the aforesaid people of taste and fashion! ... I will venture to affirm that this *Humbug* is neither an English word, nor a derivative from any other language. It is indeed a blackguard sound, made use of by most people of distinction! It is a fine make-weight in conversation, and some great men deceive themselves so egregiously as to think they mean something by it.

In *The Virginians*, which begins 'one summer morning in the year 1756', the vogue for this word is duly mentioned. It is an instance of Thackeray's remarkable knowledge and sense, in those pre-*OED* days, of the history of the language in the century previous to his own:

> A certain cant word called *humbug* had lately come into vogue. Will it be believed that the General used it to designate the family of this virtuous country gentleman? (*V* II ch. 10)

The novelist must have been aware that this process of promoting a slang word to greater currency and acceptability, and its regulation from a vague to a more precise meaning, was a good illustration of the way that philological history is apt to repeat itself. Indeed it must have afforded a flattering parallel to his own achievement in elevating one slang word to an indispensable place in standard English. I refer to Thackeray's greatest contribution to the language, the promotion and development of the word *snob*.

It was not his invention. Originally a slang word of obscure etymology, it meant in the later eighteenth century a shoe-maker or a cobbler, or a cobbler's apprentice. 'There is Sir Humphrey Howard, who served with me second lieutenant . . . but his father was a shoemaker, and we always called him Humphrey *Snob* in the gunroom' (*DD* ch. 1). Thence it was extended by Cambridge undergraduates as a contemptuous term for a townsman, one not of the University; and thence it had come more generally to mean a member of the lower orders. But this last stage had occurred at least a decade and a half before 1846, when Thackeray inaugurated what was eventually to be a permanent change in the meaning of the word with a series of articles in *Punch*, entitled 'The Snobs of England, by one of Themselves'. Often the word had been used in contrast to *nob*, for a member of the aristocracy.[1] Throughout his career, the novelist continued to use *snob* in its earlier meaning of 'one having no pretensions to rank or gentility', as well as in more innovatory meanings:

> I like a sanded floor in Carnaby Street better than a chalked one in Mayfair. I prefer *Snobs*, I own it. (*P* I ch. 30)

But already, in his article 'On University Snobs', which first appeared in 1846, Thackeray recognized the difference in meaning which he was bringing about:

> We *then* used to consider Snobs raw-looking lads, who never missed chapel; who wore highlows and no straps . . . who carried off the college scholarships. . . . We were premature in pronouncing our verdict of youthful Snobbishness. The man without straps fulfilled his destiny and duty. . . . No, no, he is

---

1 Ironically, the wheel has now come full circle: in a recent television programme on class distinction in education mention was made of a colloquial distinction between *the snobs* and *the yobs*, from the upper and lower classes respectively.

not a Snob. . . . My son, it is you who are a Snob if you lightly despise a man for doing his duty and refuse to shake an honest man's hand because it wears a Berlin glove. (*BS* ch. 15)

Nevertheless, J. Y. T. Greig is right (in *Thackeray: a Reconsideration*, p. 91), when he says that, at first at least, the novelist had 'no clear notion of what the word meant to him or anybody else'. Although, looking at this last passage with hindsight, we can see that the new sense-development marks a step, if a small one, in the rise of a meritocracy and the decline of mere privilege, at the time and in the context of their composition the essays, which in 1848 were published in book form as *The Book of Snobs*, typify a certain cavalier indiscriminateness of invective, a random machine-gunning of various targets, which was characteristic of the early numbers of *Punch*:

Stinginess is snobbish. Ostentation is snobbish. Too great profusion is snobbish. Tuft-hunting is snobbish. (*BS* ch. 19)

What, then, was the meaning of the word? A remark which is thrown out at the beginning of the book has often been quoted: 'He who meanly admires mean things is a Snob' (*BS* ch. 2); but this, despite the superficial precision implied by the repetition, is too vague as a definition. Snobbery was easier to exemplify than to define; even in a list of topical instances like the following, most of which do succeed in imparting a new precision, the additional emphasis in the second example on what Carlyle (importing the word from Germany) was beginning to call *Philistinism*, suggests the special pleading of the professional artist:[1]

A Court system that sends men of genius to the second table, I hold to be a snobbish system. A society that sets out to be polite, and ignores Arts and Letters, I hold to be a Snobbish society. You, who despise your neighbours, are a Snob; you, who forget your own friends, meanly to follow after those of a higher degree, are a Snob . . . as are you who boast of your pedigree, or are proud of your wealth. (*BS* ch. 45)

[1] The German University slang word from which Carlyle derived the term occurs in the Pumpernickel episodes in *Vanity Fair*: 'A conversation . . . mainly about "Fuchs" and "Philister", and duels and drinking-bouts at the neighbouring University of Schoppenhausen' (*VF* p. 639). (A *Fuchs* is a freshman, the *Philister* are the townspeople.)

It is possible to come nearer to a definition if we consider what the word partially replaces: *toady* (formerly also *toad-eater*), *lackey*, *tuft-hunter* — these are the words which Thackeray's new use of *snob* was eclipsing, and has continued to eclipse ever since: 'Toadyism, organized: — base Man-and-Mammon worship, instituted by command of law: — *Snobbishness*, in a word, perpetuated' (*BS* ch. 3).[1] The *OED*, however, unlike Thackeray, cannot shirk a definition, and the following (*snob* n. 3c), which no doubt cost the editors much thought, is their conclusion: 'One who meanly or vulgarly admires and seeks to imitate, or associate with, those of superior rank or wealth; one who wishes to be regarded as a person of social importance'. The first illustrative quotation comes, as of right, from Thackeray. The word is now standard English, and seems likely to remain so as long as the English language endures and pride continues to be the first of the seven deadly sins. As the brothers Fowler put it in *The King's English* (p. 53): 'When it doth prosper none dare call it slang.'

1 The word *snobbery* is not a coinage of Thackeray's. It is first recorded in the *OED* from *Blackwood's Magazine* for 1843, with what seems to be the earlier meaning of 'vulgarity', three years before Thackeray's articles began to appear in *Punch*.

CHAPTER 4

Register

🉐🉐🉐🉐🉐🉐

PEOPLE as conscious of class-distinctions as the early Victorians were very alive to differences of speech-level. Levels of speech reflected levels of society in being more rigidly demarcated than they are today; and the higher levels of language, parliamentary and sermon rhetoric for example, had, like the higher echelons of society, a more assured place. Correspondingly, vulgar language was more strictly taboo in certain ranks and certain circumstances of society than it is now. In the pursuit of refined levels of speech, grammars of English were read assiduously in the early nineteenth century. The most popular of these, Lindley Murray's *English Grammar*, published in 1795, went into two hundred editions before 1850. There must have been many, like Mrs Garth in *Middlemarch* (ch. 24), who 'in a general wreck of society would have tried to hold her "Lindley Murray" above the waves'.

It was often, indeed, the ladies on whom the responsibility fell 'to purify the dialect of the tribe'; especially if, like Miss Pinkerton of Chiswick, they were educators of the young by profession. Here she attempts, not with entire success, to correct her younger sister, Miss Jemima:

> 'Have you completed all the necessary preparations incident to Miss Sedley's departure, Miss Jemima?' asked Miss Pinkerton. . . .
> 'The girls were up at four this morning, packing her trunks sister,' replied Miss Jemima; 'we have made her a *bow-pot*.'
> 'Say a *bouquet*, sister Jemima, 'tis more genteel.'
> 'Well, a *booky* as big almost as a hay-stack.' (*VF* p. 11)

A careerist like Rebecca Sharp must adjust her level of language at times, as in this speech which she makes to Sir Pitt Crawley in an attempt to retrieve her reputation after her affair with Lord Steyne has been discovered. The two dashes in the following passage speak volumes: *esteem* is the word chosen in a last effort to suggest that her relationship with Steyne is respectable; and *bailiff's house* is preferred to the unfinished word that is first mooted – *spunging-house*:

> I saw Lord Steyne's partiality for me. . . . I own that I did every-thing in my power to make myself pleasing to him, and as far as an honest woman may, to secure his – his *esteem*. It was only on Friday morning that the news arrived of the death of the Governor of Coventry Island, and my Lord instantly secured the appointment for my dear husband. It was intended as a surprise for him. . . . My Lord was . . . saying that my dearest Rawdon would be consoled when he read of his appointment in the paper, in that shocking *spun – bailiff's house*. (*VF* p. 530)

On at least one occasion, however, Becky miscalculates in this matter of register. In an attempt to re-instate her husband Rawdon in his wealthy aunt's affections, Becky dictates to him an ingratiating letter for Miss Crawley, unwisely ignoring his suggested emendation:

> 'Before quitting the country and commencing a campaign, which very possibly may be fatal . . . I have *come hither*' – 'Why not say come here, Becky; come here's grammar,' the dragoon interposed.
> 'I have come hither,' Rebecca insisted, with a stamp of her foot, 'to say farewell to my dearest and earliest friend . . .' (*VF* p. 243)

'She won't recognize my style in *that*,' said Becky, 'I made the sentences short and brisk on purpose.' Miss Crawley, however, is not deceived for a moment: 'He never wrote to me without asking for money in his life, and all his letters are full of bad spelling, and dashes, and bad grammar. It is that little serpent of a governess who rules him;' she concludes.

To be able to spell correctly was a necessary mark of gentility. It was well enough for Lady Maria Esmond, in *The Virginians*, set in the middle of the eighteenth century, to comment, of a letter: ''Tis quite well enough spelt for any person of fashion' (*V* I ch. 18); and for the novelist himself, secure in his mastery of English, to resort to facetious spellings in letters, recalling the Wellers ('Wanety Fair') or Mrs Gamp ('peace, *repoge* and honest labour');

but by the nineteenth century, and for the serious purpose of issuing a challenge to a duel, even Rawdon Crawley felt compelled to consult Johnson's Dictionary in matters of orthography (*VF* p. 525); and a similar young man-about-town, Jack Belsize, composing a love-letter, 'looked into the dictionary to see whether *eternal* was spelt with an *e*, or *adore* with one *d* or two' (*N* I ch. 28). Major Pendennis is trying to defuse an emotional situation when he tells his sister-in-law, Pen's mother, that a letter from Fanny Bolton to her son is 'spelt . . . in a manner to outrage all sense of decorum', and he accordingly overstates the case (*P* II ch. 16); even so, by the beginning of Victoria's reign, faulty spelling had begun to carry a social stigma that it has never since lost.

This was one of the penalties that was paid for increasing literacy; but there were bonuses also – at least for one profession. A growing educated public, hungry for the information provided by the written word, were ready to accord a higher status to the journalist. Gordon Ray (*Age* p. 242) argues that *Pendennis* played a part in enhancing the status of the professional writer, as *The Newcomes* did that of the artist. One senses something of the increased prestige of the press in the famous rumination of George Warrington, Pen's journalist colleague, at the end of the thirtieth chapter of *Pendennis*:

> Look at that, Pen, . . . There she is – the great engine – she never sleeps. She has her ambassadors in every quarter of the world – her couriers upon every road. Her officers march along with armies, and her envoys walk into statesmen's cabinets. They are ubiquitous. Yonder journal has an agent, this minute, giving bribes at Madrid; and another inspecting the price of potatoes in Covent Garden. Look! here comes the Foreign Express galloping in. . . . [etc.]

Even today, a column appears in one of the serious Sunday papers, *The Observer*, over the name 'Pendennis'.

Neverthless, the tradition of Grub Street died hard. There was still great admiration for the vituperatively critical article known alternatively as *the slasher* or *the smasher*. A character in *Pendennis*, Captain Shandon, is based on a real-life journalist, whom as a young man Thackeray had greatly admired, Dr William Maginn. Maginn was a gifted Irishman who, like Shandon, could not keep out of debtors' prisons, and who ended in drunken obscurity.

Like Shandon, the unscrupulous Maginn could doubtless write 'the best *slashing* article in England' (*P* I ch. 32). Shandon's associates admit that 'when the Captain puts his hand to it he's a tremendous hand at a *smasher*' (*P* I ch. 30). But the novelist himself was proficient in this line. He wrote to his publishers, Bradbury and Evans, in 1844: 'Will you bring me to London and put me at the head of a *slashing* brilliant gentlemanlike, sixpenny, aristocratic, literary paper?' (*L* II p. 163). A variant of these verbs *to slash* and *to smash* was *to tomahawk*. Under this verb in the OED there is a reference to a book 'which Thackeray *tomahawked*'. The *Tomahawk* is the name of a 'slashing' newspaper in the long short story *Ravenswing* (ch. 7). Two rival newspapers in *Pendennis* are the *Dawn* and the *Day*, Liberal and Conservative respectively. Catering for a different level of the public was the sporting paper mentioned in *Cox's Diary* for April, the *Flare-up*. Probably the *Stoke Poges Sentinel* (*V* II ch. 8) would be less sensational! Already the word *spicy* (*Ph* II ch. 15) was beginning to be used of writing which was pungent and perhaps salacious. It is obvious that Thackeray would be worth his considerable weight in gold today as a writer of advertising copy, as James Hannay early recognized (*Studies on Thackeray*, p. 58): 'If he had undertaken to write an advertisement, it would have been as neat as one of his ballads'.[1]

1 It is astonishing to learn that Thackeray is in effect a modern advertising copywriter. Brighton, for example, is still sometimes referred to in publicity hand-outs for the town as *Dr Brighton,* a title conferred by Thackeray ('Kind, cheerful, merry Dr Brighton' *N* I ch. 9); and George Osborne is credited with 'a pale interesting countenance' (*VF* p. 52), a phrase which must surely be at the back of the 'pale interesting look', an achievement recently claimed for one of their cosmetics by Max Factor. But the most well-known and best-authenticated instance is the brand of cigarettes, *The Three Castles*. On inquiry from Messrs W. D. and H. O. Wills, of Bristol, I received this reply:

> The name was originally suggested by an Edinburgh tradesman, George Waterston, who used to supply Wills with sealing wax. In those days the small number of cigarette smokers used to roll their own cigarettes and Mr Waterston asked George Wills if he could manufacture a light shredded tobacco for this purpose. The reply he received was that Wills already had an excellent tobacco which only required a good name to promote sales. In December 1876 Mr Waterston, who had been reading Thackeray's novel *The Virginians*, sent a copy of the famous quotation to Wills and suggested that no name could be more appropriate than The Three Castles. Mr Wills was delighted with the suggestion and immediately proceeded with a label design.

The quotation, used in advertising the brand of cigarettes, is: 'There's no sweeter tobacco comes from Virginia, and no better brand than the Three Castles' (*V* I ch. 1).

If nothing else, his brilliant coinages of names would assure him success in this line. He is a master, too, of the choice of the appropriate title for a tract or song, with the addition of a slightly ridiculous burlesque element: the tracts that the Dowager Countess of Southdown peddles include *The Washerwoman of Finchley Common, The Sailor's True Binnacle* (*VF* p. 437) and, for the servants' hall, *The Livery of Sin* (*VF* p. 325). Popular ballads include 'When the Gloom is on the Glen' (*Travels in London* 'A Night's Pleasure') and the poem written by Jeames de la Pluche 'When Moonlight o'er the Hazure Seas' (*DJ* p. 139).

Skill in such matters implies an assured sense of the correct language to use in different circumstances, and a keen enjoyment of the ridiculous. These qualities the novelist had, and he made good use of them; as, for instance, the report sent back from England to the *New York Demagogue* by the unsophisticated Mr John Paul Jefferson Jones, attached to the American Embassy, of a dinner at Lord Steyne's house:

> He mentioned the names and titles of all the guests, giving biographical sketches of the principal people. He described the persons of the ladies with great eloquence; the service of the table; the size and costume of the servants; enumerated the dishes and wines served; the ornaments of the side-board, and the probable value of the plate. Such a dinner he calculated could not be dished up under fifteen or eighteen dollars per head. . . . He was most indignant that a young and insignificant aristocrat, the Earl of Southdown, should have taken the *pas* of him in their procession to the dining-room. 'Just as I was stepping up to offer my hand to a very pleasing and witty fashionable, the brilliant and exclusive Mrs Rawdon Crawley,' he wrote, 'the young patrician interposed between me and the lady, and whisked my Helen off without a word of apology. I was fain to bring up the rear with the Colonel, the lady's husband, a stout red-faced warrior who distinguished himself at Waterloo, where he had better luck than befel some of his brother red-coats at New Orleans.' (*VF* p. 472)

It is not easy to say in detail why this is all wrong, for Thackeray's sense of solecism is very subtle – as subtle as Henry James's in recording that other American journalist in Europe, Henrietta Stackpole in *The Portrait of a Lady*. We note, however, the combination

of the mercenary and the naively colloquial in 'Such a dinner
... could not be *dished up* under fifteen or eighteen dollars
per head'; the use of *stepping up*, the verb *to step* in the sense of 'to
go' having taken the downward path since the eighteenth century;[1]
phrases like 'the young patrician' and 'my Helen' with their
mingled ingenuousness and journalese; the self-congratulatory
'knowingness' and shoppy phrasing of 'a very pleasing and witty
fashionable, the brilliant and exclusive Mrs Rawdon Crawley'; the
still-rankling inferiority feelings of a young nation, seen in the
harking back to the War of Independence; and over and above
this, the ironic suggestion that this kind of coy and snobbish
gossip would have gone down well with readers of the *New York
Demagogue*.

More than one professional man in *Vanity Fair* adopts a
grandiloquent register to impress his clients. Such a man is the
Reverend Mr Veal, at whose select boarding-school young Georgy
Osborne is educated:

> Whenever he spoke (which he did almost always), he took
> care to produce the very finest and longest words of which
> the vocabulary gave him the use; rightly judging, that it was
> as cheap to employ a handsome, large, and sonorous epithet,
> as to use a little stingy one.
>
> Thus he would say to George in school, 'I observed on my
> return home from taking the indulgence of an evening's
> scientific conversation with my excellent friend Dr Bulders – a
> true archaeologian, ... that the windows of your venerated
> grandfather's almost princely mansion in Russell Square were
> illuminated as if for the purposes of festivity. Am I right in my
> conjecture, that Mr Osborne entertained a society of chosen
> spirits round his sumptuous board last night?' (*VF* p. 545)

So, too, Mr Clump the apothecary, attendant upon the wealthy
Miss Crawley, adopts impressively flowery language in quoting
the advice of Dr Squills on the patient to whom they jointly
administer:

> Dr Squills and I were thinking that our amiable friend is not
> in such a state as renders confinement to her bed necessary. ...

---

[1] We may compare Foker's description of Pen: 'He's as good a fellow as ever
stepped' (P I ch. 10); and see Fowler's *Modern English Usage* s.v. *genteelisms*.

She should have change, fresh air, gaiety; the most delightful remedies in the pharmacopœia. . . . Persuade her to rise, dear Madam; drag her from her couch . . . insist upon her taking little drives. They will restore the roses too to your cheeks, if I may so speak to Mrs Bute Crawley. (*VF* p. 184)

What Dr Squills actually said to Clump is quoted on the next page, where virtually the same advice is conveyed in more down-to-earth terms:

'That Hampshire woman will kill her in two months, Clump, my boy, if she stops about her. . . . Old woman; full feeder; nervous subject; palpitations of the heart; pressure on the brain; apoplexy; off she goes. Get her up, Squills; get her out; or I wouldn't give many weeks' purchase for your two hundred a year.'

And it was acting upon this hint that the worthy apothecary spoke with so much *candour* to Mrs Bute Crawley.

The word *candour* here, incidentally, illustrates Thackeray's subtle use of language at its best. Is *candour* used in the eighteenth-century sense of benignity or the modern sense of frankness? Whichever way we take the word (if indeed we have to choose) it is ironic; the contrast in register with what precedes shows that Squills's motives towards Mrs Bute and her patient are neither wholly frank nor wholly kind.

Clerical characters, with one exception, do not loom large in the novels. Dr Portman, in *Pendennis*, the elderly vicar of Clavering, is as his name implies a dignified man whose language from time to time recalls, as we have seen elsewhere (p. 52), a period before the Victorian era; but his clerical role is not stressed. One clergyman who is treated in more depth is the Rev. Charles Honeyman, in *The Newcomes*. From his name we gather that he is a smooth man; and he has a fashionable pulpit, Lady Whittlesea's chapel, in Mayfair. It is interesting to compare him with Dickens's most famous clergyman, Mr Chadband in *Bleak House*. Unlike Honeyman, Chadband is unattached to any particular denomination but ministers chiefly to the lower middle classes, people like the Snagsbys who produce, and are tolerant of, eccentrics. Consequently he can talk in a prolix way that, as Brook suggests (*Dickens* pp. 81–2), verges on the grotesque:

95

I say, my friends . . . why can we not fly? Is it because we are calculated to walk? It is. Could we walk, my friends, without strength? We could not. What should we do without strength, my friends? Our legs would refuse to bear us, our knees would double up, our ankles would turn over, and we should come to the ground. (*Bleak House* ch. 19)

Honeyman, moving in the higher strata of society, cannot run to Chadbandian extremes. Instead, he makes a parade of self-control:

'Poor poor Emma!' exclaimed the ecclesiastic, casting his eyes towards the chandelier, and passing a white cambric pocket-handkerchief gracefully before them. No man in London understood the ring business or the pocket-handkerchief business better, or smothered his emotions more beautifully. 'In the gayest moments, in the giddiest throng of fashion, the thoughts of the past will rise; the departed will be among us still. But this is not the strain wherewith to greet the friend newly arrived on our shores. How it *rejoices me* to behold you in old England! How you must have *joyed* to see Clive'! (*N* I ch. 8)

Honeyman is a more subtle, less extravagant, figure than Chadband and his speech illustrates the general fact that the language of Thackeray's characters is less inclined to extreme distortions. Putting their respective techniques into medieval rhetorical terms, we see that Honeyman works by *exclamatio* rather than Chadband's *ratiocinatio* (answering questions that the speaker has asked himself). But such usage as *rejoice* as a reflexive verb and the noun *joy* converted to a verb conveys an equally unmistakable, albeit more refined, unctuousness.

We can see a parallel moderation in comparing Dickens's and Thackeray's 'men-about-town'. The languid drawl of debilitated members of the upper classes like Edmund Sparkler in *Little Dorrit* and Sir Leicester Dedlock's cousin in *Bleak House* is conveyed by caricatured dialogue: in the former case by a very disjointed utterance; in the latter by language so slipshod that it deliberately verges on unintelligibility: 'The debilitated cousin only hopes some fler'll be executed – zample. . . . Hasn't a doubt – zample – far better hang wrong fler than no fler' (*Bleak House* ch. 53). Barnes Newcome, too, has acquired an aristocratic drawl, characterized by what A. O. J. Cockshut calls the 'subtle note of informal formality of the English upper classes at work' (*The Imagination of Charles Dickens*, London, 1961, p. 60):

> Oh, of course. It's very good society and that sort of thing – but it's not, you know – you understand. I give you my honour there are not three people in the room one meets anywhere, except the Rummun. What is he at home, sir? I know he ain't a Prince, you know, any more than I am. (*N* I ch. 8)

We note here the repeated 'you know', with its mixture of an ingratiating tone and an assumption that what is being said must be 'received opinion' in every sense; and the upper-class use of the pronoun *one*,[1] with its suggestion that it is possible to extrapolate from the speaker's opinion or choice to that of all right-thinking men. The imprecision of *that sort of thing* combines with the informal but at this date not necessarily déclassé *ain't*, to produce an air of studied indifference. It is especially interesting to note what happens to Barnes Newcome's language in the next speech he utters, not in the role of upper-class *flâneur*, but of practical banker and man of affairs. Colonel Newcome continues, and Barnes replies, as follows:

> 'I believe he is a rich man now,' said the Colonel. 'He began from very low beginnings, and odd stories are told about the origin of his fortune.'
> 'That may be,' says the young man; 'of course, as business men, that's not our affair. But has he got the fortune? He keeps a large account with us; and, I think, wants to have larger dealings with us still. As one of the family we may ask you to stand by us, and tell us anything you know. My father has asked him down to Newcome, and we've taken him up; wisely or not I can't say. I think otherwise; but I'm quite young in the house, and of course the elders have the chief superintendence.'
> The young man of business had dropped his drawl or his

---

1 In a *Punch* burlesque of a series of absurdly snobbish articles by Lady Londonderry, 'Journal of a Visit to Foreign Courts', Thackeray ridicules the excessive use of this indefinite pronoun, never really naturalized into English: 'How pretty that way of saying "annoying one with one's maid by one's bedside" – one only finds people of fashion ever use one's language in the proper way – does one? . . . I call it the unique way' (*Punch* V pp. 52–3, January 1844).

languor, and was speaking quite unaffectedly, good-naturedly, and selfishly.

– and, we might add, with a nervous precision and terseness which is the antithesis of Barnes's previous speech. In both the assumption and the shedding of this drawl, one senses that Thackeray reflects the reality of nineteenth-century upper-class speech more faithfully, if less amusingly, than the distorting mirror of Dickens does.

Inarticulacy may have many causes and be represented for many purposes. Sometimes an over-laconic utterance, with omitted subjects, results from ill manners and faulty upbringing:

> 'Ain't at home, John. Gone out to pay some visits. Had a fly on purpose. Gone out with my sister. 'Pon my word they have, John.' And from this accurate report of the boy's behaviour, I fear that the young Baynes must have been brought up at a classical and commercial academy, where economy was more studied than politeness. (*Ph* II ch. 4)

At other times an officious parade of confidentiality and pre-occupation may cause a man to assume incoherence, as with the banker, Sir Brian Newcome:

> 'How well India has agreed with you! how young you look! the hot winds are nothing to what we endure in Parliament. Hobson,' in a low voice, 'you saw about that hm. I am sorry about that hm – that power of attorney – and hm and hm will call here at twelve about that hm. I am sorry I must say good-bye – it seems so hard after not meeting for so many years.' (*N* I ch. 6)

The commonest reason for inarticulacy, however, is mental incapacity and the lack of confidence that proceeds from it. The outstanding example of this is the Marquis of Farintosh, who aspires to Ethel Newcome's hand in marriage and whom heaven has supplied with 'a large estate, and ancient title, and the pride belonging to it', but with 'no great quantity of brains'. His laziness of mind, bordering on effeteness and deficiency, appears in every sentence – the word *thing*, for instance, doing duty for more precise nouns:

As you weren't there . . . the Miss Rackstraws came out quite strong; really they did now, upon my honour. It was quite a quiet *thing* ... Lady Ann, you shirk London society this year ... : we expected you to give us two or three *things* this season; we did now, really. I said to Tufthunt, only yesterday, why had not Lady Ann Newcome given *anything*? You know Tufthunt? They say he's a clever fellow and that – but he's a low little beast and I hate him. (*N* II ch. 4)

The phrase *and that* usually tells a tale of inferiority in matters of inarticulate speech: 'She sneers at her mother because I haven't had learning *and that*' the parvenue Lady Clavering complains of her daughter, Blanche (*P* II ch. 6); 'Hang it, you know, she's so clever,' says Rawdon Crawley of Becky, 'and I'm not literary *and that*, you know' (*VF* p. 370). Harry Foker regrets that the short-comings in his education have made him unworthy of Blanche Amory: 'He was sorry that he had not been good at his books in early life, that he might have cut out all those chaps who were about her, and who talked the languages, and wrote poetry, ... and – *and that*' (*P* II ch. 1).

This last sentence exemplifies an important feature of reported speech in Thackeray. It begins as indirect reporting of Foker's thoughts, but in the course of it the actual language that the speaker would use emerges. One cannot strictly describe this as either direct or indirect speech. Indeed the normal school distinction between direct and indirect speech, to some extent a legacy from Latin *oratio recta et obliqua*, is in many ways an over-simplification of the varied techniques employed by the best English novelists to reflect the finer nuances of dialogue. Thackeray constantly varies and combines these two methods of direct and reported speech; often with a special purpose in mind. Thus in the following passage speech is half recorded and half reported; the quotes, normally indicating the exact words spoken, are belied by the converted tenses, more usually associated with indirect speech. The scene is a Mayfair dinner-party, at which the sharp-tongued Ethel Newcome is conversing with Arthur Pendennis, narrator of *The Newcomes*, about Clive Newcome. Over and above the impression of strain and artificiality which the muted tenses convey, the condescension and covert hostility of the arrogant heroine also emerge:

Miss Ethel asked me several questions regarding Clive, and

also respecting Miss Mackenzie; perhaps her questions were rather downright and imperious, and she patronized me in a manner that would not have given all gentlemen pleasure. I was Clive's friend, his schoolfellow? had seen him a great deal? knew him very well – very well indeed? 'Was it true that he had been very thoughtless? very wild?' 'Who told her so?' 'That was not her question' (with a blush). 'It was not true, and I ought to know? He was not spoiled?' 'He was very good-natured, generous, told the truth. He loved his profession very much, and had great talent.' 'Indeed, she was very glad. Why do they sneer at his profession? It seemed to her quite as good as her father's and brother's. . . . Is Miss Mackenzie as good-natured as she looks? Not very clever I suppose? Mrs Mackenzie looks very – No, thank you, no more.' (*N* I ch. 24)

Through the chequered dialogue, the reader may also be alerted to the undercurrent of interest that Ethel shows in Clive's career and matrimonial prospects, and may guess at the final outcome of the novel.

We have no word for this blend of direct and indirect speech in English, but must have recourse to German (*erlebte Rede*) or French (*parole indirecte libre*). Another good example of the constraint which this method of rendering speech can convey occurs in *Vanity Fair* when old Osborne, who has heard of Sedley's imminent bankruptcy, is mortified to find Amelia Sedley still dining at his house and hoping to marry his son, George. To make matters worse, George arrives late for dinner:

Mr Osborne . . . lapsed into silence, and swallowed sundry glasses of wine, till a brisk knock at the door told of George's arrival, when everybody began to rally.

'He could not come before. General Daguillet had kept him waiting at the Horse Guards. Never mind soup or fish. Give him anything – he didn't care what. Capital mutton – capital everything.' His good-humour contrasted with his father's severity; and he rattled on unceasingly during dinner, to the delight of all – of one especially. (*VF* p. 122)

But one senses the displeasure of old Osborne as his son enlivens the company with his disjointed sentences; and this constraint is partly suggested by the converted personal pronouns and tenses.

Occasionally the tedium of a desultory or predictable conversation is conveyed by quoting salient phrases between dashes. It is a device which we associate (though employed by Dickens for a different purpose) with Mr Jingle; but in fact earlier it had been used by Jane Austen to indicate Mrs Elton's prolix talk as she picked strawberries at Donwell Abbey (*Emma* ch. 42). Here is Colonel Newcome introducing his son Clive to his banker:

> Before going away, he introduced Clive to F. and M.'s corresponding London house, Jolly and Baines, Fog Court – leading out of Leadenhall – Mr Jolly, a myth as regarded the firm, now married to Lady Julia Jolly – a park in Kent – evangelical interest – great at Exeter Hall meetings – knew Clive's grandmother – that is, Mrs Newcome, a most admirable woman. (*N* I ch. 27)[1]

The staccato phrases here are not chosen at random. They substantiate the frequently-asserted connection between money and the evangelical religion, thus underlining the subtitle of *The Newcomes*: 'The Memoirs of a Most Respectable Family'. To quote Juliet McMaster: 'Money, as a determinant of respectability, is a central principle that holds together at once the Newcome family and the novel, permeating language and imagery and dominating character and action' (*Thackeray: The Major Novels*, p. 155). A further impression, and one that is particularly strong in *The Newcomes*, is that of a London still small enough for everyone of note to know everyone else. Gordon Ray (*Age* p. 25) quotes Sir William Fraser's biography, *Disraeli and his Day*, to the effect that London society in 1847 'consisted of from 300 to 500 persons; not more'. The total effect of many such passages is to give the impression of a crowded canvas, such as one of Frith's.

By this bold and subtle use of *erlebte Rede*, often admitting into the narrative a few words of a contrasting register or speech-level, Thackeray, like Dickens, is able to suggest a scene more rapidly and more immediately than by the explicit use of quotes. Here, for example, is a brief but vivid realization of an occasion when young Pen is slightly tipsy. The words spoken emerge

---

1 This conflatory device is discussed at some length by Norman Page in *Speech in the English Novel*, pp. 29–30. For a further discussion of Thackeray's unusual representation of speech, with two brilliant examples (*N* II ch. 28; *LW* ch. 6), see Geoffrey Tillotson, *Thackeray the Novelist*, pp. 25–32.

unobtrusively out of, and return back again into, a straight-forward narrative:

> Pen came home . . . with half a score of the Clavering voters yelling after him the Blue song of the election. He wanted them all to come in and have some wine – some very good Madeira – some capital Madeira – John, go and get some Madeira – and there is no knowing what the farmers would have done, had not Madam Pendennis made her appearance. (*P* I ch. 3)

Sometimes a single word may be a slight and remote echo of direct speech and may colour the narrative with a conflicting or alien thought-process. Thus, in the masterly opening of *Pendennis*, young Arthur's sensitive and close relationship with his mother and the fact that his more practical and prosaic father, founder of the family fortunes, has no part in this relationship is hinted at by the one word *business*. A less subtle novelist would have rendered the contrast by a direct representation of what the elder Pendennis was thinking; and consequently the essential inarticulacy of the father in such matters would have been lost.

> Little Arthur's figure and his mother's cast long blue shadows over the grass: and he would repeat in a low voice (for a scene of great natural beauty always moved the boy, who inherited this sensibility from his mother) certain lines beginning, 'These are Thy glorious works, Parent of Good . . .' As for John Pendennis, as the father of the family . . . everybody had the greatest respect for him. . . . After dinner he always had a nap. . . . And so, as his dinner took place at six o'clock to a minute, and the sunset *business* alluded to may be supposed to have occurred at about half-past seven, it is probable that he did not much care for the view in front of his lawn windows, or take any share in the poetry and caresses. (*P* I ch. 2)

Perhaps the most frequent reason for a versatile use of *erlebte Rede* in reproducing speech-effects is the representation of sub-standard language, often that of servants and hangers-on. Thackeray is especially good at depicting servants, and their point of view is often put briefly but forcibly, evoking echoes, un-heralded by quotes, of the actual language they use:

> If you and the Captain have high words upon any subject . . . and if Mrs Smith's maid should by chance be taking a dish of

tea with yours . . . the next day her mistress will probably know that Captain and Mrs Jones have been *a quarrelling* as usual. (*P* I ch. 36)

The country people vowed my lady was not handsome, to be sure, but pronounced her to be *uncommon* fine dressed, as indeed she was – with the finest of shawls, the finest of pelisses, the brilliantest of bonnets, . . . and *a power of* rings. (*P* I ch. 22)

The luxuriance of the establishment was greatly . . . reduced. One of the large footmen was cashiered, upon which the other gave warning, not liking to serve . . . where *on'y* one footman was *kep'*. (*P* II ch. 22)

The last sentence exemplifies a favourite ploy of Thackeray's: a deliberate clash of registers for anticlimax and humorous effect. It is a device that can occur in the narrative, as when the Chevalier Strong in *Pendennis*, is 'waited on by a former Spanish legionary of his whom he had left at a breach of a Spanish fort, and found at a crossing in Tottenham-court Road' (*P* I ch. 37); or in dialogue, as when Harry Foker replies to Pen's excessive protests of affection with the Victorian slang exclamation *gammon*, meaning 'stuff and nonsense':

'Henry, friend of my youth . . . were I in a straight of poverty, I would come to my Foker's purse. Were I in grief, I would discharge my grief upon his sympathising bosom – '
'*Gammon*, Pen – go on,' Foker said. (*P* II ch. 7)

Presumably Pen's language here is derived from his reading; as is Miss Clapp's, daughter of the Sedleys' landlady in *Vanity Fair*, who was sure when Amelia left her lodgings that she would never be so happy as she had been 'in their *humble cot* as Miss Clapp called it in the language of the novels which she loved' (*VF* p. 575). Young Harry Warrington, too, in *The Virginians*, has acquired certain formulaic protestations of love from his reading of the novels of his day; and Thackeray suggests very cleverly the way his fluency deserts him and he becomes a plain-speaking, rather callow youth once his literary inspiration is exhausted:

'Incomparable Maria! I prefer thee to all the women in the world and all the angels in Paradise – and I would go anywhere, were it to dungeons, if you ordered me!' . . .

'Men always talk in that way – that is – that is, I have heard so,'
said the spinster, correcting herself . . .
'But I think I never want to go away as long as I live,' groaned
out the young man. 'I have tired of many things; not books
and that, I never cared for study much, but games and sports
which I used to be fond of . . . now, I only care for one thing in
the world, and you know what that is.' (*V* I ch. 18)

Skill in manipulation of speech-levels comes partly, no doubt,
from the novelist's apprenticeship in *Punch*, where his gift for
parody found its full expression and was improved by practice.
Indeed, while the first numbers of *Vanity Fair* were appearing he
was also writing a series, 'Punch's Prize Novelists', burlesquing
various kinds of popular novel. Doubtless with this preoccupation
in mind, in the sixth chapter of his masterpiece he pretends to
hesitate as to how the affair between Jos Sedley and Rebecca
shall be dealt with: shall it be a high-life 'silver-fork' treatment; or
a 'below-stairs' account; or is it to be in the sordid Newgate
style?

Suppose we had laid the scene in Grosvenor Square. . . . Suppose we had shown how Lord Joseph Sedley fell in love, and
the Marquis of Osborne *became attached* to Lady Amelia . . .; or
instead of the supremely genteel, suppose we had resorted to
the entirely low, and described what was going on in Mr
Sedley's kitchen; – how black Sambo was *in love with* the
cook. . . . Or if, on the contrary, we had taken a fancy for the
terrible, and made *the lover* . . . a professional burglar, who . . .
carries off Amelia in her night-dress. (*VF* p. 54)

My italics here show how cleverly Thackeray chooses precisely
the right terminology for the level at which the affair is to be
carried on; the Richardsonian *become attached* contrasting with the
plainer *in love with*, and the more sensational and risqué *lover*. These
in turn all differ from the intermediate language of the middle
classes, as when, three chapters later, with more serious intent the
novelist shows us Rose Dawson, the ironmonger's daughter,
forsaking her respectable origins for the dubious honour of Sir
Pitt Crawley's bed: 'She gave up Peter Butt, a young man who
kept company with her, and in consequence of his disappointment
in love took to smuggling' (*VF* p. 82).

It is the more surprising, in view of such expertise, that in the later novels Thackeray cannot resist making the letters and conversations of certain characters the vehicles of full-scale authorial digressions, often inappropriate to the person who speaks them. Is it likely, for example, that Pendennis, skilled journalist though he is, would end a conversation with his friend George Warrington in a rapturous purple passage on the dawn (*P* II ch. 6)? It is in *The Newcomes* that this flaw is most obvious. In the following passage the casual talk of the youthful Clive Newcome is temporarily transformed into the mannerism of the middle-aged stylist who created him, with such favourite Thackerayan devices as apostrophizing, the repetition of words of similar sound ('lowly, slowly'), and the use of a normally adjectival form with weightier adverbial function ('to walk stately'). Such fine language is quite out of keeping with Clive's normal speech which, as we have seen, is often vividly realized:

> Some women ought to be stupid. . . . Why shouldn't the Sherrick be stupid, I say? About great beauty there should always reign a silence. As you look at great nature, the great ocean, any great scene of nature, you hush, sir. . . . When I saw the great Venus of the Louvre, I thought – Wert thou alive, O goddess, thou shouldst never open those lovely lips but to speak *lowly, slowly*; thou shouldst never descend from that pedestal but to walk *stately* to some near couch, and assume another attitude of beautiful calm. To be beautiful is enough . . . [etc.] (*N* I ch. 25)

It is still more gratuitous that a letter of Clive's, written from Rome, should develop into a full-scale apologia, rather in the style of one of the *Roundabout Papers*, for the Catholic church (*N* I ch. 35). But perhaps the most blatant instance occurs in the thirtieth chapter. Clive and Lord Kew are in conversation about love and marriage, when all of a sudden the latter 'kindling as he spoke,' as Thackeray puts it, 'and forgetting the slang and colloquialisms with which we garnish all our conversation,' launches into an authorial dissertation on coming to terms with the practicalities of marriage, and on the marriage-market generally. The passage is germane to the theme of the whole book, but the language is totally out of character; Lord Kew has no other bursts of eloquence in this vein. The reader is in sympathy with

Juliet McMaster's attempt (*op. cit.*, ch. 4) to defend *The Newcomes* against Henry James's charge that it is a 'loose baggy monster'; but these long digressions do not help her case.

Like Dickens, Thackeray enjoyed finding ways of representing both affected and substandard pronunciation. The affectations of the fashionable man-about-town could include a lisp, a failure to pronounce the letter *r*, a tendency to emphasize and modify the last syllable of a centring diphthong, and the pronunciation of words containing the spelling *er* with the sound [aː], now standardized in only a few words such as *clerk* and *Derby*:

'Hullo, *here'th* a go!' exclaimed Lord Viscount Cinqbars . . . '*cuth* me, *there'th* only one man!' (*SGS* ch. 9)

'Notorious old rogue,' Pop said, wagging his head. ('*Notowious* old *wogue*,' he pronounced the words, thereby rendering them much more emphatic.) (*P* I ch. 36)

His lordship has been heard to say he had been taken to 'a monsus *queeah* place, *queeah* set of folks.' (*N* I ch. 25)

Cuth me if I didn't meet the *infarnal* old family *dwag*, with my mother, *thithterth*, and all, *ath* I *wath dwiving* a hack-cab. (*SGS* ch. 8)

'These things belong only to pronunciation,' one might be tempted to say with Mrs Garth in *Middlemarch* (ch. 24), 'which is the least part of grammar!' Here, however, Mrs Garth was wrong; for we generally hear people speak before we have the opportunity to observe their orthography or discover whether they write grammatically. As Thackeray well knew, there is no more immediate, and often no surer, way of 'placing' a person socially than by noting, and if one is a novelist attempting to note down, his or her pronunciation. The omission, or the improper inclusion, of the consonant *h*, the intrusive *r*, the phrase *this here*, substandard in itself and doubly so when a semi-vowel appears between the two syllables, these are matters of moment in social novels, as they doubtless were in the polite society of Victorian times.

Thus one of the arguments adduced by Major Pendennis against Pen's alliance with the Fotheringay is the social consequences of marrying into a family whose English is below par:

'Fancy your wife attached to a mother who dropped her h's, or called Maria *Marire*!' He cites the dreadful example of one Lady Brouncker 'who was a druggist's daughter, or some such thing, and as Tom Wagg remarked of her, never wanted medicine certainly, for she never had an *h* in her life' (*P* I ch. 7).[1] Failure to pronounce *h* was especially characteristic of newly-rich people 'who, if there was talk of a statue to the Queen or the Duke, would come down to the Town 'All and subscribe their one, two, three 'undred apiece (especially if in the neighbouring town of Slowcome they were putting up a statue)' (*N* II ch. 17). Typical of this class is Mr Mugford, Philip Firmin's employer, who says ' "Look year, Firmin", or scratches one of his pigs on the back and says, "We'll 'ave a cut of this fellow on Saturday" ' (*Ph* II ch. 14). Lady Clavering, in *Pendennis*, manifests her uncertain social origins in her speech: 'If Lady Clavering talked about *Sparrowgrass* instead of Asparagus, or called an object *a hobject*, as this unfortunate lady would sometimes do, Missy calmly corrected her' (*P* I ch. 23).

The addition of an *h* where it is not required, as in Lady Clavering's usage here, also represents an over-adjustment of register, a false gentility that is especially characteristic of footmen, butlers and upper domestics generally (Thackeray sometimes spells the word *hhonest* with two *h*'s to exemplify this striving for the genteel). The same tendency can lead to an adjustment of vocabulary, as in this speech of the valet, Morgan, to his master, Major Pendennis:

> But Chevalier Strong, sir, came up and stopped the *shindy* – I
> beg pardon, the holtercation, sir. (*P* I ch. 36)

An uneasy awareness that it was incorrect to pronounce the final consonant in present participles as [n] (crossin'), led to the substitution of [ŋ] for [n], inappropriately: Morgan boasts, 'We have lived in the fust society, both at 'ome and *foring*' (*P* II ch. 22); and Sir Brian Newcome's valet announces that the family is at *Brighting* (*N* II ch. 2). An excrescent consonant can sometimes be a mark of over-refinement: a housekeeper declares that her absent family have 'gone up the *Rind*' (*BS* ch. 18). Also characteristically

---

[1] Given the Major's old-fashioned pronunciation, this was a rather better pun that it now appears to be. The noun was pronounced [eik] as now with a final plosive, whereas the verb was pronounced [eitʃ] with a final affricate. One can compare *bake* and *batch*, or *speak* and *speech*. See *OED ache* (v. and sb.), and E. J. Dobson, *English Pronunciation 1500–1700*, vol. II, Oxford, 1957, p. 949.

over-refined is a too-elaborate syntax in which the relative pronoun is followed by a redundant personal pronoun; especially
common when the speaker is called upon, like the butler
J. J. Ridley in *The Newcomes*, to make 'a speech which evidently
was a studied composition':

> He said he never could forget the kindness with which the
> Colonel have a treated him. His Lordship have taken a young
> man, *which* Mr Ridley had brought *him* up under his own eye,
> and can answer for him . . . and *which he* is to be his lordship's
> own man for the future.' (*N* I ch. 26)

With this we can compare the portentous usage of Firkin,
Miss Crawley's housekeeper:

> And so impressed was Mrs Firkin with the news, that she
> thought proper to write off by that very night's post, 'with
> her humble duty to Mrs Bute Crawley and the family at the
> Rectory, and Sir Pitt has been and proposed for to marry
> Miss Sharp, *wherein* she has refused *him*, to the wonder of all.'
> (*VF* p. 145)

The representation of substandard speech, particularly when,
from a character's status or pretensions, more correct English
might have been expected, was a way of caricaturing and poking
fun; although, as P. J. Keating has suggested (*The Working Classes
and Victorian Fiction*, p. 254), the joke does sometimes wear rather
thin; in such a production as *The Yellowplush Papers* where the
'comic' spellings of the footman Charles Yellowplush (often
spellings like *stomick* or *convulshuns*, which suggest no very different
pronunciation from standard English) are intended as a staple
source of humour throughout. On the whole, however, provided
one does not allow oneself to be too class-conscious on the subject,
Thackeray's representations of lower-class speech often have the
sharpness of observation, if not the gusto, of Dickens:

> Artises come and take hoff the church from that there tree –
> It was a Habby once, sir. (*P* I ch. 15)

> Ladies, your humble. . . . I'm glad you ain't got that proud gent
> with the glass hi . . . he's the most hillbred, supercilious beast
> I ever see. (*SGS* ch. 3)

When substandard language is intended to move us to tears rather than laughter, however, Thackeray is on much less firm ground; he then displays a tendency to patronize which becomes embarrassing. This condescension at its worst is embodied in the character known as Caroline Gann (in *A Shabby Genteel Story*) and (in its sequel, *Philip*) variously as Mrs Brandon, Nurse Brandon and the Little Sister. Part of the trouble is that, given her profession, we inevitably compare her with the most famous nurse in English fiction. For this is very much Dickens territory, and we are bound to imagine what he might have made of her; something like Miss Pross in *A Tale of Two Cities* and Mrs Gamp rolled into one. Nurse Brandon has been seduced by Philip's callous father before he marries Philip's mother, but in spite of this she appoints herself Philip's guardian angel and resolute supporter through thick and thin. What with her past, and the fact that she works for a living, she cannot be unequivocally a lady. Moreover, she is called upon by the exigencies of plot to chloroform a clergyman (one villainously given to blackmail, admittedly) and rob him of a 'bill' which would involve Philip in his father's debts. But over and above this, as Thackeray painfully and repeatedly insists, her bad grammar prevents her real acceptance into polite society; and yet her grammar is also said to be one of her charms: 'her voice, with its gentle laugh, and little sweet bad grammar, has always seemed the sweetest of voices' (*Ph* II ch. 11). 'Except her h's, that woman has every virtue' (*Ph* II ch. 19). The narrator, Pendennis, who also plays a part in the tale, at one point receives a letter from 'the Little Sister, in her dear little bad spelling, about which there used to be somehow a pathos which the very finest writing does not possess' (*Ph* II ch. 17).[1]

When Thackeray uses the word *little*, it is generally a sign that he is unsure of himself. In the scene leading up to the

---

[1] 'How could anyone be so sentimental about bad grammar and spelling?' one is tempted to ask, 'surely no-one in real life found such things romantic?' So one would have argued before 1972, when the diary of A. J. Munby (1828–1910) appeared under the title *Munby, Man of Two Worlds*. Munby, like Marlow in *She Stoops to Conquer*, was only at ease with women of a class in society below his own. He secretly married a working-class woman, Hannah Cullwick, who refused to become a 'lady'; and he sentimentalizes over her 'kitchen errors' of speech in a way that strongly recalls the treatment of the Little Sister in *Philip*: 'When she says . . . "I'd as lief do it" or "never did nothing" or the familiar "she says, says she", the phrase sounds precious as an epigram.' *Munby, Man of Two Worlds*, ed. Derek Hudson, London, 1972, pp. 184–9.

chloroforming just mentioned which, incidentally, the Little Sister performs in an arch, 'cute' way that is disquieting if we stop to think about it,[1] the word occurs at least a dozen times. Nurse Brandon falls a casualty, in fact, to mid-Victorian anxiety concerning the social use of language. It is an anxiety that has been wittily hinted at by G. M. Young, in *Portrait of an Age* (Oxford, 1936), p. 2:

> The world is very evil. An unguarded look, a gesture, a picture, or a novel, might plant a seed of corruption in the most inno-cent heart, and the same word or gesture might betray a lingering affinity with the class below.

In view of such considerations, Nurse Brandon cannot be comically treated; for in spite of everything she is almost accept-able, talking on almost equal terms with the impeccable Mrs Pendennis; and the manifestations of her bad grammar must not be overplayed. *You was, he have, what on hearth* and a general tendency to a repetitive, short-breathed, aggrieved sort of utterance – such things seem minor linguistic peccadilloes, on a par, perhaps, with her indulgence (before the chloroforming) in 'a glass – a little glass – of something comfortable' (*Ph* II ch. 19). As to the 'dear little bad spelling', we are vouchsafed only a glimpse of it (*Ph* II ch. 17): she spells *spirit* as *sperit*; but otherwise her orthography is not 'pathetic' in any sense.

Linguistic usage is a source of anxiety also to Philip Firmin, the hero, a gentleman-born despite his disreputable father. Nurse Brandon is worried about his status: 'A gentleman like Philip oughtn't to have a master. I couldn't bear to think of your going down of a Saturday to the publishing office to get your wages like a workman'; to which Philip replies, proudly, 'But I am a work-man' (*Ph* II ch. 17). He is proud of his position as a sub-editor; but not of his patron, the owner of the newspaper, a Mr Mugford, nor Mr Mugford's *nouveau-riche* wife, with her intrusive *r*'s:

> But how can Char [Philip's wife, Charlotte] frankly be the friend of a woman who calls a drawing-room a *droaring-room*? With our dear little friend in Thornhaugh Street [Nurse Brandon], it is different. Here is a patron and patroness, don't

1 See Joseph Baker, 'Thackeray's Recantation', in *PMLA*, vol. LXXVII (1972), pp. 586–94.

you see? When Mugford walks me round his paddock ...
scratches one of his pigs on the back, and says, 'We'll 'ave a
cut of this fellow on Saturday' – (explosive attempts at insub-
ordination and derision on the part of the children again are
severely checked by the parental authorities) – I feel inclined to
throw him ... into the trough. (*Ph* II ch. 14)

Even allowing that the views of the narrator, Pendennis, are not
entirely Thackeray's own, and that he is clearly critical of the
headstrong hero, I think that Thackeray had in practice come to
accept many of the social attitudes displayed here; and they
represent a decline from the radical criticism of society found in
earlier work like *The Book of Snobs*.

Philip represents a decline in technique, also, compared to
Pendennis of twelve years before and the much subtler treatment of
the Fanny Bolton affair, in which some four gradations of class
are both neatly marked in linguistic usage and treated in a
detached way that is conducive to thoughtful amusement rather
than embarrassment. The hero, Arthur Pendennis, or Pen, is
thrown by chance into the company of Fanny Bolton, 'the poor
little Ariadne of Shepherd's Inn', as she is later called (*P* II ch. 26).
After an illness in which Fanny tends him, thus compromising
herself in the eyes of Pen's mother, Pen discovers that he no
longer loves her, although he continues to have affectionate
memories of the affair: 'She dropped her h's, but she was a dear
little girl' (*P* II ch. 16). Pen's condescension is indicated in some
fine ironic dialogue, in which also Fanny's lowlier origins are
hinted at in her own speech, and emphasized more strongly in
that of her still less refined mother:

'And she went and ast for it [the novel Pen has written] at the
libery,' Mrs Bolton said ... 'and some 'ad it and it was hout,
and some 'adn't it. And one of the liberies as 'ad it wouldn't
let 'er 'ave it without a sovering; and she 'adn't one, and she
came back a-crying to me ... and I gave her a sovering.'
'And, oh, I was in such a fright lest any one should have come
to the libery and took it while I was away,' Fanny said. (*P* II
ch. 11)

Thackeray mingles humour with pathos in the portrait of this
Ariadne and successfully implies that she is not without resource

or ambition despite her apparent guilelessness. She may be forsaken by the gentry, but by well-timed smiles and tears she secures Sam Huxter, the son of a successful apothecary, who has appreciated her from the beginning as 'a pretty bit of *muslin*' (*P* II ch. 12). Sam is not in the Pendennis class (his black gloves leave marks on Pen's lavender ones, and he has a few linguistic vagaries); even so, it is a promotion for Fanny. As Sam says: 'Fanny ain't of a good family, I know, and not up to us in breeding and that – but she's a Huxter now' (*P* II ch. 34). Accordingly, her new position necessitates that Fanny be groomed by lessons in grammar from her husband-to-be:

> 'Mar had actially refused him twice, and had had to wait three months to get seven shillings which he had borrered of 'er.'
> 'Don't say 'er, but her; borrer, but borrow; actially, but actually, Fanny,' Mr Huxter replied – not to a fault in her argument, but to grammatical errors in her statement.
> 'Well then, her, and borrow, and hactually – there then, you stoopid.' (*P* II ch. 23)

On the whole, the reader feels the justice of this; such upward-striving is bound to bring its attendant obligations!

As a final example, perhaps the best, of the novelist's skilful manipulation of speech-levels, we might consider the brilliant portrait of Milly Costigan, or to give her her stage name, the Fotheringay. Her acting skills are shown eventually to be mechanical, trained as she has been down to the last detail by the cripple, Bows. But the contrast between her romantic roles and her homely, even stupid amiability, her refined sensibilities on stage and her hearty appetite for veal and ham 'poys' off stage, produces some of the novelist's funniest pages. The effect is partly achieved by linguistic means, for Milly Costigan reverts to her Irish brogue when not acting, and in the narrative the contrast in style between the highflown and the humdrum is fully exploited:

> After she had come out trembling with emotion before the audience, and looking so exhausted and tearful that you fancied she would faint with sensibility, she would gather up her hair the instant she was behind the curtain, and go home to a mutton chop and a glass of brown stout. (*P* I ch. 6)

She brought in a pair of ex-white satin shoes with her, which she proposed to rub as clean as might be with bread-crumbs; intending to go mad with them next Tuesday evening in Ophelia. (*P* I ch. 12)

'You are as pathetic as Miss O'Neill,' [Major Pendennis] continued, bowing and seating himself, 'your snatches of song remind me of Mrs Jordan in her best time . . . and your mother reminded me of Mars. Did you ever see the Mars, Miss Fotheringay?'
'There was two Mahers in Crow Street,' remarked Miss Emily: 'Fanny was well enough, but Biddy was no great things.'
'Sure, the Major means the god of war, Milly, my dear,' interrupted the parent.
'It is not the Mars I meant, though Venus, I suppose, may be pardoned for thinking about him;' the Major replied with a smile. (*P* I ch. 11)

The Fotheringay's ideas of beauty are catholic: she applies the epithet *beautiful* to some poems Pen has written in her honour, to some filberts she is eating and to punch. Nor is she intellectually equipped to discuss Shakespeare:

Pen tried to engage in conversation about poetry and about her profession. He asked her what she thought of Ophelia's madness, and whether she was in love with Hamlet or not? 'In love with such a little ojus wretch as that stunted manager of a Bingley?' She bristled at the thought. (*P* I ch. 5)

Pen reconciles this contradiction of her nature in a manner flattering to her – using for this purpose the rather threadbare language of the romance: 'How beautiful she is,' thought Pen . . . 'How simple and how tender! How charming it is to see a woman of her genius busying herself with the humble offices of domestic life!' (*P* I ch. 5). Major Pendennis, however, concerned to cure his nephew of his infatuation, has no such illusions. He wonders 'how she should be so stupid and act so well' (*P* I ch. 11). But Milly's head has not been turned either; and there is more than one kind of *intelligence*, as Thackeray shows a few lines later, when he recounts her down-to-earth practicality with polysyllabic irony:

'Some of the old Madara, Milly, love,' Costigan said, winking to his child – and that lady, turning to her father a glance of *intelligence*, went out of the room, and . . . softly summoned her little emissary Master Tommy Creed: and . . . ordered him to go buy a pint of Madara wine at the Grapes, and sixpennyworth of sorted biscuits at the baker's.

CHAPTER 5

Grammar, Word-Formation, Lexis

🀫🀫🀫🀫🀫🀫

GENERALLY speaking, there is little difference between Thackeray's grammatical usage and our own, and a full-length study of his grammar would be unprofitable. But of course, such a well-read man whose heart was attached in so many ways to the eighteenth century could not fail, not only in *Esmond, Barry Lyndon, Catherine* and *The Virginians,* but also in the novels set in his own day, to call up echoes of earlier usage. I give below some of the more noteworthy instances and many of these points are discussed in more detail in my book, *Jane Austen's English,* under the pages indicated.

1 A preterite tense used in the vicinity of the adverb *never,* where now a perfect, sometimes known as the 'perfect of experience', is usual (*JAE* p. 109):

I never *saw* an actress in my life. (*P* II ch. 2)

The hotel seems comfortable. I never *was* in it before. (*N* I ch. 12)

2 The earlier form of the negative and interrogative without auxiliary *do;* much rarer than in Jane Austen (*JAE* pp. 117–18):

But Pen *spoke not* on this matter to Mr Warrington. (*P* II ch. 26)

As for my health, what *matters it*? (*VF* p. 184)

3 The past tense of *may* (*might*) where now *may have,* indicating more explicitly present supposition about past action, is preferred (*JAE* p. 121):

It never entered his head while conversing with Jack and Tom that he was in any respect their better; although, perhaps, the deference which they paid him *might* please him. (*P* I ch. 30)

So, probably, 200 and 202 in Curzon Street *might* know what was going on. (*VF* p. 361)

4 The use of *must have* not, as today, of present supposition about the past, but to indicate necessity in the past (*JAE* p. 124):

If we'd gone on to Rouge et Noir, I *must have* won. (*P* II ch. 5)

One evening, at the close of 1854, as Charlotte Nicholls sat with her husband . . . she suddenly said . . . 'If you had not been with me, I *must have* been writing now'. (*RP* 'The Last Sketch')

5 The collocation *was used to* + infinitive, where *used to* is now normal. This is Jane Austen's regular usage, but it is rare in Thackeray (*JAE* p. 124):

Mr Bolton, grumbling as he *was used to do* every morning. (*P* II ch. 17)

6 Thackeray shares with Dickens a curious use of the auxiliary *shall*, expressing a kind of hypothetical situation. Visser (*An Historical Syntax of the English Language*, III ii, p. 1597) typifies this usage with a sentence-pattern from *The Newcomes*, the first quoted below. As he says, the clause containing this kind of *shall* is often followed by another clause opening with *and*. Fowler (*Modern English Usage* s.v. *shall* 6) advises caution before using 'this decorative second or third person *shall*'. He calls it 'an archaism, before using which, as before using other archaisms, a writer should be very sure that his style in general will stand comparison with that of the few who have archaized to good purpose'. One of these, unquestionably, is Thackeray:

A company of old comrades *shall* be merry and laughing together, and the entrance of a single youngster will stop the conversation. (*N* I ch. 21)

Rather more promissory than hypothetical, but equally characteristic of Thackeray, is the following use of the auxiliary:

There is now hardly a town of France or Italy in which you *shall* not see some noble countryman of our own. (*VF* p. 356)

As you see a pauper's child . . . able to haggle at market . . . you *shall* find a young beauty . . . as wise and knowing as the old practitioners. (*N* II ch. 7)

7 The collocation *the* + gerund = object, now generally either with no definite article, or with the gerund preceded by the article and followed by the preposition *of* (*JAE* p. 131):

> *The* very *missing her* at her coach had something fatal in it. (*P* I ch. 16)

8 The use of the *to be to* construction in the sense of 'is likely to' and without the present-day suggestion of compulsion or pre-ordination. Again this is much commoner in Jane Austen than in Thackeray (*JAE* pp. 137–9):

> It is a conspiracy of the middle classes against gentlemen; it is only the shopkeeper cant which *is to go* down nowadays. (*BL* ch. 9)

> 'He *is to make* fun of me, is he?' thought Rebecca. (*VF* p. 63)

9 Verbs are sometimes found to be (a) transitive or (b) intransitive, contrary to modern practice (*JAE* pp. 152–4):

> (a) Some of his comrades . . . *joked* him about the splendour of his costume. (*VF* p. 205)
>
> Lord Sextonbury . . . seems to have *recovered* her ladyship's death. (*BS* ch. 43)
>
> He *pays* their dinners at Greenwich, and they invite the company. (*VF* p. 136)
>
> Everything might still be *hoped* from his youth. (*P* II ch. 14)
>
> Invite your mother . . . to *stay* Christmas there. (*N* II ch. 14)
>
> Come away! . . . You have no right to be *spying* the young fellow. (*V* I ch. 32)

To protest as a transitive verb, which has a very contemporary ring (see S. Potter, *Changing English*, p. 141), has always been the correct usage in certain financial contexts, as here: 'The India bills had arrived, and been *protested* in the City' (*N* II ch. 33).

> (b) I cannot *consult* to-night; I must go to bed. (*FG* p. 106)
>
> A young fellow can make himself happy even out of the season; and Mr Harry was determined to *enjoy*. (*V* I ch. 40)

The absolute use of *to preserve*, meaning 'to keep game undisturbed for personal use in hunting, shooting and fishing', probably not yet obsolete but now much rarer, should also be included here: 'Pendennis don't *preserve*, then?' (*P* I ch. 25).

10 There is a tendency for the subjunctive mood to be used more frequently than today: *had* in the sense 'would have', and *were* in the sense 'would be' are both commoner. One could even argue that the latter usage in principal clauses is a sort of shibboleth, in nineteenth-century fiction, for old-fashioned or pompous clergymen, from Mr Collins (*JAE* p. 155) to Dr Casaubon, who spoke with 'that air of formal effort which never forsook him even when he spoke without his waistcoat and cravat' (*Middlemarch* ch. 37). One remembers, too, the Reverend Josiah Crawley's rebuke to Mrs Proudie in *The Last Chronicle of Barset* (ch. 18): 'Madam, you should not interfere in these matters. You simply debase your husband's high office. The distaff *were* more fitting for you'. We are not surprised that Thackeray's unctuous clergyman, the Rev. Charles Honeyman, has the usage: 'He *were* a brute – a savage, if he did!'; 'That . . . *were* scarcely clerical' (*N* I ch. 23).

11 In matters of concord, the only noteworthy fact is that the word *news* is often plural:

'Papa, papa!' Emmy cried out, 'here *are news*!' (*VF* p. 565)

What famous *news are* these. (*V* II ch. 36)

12 Abstract nouns tend to occur more frequently in the plural, and also with the indefinite article in the meaning 'an act of, instance of (the quality in question)' (*JAE* pp. 159–62):

Jack . . . had had one or two *helps* from the good-natured prodigal. (*P* I ch. 32)

Our little siren was at her piano, singing with all her might and *fascinations*. (*P* II ch. 35)

Do his *intellects* brighten after a sermon from the dull old vicar? (*V* II ch. 37)

I hope no one has offered you *a rudeness*. (*LW* ch. 5)

After *a generous and manly conduct* . . . he has met from some friends of his with a most unkind suspicion. (*P* II ch. 19)

I can't fancy *a behaviour* more unmanly. (*FG* p. 113)

13 In regard to the genitive, the elliptical partitive genitive is commoner in Thackeray than it is today, though not so frequent as in Jane Austen's time (*JAE* p. 164):

Arthur eagerly pressed his friend to be *of the party*. (*P* II ch. 16)

Major Pendennis vowed that he liked snug dinners *of all things* in the world. (*P* I ch. 37)

To suggest bucolic overtones when a rustic guide conducts a party over a stately home, the novelist revives that Tudor phenomenon, which Jespersen (*Progress in Language with Special Reference to English*, pp. 318–27) calls the quasi-genitive, as in John Smith his mark':

The upper part by Inigo Jones; the lower was altered by the eminent Dutch architect, Vanderputty, in *George the First his time*. (*P* I ch. 22)

14 Among uses involving personal pronouns, we might mention (a) the 'shoppy' omission of a pronoun subject, where intervening alternative pronouns make the repetition of the first pronoun usual; (b) the use of *it* for persons, commonest either when talking of and to children and therefore a childish affectation with Blanche Amory and Pen or when, being contemptuous and therefore appropriate, Becky Sharp, revisiting Belgium, recalls Amelia Sedley's conduct before Waterloo; (c) Thackeray's awareness that usage may override grammatical precision in the choice of pronouns (*JAE* pp. 164–7):

(a) Sorry I'd no better news to bring you, Mr T, and as you are dissatisfied, again recommend you to employ another law agent. (*P* I ch. 13)

(b) I can buy a hatful at Fortnum and Mason's for a guinea. And *it* shall have *its* bonbons, *its* pootty little sugarplums. (*P* II ch. 26)

'Foolish boy,' she said, '*it* shall be loved as it deserves.' (*P* II ch. 35)

I wonder whether little Emmy is alive. *It* was a good little creature. (*VF* p. 624)

(c) 'Is that *him*?' said the lady in questionable grammar. (*Ph* I ch. 16)

'You are a good fellow, William,' said Mr Osborne . . . ,
'and *me* and George shouldn't part in anger, that is true.'
(*VF* p. 220)

15 As to relative pronouns, we have noted elsewhere [p. 108) that
it is characteristic of substandard nineteenth-century speech to
subordinate adjective clauses imperfectly ('wantin' to fight Tom
the post-boy, *which* I'm thinking he'd have had the worst of *it*' *P*
I ch. 5). Otherwise, all that seems noteworthy is a rather osten-
tatious carelessness in the matter of relatives:

That charming young creature who has just stepped into her
carriage from Mr Fraser's shop, and *to whom and her mamma* Mr
Fraser has made the most elegant bow. (*SGS* ch. 5)

A gentleman, in a shaky steamboat, on a dangerous river, in a
far-off country, *which* caught fire three times during the voyage
– (of course I mean the steamboat, not the country). (*RP* 'A
Mississippi Bubble')

16 There are only a few points of difference of usage with our
own in the matter of definite and indefinite articles (*JAE* pp.
172–6): we are less likely now to use the definite article with
names of diseases, as '*the* bronchitis' (*P* I ch. 13); '*the* scarlet fever'
(*VF* p. 12); or in such phrases as 'great personages of *the* fashion'
(*P* I ch. 32); 'she . . . comes up to *the* scratch' (*Ph* II ch. 5); 'certain
other personages in *the* creation' (*EH* p. 154); and Thackeray
reminds us of the date at which *Vanity Fair* was supposed to have
occurred when he talks of '*the* Regent's Park' (*VF* p. 582). The
indefinite article is omitted where we now find it desirable in *for
change of air* and *out of window*, and included occasionally before
the pronoun *something*, the latter usage being much more common in Jane Austen (*JAE* pp. 172–6): 'All the party had gone to
Richmond for *change of air*' (*P* II ch. 15); 'I . . . long to kick him
out of window' (*N* I ch. 30); 'pitchin' him *outawinder*' (*P* I ch. 36);
'The young gentlemen in Hart Street might learn *a something* of
every known science' (*VF* p. 545).[1]

1 Even an indefinite article can contribute, as here, to satirical purpose. These
young gentlemen, who include Georgy Osborne, are being educated at the school
run by the Reverend Lawrence Veal, whose system does not 'embrace the degrad-
ing corporal severities, still practised at the ancient places of education'; but who
also, this indefinite article implies, gives the boys an inadequate smattering of
many subjects, and no substantial education.

17 Adjectives, though polysyllabic, are still occasionally compared with suffixes (*JAE* p. 176). The adjective *other*, now normally occurs next to the noun qualified; in Thackeray, as a stylistic archaism, intervening qualifiers occur:

> George though he was one of the *generousest* creatures alive. (*VF* p. 187)

> My friend Crocky Doyle was . . . deemed . . . the *honestest* fellow. (*VF* p. 211)

> The Marquis of Steyne made *other two* profound bows to Lady Clavering. (*P* II ch. 7)

> He . . . went into the kitchen on his way to the dog-kennel, the fowl-houses, and *other his* favourite haunts. (*P* I ch. 2)

18 The eighteenth-century grammarians insisted, as far as they could, on the suffix *-ly* being the mark of adverbial function. In the novels which recall the eighteenth century, Thackeray is fond of retaining the earlier custom of using suffixless forms in such grammatical contexts:

> They led the happiest, simplest lives *sure* ever led by married couple. (*FG* p. 76)

> Everyone knew I was *bitter* poor; and . . . I was *bitter* proud too. (*BL* ch. 1)

19 In the matter of negation, J. W. Clark's observation (pp. 36–8) on the usage of Trollope is broadly true for Thackeray also: '*Ain't* was common and entirely acceptable . . . in the familiar speech of the educated and upper classes . . . but *not* in their formal, especially public, speech or in their writing . . . This is not to say that it is usual in such speech; it is much less common than the correct forms.' The distribution for *don't*, Clark later adds, is essentially the same as for *ain't*. The eponymous hero of *Philip*, a 'gentleman born', has such usage as 'My father *don't* like it' (*Ph* I ch. 7); and 'I want shelter; *ain't* I in good quarters?' (*Ph* I ch. 17).

20 As to what the Germans call *Präpositionslehre*, Thackeray is apt, as always, to retain occasionally usage that was probably felt in his own day to be archaic or obsolescent. Thus he avails himself of such Austenian and earlier usage (*JAE* pp. 190–6) as the

following: 'He was *for* carrying her off' (*P* II ch. 37); 'The black man is safe *for* me' (*RP* 'A Mississippi Bubble'); 'I'd leave my money *from* him' (*VF* p. 157); 'She's five thousand pound *to* her fortune' (*VF* p. 563); 'He was tender about his children *to* weakness' (*V* II ch. 30). *In behalf of* (*P* II ch. 28) and to be interested *about* (*VF* p. 438) are still regular idioms. One can also observe how the phrase *in course*, which was acceptable in the eighteenth century, unacceptable in the nineteenth, and superseded entirely by *of course* in the twentieth, took the downward path. It occurs in reputable conversation in *The Virginians* ('He was smaller than me, and *in course* younger' *V* I ch. 43), and is last illustrated in the *OED* (*course* 34c) from *Catherine*. In *A Shabby Genteel Story* the phrase has been demoted:

> 'The finest wine I ever tasted in my life – at a commoner's table, that is.'
> 'Oh, *in course*, a commoner's table! . . . Mr Gann, I will trouble you for some more crackling.' (*SGS* ch. 3)[1]

21 Perhaps only two archaic uses of conjunctions are noteworthy: (a) *for that* as the equivalent of *because*; (b) *whether* in what the *OED* describes as a rare archaic or obsolete use (*whether* B II 1), to introduce a disjunctive direct question, expressing a doubt between two alternatives:

> I said I should die happy, *for that* to please those two ladies was . . . the great aim of my existence. (*P* II ch. 6)

> *Whether* is it the more mortifying to us, to feel that we are disliked or liked undeservedly? (*N* II ch. 18)

> *Whether* was it better for him to be slighted in a fashionable club, or to swagger at the head of a company in a tavern parlour? (*Ph* II ch. 12)

Thackeray was able to employ the usages of grammar with precision, or with deliberate imprecision, to make a satirical point or to indicate an aspect of character. Note the clever use of relative pronouns here:

> The great rich Miss Crawley, with seventy thousand pounds in the five per cents., *whom*, or I had better say *which*, her two brothers adore. (*VF* p. 98)

1 It is one of the substandard phrases assumed, in haughty mockery of the language of servants, by Mr Rochester in *Jane Eyre* (ch. 21).

A good example of deliberate imprecision occurs in the post-script to a letter written by Ethel Newcome to Laura Pendennis, apropos of Ethel's brother Barnes, the villain of *The Newcomes*:

> They have put up a dreadful caricature of B. in Newcome: and my brother says *he* did it, but I hope not. It is very droll, though: *he* used to make them very funnily. (*N* II ch. 30, my italics)

When he has been shown this postscript, Arthur Pendennis comments: 'He says he did it. . . . Barnes Newcome would scarcely caricature himself, my dear!' To which Laura replies in an off-hand manner: ' "He" often means – means Clive – I think.' In this way Ethel's divided loyalties, to her brother and to the man she would have liked to marry, are indicated. The classicist will be quick to point out that this ambiguity cannot arise in Latin, where *se* or *eum* or, with the possessive, *suus* or *eius* would differentiate.[1] There is, however, in the following passage from *The Virginians*, a subtle and deliberate failure to follow the normal sequence of mood which has many Latin precedents:

> 'Could we have moved, sir, a month sooner, the fort *was* certainly ours, and the little army had never been defeated,' Mr Warrington said. (*V* II ch. 60)

Classical grammarians would class this statement as an assertion of unreal condition. In Latin all three verbs in protasis and apodoses would appear in the subjunctive mood. But the use of the indicative *was* here, with its implication of fact rather than hope, wish or supposition, indicates how tantalizingly near to fulfilment the desires of the speaker were. There are parallels to this abnormal use of the indicative in Latin (e.g. Virgil, *Aeneid* II 55).

A half-way stage between the study of grammar and that of word-formation is provided by the phenomenon of grammatical conversion, the use of what was originally one part of speech in the function of another part of speech. Since English has lost

---

1 There is no doubt that this is a defect of English, as compared with Latin and Greek. The ambiguity does not often occur; but when it does it can cause amusement, as with a child's alleged misunderstanding of Cowper's well-known hymn:

> And Satan trembles when he sees
> The meanest saint upon *his* knees.
> (*Olney Hymns*)

nearly all its inflexions, there has been a good deal of freedom in this matter of conversion, though over the centuries various and varying restrictions to the process have obtained. For example, we should be less likely today to use the word *amaze*, now normally a verb, as a noun in the sense of 'amazement', as Milton does in 'The Nativity Ode' ('The stars, with deep *amaze*, stand fix'd in steadfast gaze'), and Thackeray still very occasionally does: 'To the *amaze* of her mamma and sisters . . . she actually inspired a passion' (*SGS* ch. 1). Nor, perhaps, should we be inclined to use *brag* as a noun, as in Shakespeare's 'Caesar's thrasonical *brag* of "I came, saw, and overcame" ' (*As You Like It*, V ii 34), or Thackeray's 'His peculiar dignity of manner, and great fluency of *brag*' (*SGS* ch. 2). Similarly *meet* as a noun is a word that still tends to be confined in England, though not in America, to the meaning of 'a meeting of hounds and men in preparation for a hunt'. But Thackeray has the word with wider meaning: 'They have an English library [in Rome] where the various *meets* for the week are placarded' (*N* II ch. 1).

The commonest conversion is not, as in these last examples, of verb to noun, but of noun to verb. Again, there are instances which we should hesitate over, preferring an established verb. Dr Johnson, in his Dictionary, noted that *compassion* as a verb is 'a word scarcely used'; yet Thackeray has it: 'An injured queen . . . who was greatly *compassioned* and patronized by Mrs James Gann' (*SGS* ch. 1). Probably the novelist is consciously recalling eighteenth-century usage when he writes in *The Four Georges* of 'the crowd at Drury Lane to look at the body of Miss Ray, whom Parson Hackman has just *pistolled*' (*FG* p. 66); as he certainly is with the verb *to pigeon*, meaning 'to cheat' from the slang noun *a pigeon*, meaning 'a dupe', in this, the last *OED* quotation for the verb: 'You sit down with him in private to cards, and *pigeon* him' (*V* II ch. 46). Contrariwise, his is the first recorded instance of the slang verb *to pill*, manifestly from the noun, meaning 'to reject by ballot; to black-ball' (*OED pill* v² 3): 'He was coming on for election at Bays' and was as nearly *pilled* as any man I ever knew' (*N* I ch. 30). We should have little use today for a verb which he is first recorded as having used, *to back-board*, meaning 'to subject to the use of the back-board, held or strapped across the back to straighten the figure': 'They have been lectured, and learning, and *back-boarded*, and practising' (*N* II ch. 15). This kind of verb might naturally arise, however, and one is surprised that it was not recorded earlier, as was *to wafer*, meaning 'to seal or fasten with a wafer, a small disc made of gum and flour used for the purpose': 'Another brought a large playbill from Chatteris, and *wafered* it there' (*P* I ch. 15). In this commercial age, but by a similar conversion, it would be *sellotaped* or *bluetacked*. One interesting difference is that the verb *to needle*, which now occurs only in the transferred colloquial sense of 'to annoy', appears with the literal meaning of 'to sew': 'Groups of women . . . *needling* away' (*FG* p. 82). Thackeray was always ready to coin self-explanatory verbs from nouns, to write that a bishop '*amen'd* the humbug' (*N* II ch. 19) or that a man is '*leading-stringed* by women' (*V* II ch. 14), or to have a character accuse the eponymous heroine of *Catherine*: 'I suppose you'd *laudanum* him' (*C* ch. 5), the last two being nonce-formations. Some of the most striking of these conversions to verbs are concerned with modes of address, reminding us of Jane Austen's 'Let me not suppose that she dares go about *Emma Woodhouse-ing* me' (*Emma* ch. 43):

> The Vicar . . . '*Sir Brians*' Papa, and '*Your Ladyships*' Mamma. (*N* II ch. 9)

> They *my-loved* and *my-deared* each other . . . , but kept apart. (*VF* p. 442)

Two conversions from adjectives to nouns that are no longer current are *ordinary* for a regular meal at a fixed price at an eating-house or tavern; and *fashionable*, meaning either a member of fashionable society or a novel of the 'high-life' or 'silver-fork' variety:

> He . . . made his appearance at the market-day and the farmers' *ordinary*. (*P* II ch. 27)

> A very pleasing and witty *fashionable*, the brilliant . . . Mrs Rawdon Crawley. (*VF* p. 472)

> It was at the period when the novel called the 'fashionable' was in vogue. (*P* II ch. 3)

Here we should also include the partial conversion[1] of the

---

1 For this distinction, see further, Valerie Adams, *An Introduction to Modern English Word-Formation*, pp. 16-20. A frequent sign of partial conversion is the fact that the converted word cannot be made plural. See also S. Potter, *Changing English*, pp. 166-7.

adjectives *entire*, short for *entire beer*, a liquor containing the combined flavours of 'ale, beer and twopenny' (*OED entire* A 2b), and *particular* for an individual's special choice of wine:

> Yonder artist who is painting up Foker's *Entire* over the public-house at the corner. (*N* II ch. 12)

> If it had been Lord Steyne's *particular*, and not public-house Cape. (*P* I ch. 11)

The sense of an omitted noun is strong in these last two examples; and still more in the following, where *threes* manifestly means 'three per cent stock'; the conversion of the numeral in this meaning is first recorded in the *OED* from Thackeray (*three* II 3d):

> I'm told she has six hundred thousand pounds in the *Threes*. (*P* I ch. 36)

He is also the first to record, judging by the *OED* quotations, a conversion that is the reverse of those hitherto illustrated in this paragraph: the noun *sensation* used attributively (*sensation* 5).

> At the theatres they have a new name for their melodramatic pieces and call them '*Sensation* Dramas.' (*RP* 'On Two Papers I Intended to Write')

The use of the personal pronoun *she* as a noun meaning 'woman' occurs only once, so far as I have observed. This was usage which was more common in our earlier literature; in Crashaw, for example: 'Whoe'er she be/That not impossible *she*/That shall command my heart and me' ('Wishes to His Supposed Mistress'); and also in Shakespeare. The increasing use, in the last two hundred years, of the prop-word *one* has virtually ousted this usage:

> No, not to be Helen, Queen Elizabeth, Mrs Coutts, or the luckiest *she* in history. (*SGS* ch. 1)

A favourite stylistic trick of the novelist's which is also a grammatical conversion is to give a word ending in -*ly* that is normally an adjective the extra weight of an adverbial function. People are apt, in Thackeray's pages, 'to perish *untimely*' for example (*P* I ch. 18), 'to walk *stately*' or 'to nod *friendly*' (*N* I ch. 25). Less common is the use of an adverb attributively, as in 'an *almost* reconciliation' (*VF* p. 364), or 'to the *almost* terror of the persons present' (*RP* 'Nil Nisi Bonum').

Perhaps the most extreme instances of conversions are the use of the relative *who* as a noun: 'They pointed out to her who was on the course; and the "*who*" was not always the person a young lady should know' (*P* II ch. 20); and the elevation of the conjunction *but* to the status of a noun and a key word:

> *But* will come in spite of us. *But* is reflection. *But* is the sceptic's familiar, with whom he has made a compact; and if he forgets it . . . , *But* taps at the door, and says, Master, I am here. . . . That is what *But* is. (*P* II ch. 33)[1]

There are, of course, rare or nonce-formations in Thackeray as in all great writers. They are particularly common in the journalistic essays collected under the title *Roundabout Papers*. The diminutives *squeezekin, princekin, lordkin, birdikin, grudgekin* and *giftling* are apparently Thackerayan formations. The frequency of the rather rare diminutive suffix -*kin* is no accident, but is a symptom of the novelist's reductive cast of mind. *Misshood*, meaning 'the condition of a young unmarried woman', seems to be his invention; as is *opinant* for 'one who forms or holds an opinion'. He extrapolates from *biographies* to *thanatographies*, meaning 'accounts of life and of death' (in the Newgate Calendar) (*C* ch. 6); and from *exhaust* to *inhaust*, the latter meaning 'to inhale or suck in'. He has two odd formations *sweeperess* for a female crossing-sweeper and *bankeress* for a banker's wife. He could rely on a reading public sufficiently versed in Latin to understand at sight new expressions like '*diffugient* snows',[2] '*concutient* cannon-balls', *impavidly* meaning 'fearlessly' and *viduous* meaning 'empty, bereft of company';

1 *But* is here equivalent to such a noun as *objection*, as in the saying 'But me no *buts*'; not a specific objection, but a generic one, compounded from the innumerable sentences where the conjunction has this adversative import. Similarly, when Kipling leads off a poem with the title 'If', we know that what follows will represent some aspect of that lamentable and oft-lamented discrepancy between the actual and the ideal. So, common conjunctions like *Until* and *Because* can stand as titles to popular drawing-room ballads. The point has been seized on by Beachcomber (J. B. Morton) of the *Daily Express*: 'Miss Janice Tullibardine is to sing four little songs by Miss Ailsa Jacobson – "Whenever", "Before", "Inasmuch As", and "Whatever".' J. B. Morton, *By The Way*, London, 1931, p. 342.

2 '*Diffugient* snows' echoes Horace (*Odes*, IV vii 1); and a still closer reference to the *Odes* (II xiv 1) occurs in the sentence: 'But the *fugacious* years have lapsed, my Posthumous' (*LW* ch. 4).

and the expressive *cornucopiosity* to describe the lavish excess in the furnishing of snobbish households (*BS* ch. 43). When he called a certain white wine *supernacular*, he perhaps had more hope than a modern novelist would have that his readers would associate it with the word *supernaculum*, a modern Latin rendering of German *auf den Nagel trinken*, meaning 'to drink off to the last drop', hence a superlative wine (*OED* s.v. *supernaculum*). He seems to have been among the first to import the Swiss German noun (though not the verb) *jödel*, now usually spelt *yodel*, and the colloquial French *poulet*, meaning a love-letter; from French *brumeux* he coins the adjective *brumous* to describe the foggy air of Britain, and from *orageux* he borrow *oragious* meaning 'stormy'. With the exception of *oragious*, *brumous*, *bankeress*, *yodel* and *inhaust* all these words are *OED* nonce-formations.

On the basis, doubtless, of *fortify*, he humorously creates to *portify*, using it figuratively; 'This claret is loaded, as it were; but your desire to *portify* yourself is amiable, is pardonable, is perhaps honourable' (*RP* 'Small Beer Chronicle'). Another bibulous metaphor is 'an *amontillado* manner' (*Ph* I ch. 17), meaning one that is dry and astringent, like amontillado sherry. He coins an onomatopoetic word *cloop*, meaning the noise a cork makes when leaving a bottle (*Ph* II ch. 2).

In *The Virginians* there occurs what the *OED* calls a 'humorously pedantic' revival of the noun *madefaction*, meaning 'a making wet' (Latin *madēre* 'to be wet'), of weeping: 'That *madefaction* of pocket-handkerchiefs' (*V* II ch. 29); and another rare Latinate revival is *rident* (Latin *rīdēre* 'to laugh'): 'Hetty was radiant and *rident*' (*V* II ch. 29). In *The Virginians*, also, there occurs the first importation into English of *cheese* in the special sense of French *faire des fromages* (*OED cheese* n. 3) 'a schoolgirl's amusement, consisting in turning rapidly round and then suddenly sinking down, so that the petticoats are inflated all round somewhat in the form of a cheese. Hence, applied sometimes to a deep curtseying': 'It was such a deep ceremonial curtsey as you never see at present. She and her sister both made these "cheeses" in compliment to the new comer, and with much stately agility' (*V* I ch. 22).

More important than these rare or nonce words is the question of words now in common use which may have been introduced, first recorded, or modified in meaning by Thackeray. As we shall see, *hangar* first occurs, meaning a covered space or shed for coaches, in *Henry Esmond*; and *snob* was a word that the novelist made his own, and in which he crystallized, if he did not bring about, a radical alteration of meaning. He seems to have been the first to use the verb *pose* in the sense (*pose* v.[1] 4c) of 'to present oneself in a particular, often an assumed, character'. He also developed a meaning of the verb that, perhaps coincidentally, had occurred much earlier in the language and had then apparently lapsed in currency: *pose* in the sense of 'to place in a specific situation or condition, to establish' (see *OED* v.[1] 1 and *Supp.*). I append the two instances, both of which seem to be innovatory:

Mr Brandon . . . '*posed*' before her as a hero of the most sublime kind. (*SGS* ch. 6)

A . . . silver-gilt dressing-case . . . looks well on a man's dressing-table at a country-house. It '*poses*' a man, you understand. (*Ph* I ch. 18)

A usage which the novelist is accredited with first recording is *loud* in the sense (*OED loud* 4 and *loudly*) of 'vulgarly obtrusive, flashy'. He was very aware of the metaphorical sense: 'Trousers that cried with a *loud* voice, "Come look at me, and see how cheap and tawdry I am" ' (*P* II ch. 8). But there is a curious antedating of the *OED* in *The Cumberland Letters*, 1775: 'He cut a flaming figure . . . with his *loud* waistcoat' (*The Cumberland Letters, 1771–84*, ed. Clementina Black, London, 1912, p. 88).

In her recent authoritative book *A History of English*, Barbara Strang has rightly alerted us to the fact that the study of word losses is of importance, but is often neglected. In this respect, Thackeray repays study; as a writer of historical novels he preserves many archaisms and, in effect, ignores both parts of Pope's two-fold advice in *An Essay on Criticism*:

Be not the first by whom the new are tried
Nor yet the last to lay the old aside.

He seems to have been almost as knowledgeable about women's fashions in the eighteenth century as about those of his own day. A *cardinal* for a lady's short cloak is last illustrated in the *OED* from *The Virginians*; and similarly with *capuchin* for a lady's cloak and hood, made in the manner of the capuchin friars. He writes, in the same novel (ch. 32): 'The girls went off straightway to get their best calamancoes, paduasoys, falbalas, furbelows, capes, cardinals, sacks, negligées, solitaires, caps, ribbons, mantuas, clocked stockings, and high-heeled shoes.' This is the last *OED* citation for *calamancoes*, women's garments made from *calamanco* 'a woollen stuff of Flanders, glossy on the surface, and woven with a satin twill and chequered in the warp, so that the checks are seen on one side only'. This kind of cloth was fashionable in the eighteenth century. A *solitaire*, a loose neck-tie of black silk or broad ribbon, was normally worn by men. A *falbala* was a trimming for women's petticoats. The last *OED* quotation for *outcry* in the sense of 'an auction sale' is from *Vanity Fair*: 'He sold it all at public *outcry*, at enormous loss to himself' (*VF* p. 381). The last instance for the spelling of *currants* in the etymological way, *corinths*, is from *The Virginians* (*V* I ch. 33). Thackeray is the last writer to be cited as using *illustration* in the sense 'an example, means or cause of distinction' (*OED illustration* 2). The sententious blue-stocking, Mrs Hobson Newcome, says: 'My maxim is, that genius is an *illustration*, and merit is better than any pedigree' (*N* I ch. 7). He seems to be the last to use *sport* in the obsolete sense (*sport* v. 9) of 'to lay out in a wager': 'The chaps will win your money as sure as you *sport* it' (*P* I ch. 19); and the last to use the word *slavey* for a male (as opposed to a female) attendant: 'The *slavey* has Mr Frederick's hot water, and a bottle of soda-water. . . . He has been instructed to bring soda, whenever he hears the word *slavey* pronounced from above' (*N* I ch. 11). His is the last *OED* instance of *moneyer* in the eighteenth-century sense of 'banker' (*moneyer* 1b), which the *OED* thinks is now probably obsolete: 'F.B., sir, has a station in the world; F.B. moves among *moneyers* and City nobs' (*N* II ch. 26); and his usage postdates the last *OED* example of *wigsby* (*P* II ch. 29), a jocular and derisive epithet for a man wearing a wig, applied to Major Pendennis. Two usages which are now dialectal but which were characteristic of earlier English, are *compliment* in the eighteenth-century sense of a complimentary gift or gratuity, and *hanker* in the sense of 'to loiter, linger':

> I had even got Mr Army-Secretary Walpole to take a hundred guineas in a *compliment*. (*C* ch. 5)

> Our friend the painter and glazier has been *hankering* about our barracks at Knightsbridge. (*N* II ch. 15)

It was eighteenth-century usage to refer to a vehicle like a sedan chair as a *machine*: 'a couple of stout reputable chairmen and their *machine*' (*BL* ch. 14); or to an evening assembly as a *drum*: 'Harry ... I have no doubt is going to the *drum* too' (*V* I ch. 32).[1] To *perform* in the sense of 'to carry out or execute (a work of art)' is also earlier usage: the last *OED* quote (*perform* v. 3) is for 1774: 'the picture of St Francis adoring the infant Saviour, *performed* by Sir Peter Paul Rubens' (*V* II ch. 10).

All these instances corroborate the evidence of *Esmond* that Thackeray's knowledge of eighteenth-century life, letters and language is nothing short of astonishing. If further proof is needed, the following two instances are surely conclusive. One is from *The Virginians*:

Have you not read of the fine lady in Walpole, who said, 'If I drink more, I shall be "muckibus" '? (*V* I ch. 38)

The *OED* illustrates this nonce-word from Walpole's letters, defining *muckibus* as 'intoxicated, tipsy, fuddled':

Lady Coventry ... said in a very vulgar accent, if she drank any more, she should be *muckibus*. 'Lord!' said Lady Mary Coke, 'what is that?' – 'Oh! it is Irish for sentimental.'

The second example is from *Pendennis*, in a general comment on novel readers. He writes of 'mischievous and prosaic people who carp and calculate at every detail of the romancer, and want to know, for instance, how, when the characters in the "Critic" are at a *dead lock* with their daggers at each other's throats, they are to be got out of that murderous complication of circumstances' (*P* II ch. 14). Now *lock* in the sense of 'a dilemma' (*OED lock* n.[2] 12) is found still in *Catherine*: 'And here, at this *lock*, we shall leave the whole company until the next chapter' (*C* ch. 4). The only survival of *lock* in this meaning today is the combination *deadlock*, the first instance of which, as Thackeray must have known, is from the third act of Sheridan's *The Critic*: 'I have them all at a *dead lock*! for every one of them is afraid to let go first.'

---

1 The *OED* suggests that in Victorian times the word could also mean an afternoon tea-party; and this seems to be the novelist's meaning in the letters: 'Tomorrow Miss Anny gives her first *drum*' (*L* IV p. 80).

CHAPTER 6

Regional Dialects

🌀🌀🌀🌀🌀🌀

WHEN Becky Sharp first goes from the Sedleys' house in Russell Square to the Crawleys' town house in Great Gaunt Street, her luggage is transferred from the Sedleys' carriage to the house, and the following dialogue ensues:

> 'This Sir Pitt Crawley's?' says John, from the box.
> 'Ess,' says the man at the door with a nod.
> 'Hand down these 'ere trunks then,' said John.
> 'Hand 'n down yourself,' said the porter.
> 'Don't you see I can't leave my hosses? Come, bear a hand, my fine feller, and Miss will give you some beer.' (*VF* p. 68)

John's interlocutor here proves to be not, in fact, the porter, but Sir Pitt Crawley of Queen's Crawley in Hampshire. The passage illustrates two of the three main types of dialect speech that Thackeray portrays; a substandard London, or at least South-Eastern urban, type spoken mainly by servants and hangers-on of the aristocracy, and best illustrated in *The Yellowplush Papers* and *The Diary of Jeames de la Pluche*, but frequent also elsewhere; and what one might call a generalized rural South-Western type, showing few if any dialectal differences between, for instance, the Hampshire of the Crawleys in *Vanity Fair* and the South-East Devonshire of the servants in *Pendennis*. The third dialect which the novelist observes, with much sharpness and humour, is a Southern Irish dialect, as with Mrs O'Dowd in *Vanity Fair* and Captain Costigan in *Pendennis*. In addition, the Anglo-Indian elements in the language of Thackeray seem worthy of mention.

With other dialects and accents, Thackeray seems to have fought shy of a full treatment, though he was adept at suggesting peculiarities and defects of speech by occasional spellings: as for example a certain type of adenoidal Jewish speech, with *beide the seeds* for 'behind the scenes' (*N* I ch. 20); or the effects on speech of inebriation, as *distiwisht officer ithe rex roob* for 'distinguished officer in the next room' (*E* II ch. 15); or of apoplexy, as 'he himself had had a slight tack – vay slight – was getting well ev'y day – strong as a horse – go back to Parliament d'reckly' (*N* II ch. 4).

He refused to tackle a Scottish accent, except very briefly:

> 'When I sailed to Rigy, Cornel,' the [Scottish] first mate was speaking – nor can any spelling or combination of letters of which I am master reproduce this gentleman's accent when he was talking his best – 'I racklackt they used to sairve us a drem before denner.' (*N* I ch. 13)

Otherwise, he approaches no nearer to the accents of Caledonia than the idiomatic insertion of the adverb *just*, familiar to all those who have lived in Edinburgh; as in the speech of Clive Newcome's formidable mother-in-law:

> I could not see the other people *just* for crying myself. Oh, but I wish we could have you at Musselburgh! (*N* I ch. 23)

> Oh, it's *just* seraphic! . . . It's *just* the breath of incense. (*N* I ch. 23)

It is interesting that Scots speech is hardly represented in Dickens, either.

On the other hand, Thackeray does not hesitate to represent a Scottish rendering of Italian:

> 'Quasty peecoly Rosiny,' says James in a fine Scotch Italian, 'è la piu bella, la piu cara, ragazza, ma la mawdry e il diav – (*N* II ch. 6)

He also differentiates between an English and a German version of French:

> 'Issy Monsieur Donnerwetter; ally dimandy ung pew d'o sho poor mwaw.'
> 'Et de l'eau de fie afec, n'est-ce-bas, Matame?' said Mr Donnerwetter. (*SGS* ch. 7)

He distinguishes, too, the broken English of a Frenchwoman:

> 'Ah!' the little French governess used to say . . . 'I like milor to come. All day you vip me. When milor come, he vip you, and you kneel down and kiss de rod. (*Ph* I ch. 4)

from that of a German:

> Sheneral Bulkeley, an English sheneral, tvice so pic as you, sir.
> I sen him back qvite tin after tree months. (*VF* p. 607)

According to a footnote by Gordon Ray in his edition of the
Letters (*L* II p. 67n.) Thackeray was fond of exhibiting his French
pronunciation in conversation, and he also loved to indicate the
inadequacy of other people's French; including, naturally, those
of the characters in his novels. Jos Sedley, giving up his military
uniform to his Belgian servant Isidor for fear of being taken for a
redcoat if the French won at Waterloo, and Harry Foker, in an
access of love for Blanche Amory, ordering his polyglot valet
to curl his hair, both demonstrate the inability of the Anglo-
Saxon to confine his preconceived notions of pronunciation within the strait-jacket of an alien phonemic structure:

> 'Ne porty ploo – habit militair – bonny – donny a voo, prenny
> dehors' – were Jos's words – the coat and cap were at last his
> property. (*VF* p. 304)

> 'Chercy alors une paire de tongs, – et – curly moi un pew,' Mr
> Foker said. (*P* II ch. 1)

Pen's French is better than this, but by no means perfect – for
instance he coins a form *intendé* for 'intended' (*P* I ch. 27). Sometimes, like Dickens, Thackeray renders the speech of French
characters, not by a French phonetic version of broken English,
but by Anglicizing Gallic idiom and syntax. Thus Becky's success
in Paris society is reported by a French duchess to Miss Crawley:

> She is of all the societies, of all the balls – of the balls – yes –
> of the dances, no; and yet how interesting and pretty this fair
> creature looks surrounded by the homage of the men, and so
> soon to be a mother! (*VF* p. 338)

'Gallicized graces' are also one of the affectations of Blanche
Amory's character; and these, similarly, are conveyed by what is in
effect an over-literal translation from French: 'One does not know
what may not arrive,' said Miss Blanche, in French, 'when a girl
has the mind. . . . Figure to yourself . . . [etc.]' (*P* II ch. 20).

The novelist's concern, of course, is not to represent a dialect
in detail and in full (indeed this cannot be done without some

form of phonetic transcription), but to hint at a dialectal flavour in vocabulary, idiom or pronunciation. A closer representation would defeat his purpose as a novelist. Thomas Hardy has said the last word on this (quoted by Norman Page in *Speech in the English Novel*, p. 69):

> If a writer attempts to exhibit on paper the precise accents of a rustic speaker he disturbs the proper balance of a true representation by unduly insisting upon the grotesque element; thus directing attention to a point of inferior interest, and diverting it from the speaker's meaning.

This corresponds to Thackeray's practice also; in his Irish dialogue, for example, two or three eccentric spellings per sentence is the norm. He is not in the least hidebound by any traditional renderings of speech; transcribing what he hears boldly, not to say facetiously at times. Doubtless he would have made a competent phonetician.

Of the three dialects mentioned above, Cockney, South-Western and Irish, I propose to discuss in detail only the third. Cockney dialect, including its specific rendering in *The Yellowplush Papers*, has already been treated very fully in William Matthews's book *Cockney Past and Present*; and the evidence of Cockney from the footmen's mis-spellings corresponds very closely to that compiled on substandard speech in the appendix of G. L. Brook's admirable volume on *The Language of Dickens*. Specimens of South-Western dialect are much scantier than the other two, although, as a native of the South-West, I have noticed a good deal of sharp observation in the representation of pronunciation.

THE SOUTH-WESTERN DIALECT

Sir Pitt Crawley's speech, according to Becky Sharp, fluctuated between 'the coarsest and vulgarest Hampshire accent' and 'the tone of a man of the world' (*VF* p. 71). The rural squire in Victorian times seems to have been occasionally bilingual in this way; we can compare Squire Hamley of Hamley in Mrs Gaskell's *Wives and Daughters* (ch. 22), with a pedigree going back, he claims, to the Heptarchy, who could both converse with his fellow gentry and speak to his farm labourers 'from time to time in their own strong nervous country dialect'. There may have been many such. Certainly when Thackeray was reproached for having made the baronet unnatural, he replied that he was 'almost the only exact portrait in the whole book'. According to Saintsbury, the original of Sir Pitt Crawley may have been Lord Rolle of Bicton in East Devon,[1] of whose eccentricities the novelist may have heard in his Larkbeare days. This may explain why the dialect of Sir Pitt sounds, if anything, more like Devonshire than anywhere further East. His shortening of *sheep* to *ship*, however ('What *ship* was it, Horrocks, and when did you kill?' *VF* p. 78), is a Hampshire characteristic. The county's most famous daughter, Jane Austen, seems facetiously to be imitating Hampshire dialect when she writes about a cloak in a letter to a friend: 'I hope you like the *sim* of it', meaning 'how it seems or appears' (*Letters*, ed. Chapman, p. 499). But when Becky writes to Amelia: 'Sir Pitt . . . pronounces avenue – *evenue*, . . . so droll' (*VF* p. 75); or when the baronet asks Becky 'Who is it *tu*, then, you're married?' (*VF* p. 143) these are most probably Devon vowels – in the latter case the vowel with front-rounded articulation of standard [u:], namely [y:], comparable with the vowel in French *lune* (see K. C. Phillipps, *Westcountry Words and Ways*, Newton Abbot, 1976, pp. 121, 61). Also Devonian is the monophthong [u:] instead of the diphthong [ou] in Sir Pitt's '*Goo* back to Mudbury' (*VF* p. 387). More appropriately, the Fairoaks servants have a Devon dialect: 'I'se *garner* and stable man, and lives in the *ladge* now' (*P* I ch. 21). The unrounding of the short [o] in *ladge*, and the omission of the medial [d] in *gardener* are still to be heard in Devon. The voicing of [f] and [s] to [v] and [z], however, is a feature which all dialects South of the Thames have traditionally shared; and it comes appropriately, therefore, not only from Devon rustics, but also from the Hampshire baronet: 'Come as Lady Crawley, if you like,' the baronet said . . . 'There! will that *zatusfy* you? Come back and be my wife. Your *vit vor't*' (*VF* p. 142).

The South-Western dialects tend to give due prominence to *r* (generally retroflex, with [r]-colouring of the preceding vowel) in the final or penultimate positions, where it is generally not pronounced in the South-East. This probably accounts for the pronunciation that the novelist seems to be hinting at in the following:

1 There are, however, at least two claimants. See Ray, *Uses*, p. 398 and n.

'The Capting is an Irishman,' Mrs Bungay replied; 'and those Irish I have always said I couldn't abide. But his wife is a lady, as any one can see; and a good woman, and a clergyman's daughter, and a West of England woman, B., which I am myself, by my mother's side – and, O Marmaduke, didn't you remark her little *gurl*?'
'Yes, Mrs B., I saw the little girl.' (*P* I ch. 33)

'What was the novelist's own pronunciation of this word?' we might incidentally ask. In *Vanity Fair* he ridicules *gal* as dandified: 'A young officer of the Life Guards ... said, "A dem fine *gal*, egad!" ' (*VF* p. 24). Probably he would have pronounced *girl* with a mid front vowel, rhyming with *hell*, now an old-fashioned U pronunciation, associated in some people's minds with Cheltenham.

THE SOUTH-EASTERN DIALECT

Both *The Yellowplush Papers* and *The Diary of Jeames de la Pluche* illustrate a dialect with a Cockney base, but with an admixture of false refinement, typical of servants with social aspirations and of upper domestics generally. We have mentioned some of the linguistic characteristics of over-refinement and social insecurity in discussing register. There is no doubt that Thackeray records the language of valets, footmen and butlers with telling accuracy. I am afraid that P. J. Keating is right to observe that often the humour is 'based on feelings of class or educational superiority' (*The Working Class in Victorian Fiction*, p. 254). The following extract from the letters suggests that in real life also the novelist was apt to assert his superiority to this class of servant:

> There was only one butler but he was very rich. I wish you could have heard him describe his residence with a family in Paris in the year when *Munseer Dulong* was shot by Marshal *Bogo* [Thomas Robert *Bugeaud* de la Piconnerie]. *Bewjawd* says I I think's the way of pronouncing the name. 'I think you'll find it *Bogo*,' says he with a solemnity which I can't describe. (*L* II p. 228)

Clearly, here was a Charles Yellowplush or Jeames de la Pluche to the life. (Both surnames, by the way, are from the plush breeches worn by footmen.) Another passage in the letters that is equally free from twentieth-century inhibitions in matters of class, and also of race, is the following:

> In one of Anny's letters she wrote we have got a black *nuss* not puss. I thought it was a natural Yellowplushism – and was in truth very much disgusted at the idea of a nigger *bonne*. (*L* II p. 222)

The footmen commonly render *-rs-* forms as *ss* or *s*, with words like *hosses* (*YP* p. 51) and *interspussed* (*YP* p. 36). As Ernest Weekley has observed (*Adjectives and Other Words*, p. 142), this was a pronunciation that had been recommended by at least one orthoepist in the eighteenth century; but by the nineteenth it had become substandard.

As Keating points out, a phrase like 'Let us draw a vail over the seen' indicates no difference of pronunciation;[1] it is the orthography that is being pilloried here, and illiteracy is the slur. At the same time, it is fair to say that this is not the only rank of society to be ridiculed in the novels; and facetious spellings like Yellowplush's 'Mrs *Siddums* in the Tragic *Mews*', 'up to *snough*' and 'the waives of the *otion*' are also part of the writer's stock-in-trade in many articles and letters. Malapropisms are common: 'he never said a *syllabub*' (*YP* p. 10); 'a *polygon* of exlens' (*YP* p. 35). Sometimes, as with many of the best Malapropisms, there is a secondary appropriateness: 'One of the younger gals . . . had seen my master come and . . . said so in a *cussary* way' (*YP* p. 15); 'He looked at her very *tendrilly*' (*YP* p. 24); 'Master's robe de *sham*' (*YP* p. 96); 'my *ventriloquism* or inward speech' (*YP* p. 109). As with the rendering of Irish and South-Western dialogue, the eccentric spellings do not come so thickly as to cause annoyance or incomprehension.

Both Yellowplush and Jeames are chauvinists and given also to the humorous misinterpretation of foreign words and phrases. Yellowplush's travels into 'foring parts' are an opportunity for Thackeray's favourite device of playing interlinguistically upon the sounds and spellings of words:

---

[1] We must not forget that *vail* in earlier centuries had meant 'a gratuity'; though the inverted commas in the following reference suggest that for the Victorians it was an archaism: 'The lacqueys rose up from their cards to open the door to him, in order to get their "vails" ' (*V* I ch. 2).

Will it be believed that they call the upper town the *Hot Veal*, and the other the *Base Veal*, which is on the contry, genrally good in France, though the beaf . . . is exscrabble. (*YP* p. 46)

Looking hard and kind at all the nussary maids – *buns* they call them in France. (*YP* p. 92)

So also with Jeames, when he becomes rich from railway speculation:

I call this *vally* my *Trent Vally*, for it was the prophit I got from that exlent line, which injuiced me to ingage him. (*DJ* p. 114)

THE IRISH DIALECT

Thackeray had some acquaintance with Ireland, and with Irish people. He had married into an Irish military family, and in 1842 he visited Ireland to write a book on the country, *The Irish Sketch Book*. Echoes of dialogue in the travel sketches were later used in his portraits of the Costigans and the O'Dowds. By the time of the novels he had become bolder, more accurate, and often more facetious in his representation in spelling of the accents of Hibernia. Thus the recorded phrase in *The Irish Sketch Book* (ch. 25) 'a complete new *shuit* from head to foot' becomes in *Pendennis* 'a new *shoot* of clothes' (*P* I ch. 6). 'Four *hunder* guineas' in the sketches (*IS* ch. 23) becomes 'the *hunther* pounds' (*P* I ch. 30). One sees the observant journalist noting phrases like: 'Tim, some hot *wather* – screeching hot, you *divil* – and a sthroke of the limin' (*IS* ch. 23), or 'Fait, and I wish dere was some tabaccy here' (*IS* ch. 32) and one finds some of the same idiosyncrasies later worked up into the Irish dialogue in the novels.

Perhaps the outstanding instance of this seminal process is an encounter which the novelist mentions in a letter to Jane Brookfield in 1853 (*L* III p. 183), and then recalls in a *Roundabout Paper* some years later:

In the novel of 'Pendennis', written ten years ago, there is an account of a certain Captain Costigan, whom I had invented. . . . I was smoking in the tavern one night – and this Costigan came into the room alive – the very man. . . . He had the same little coat, the same battered hat, cocked on one eye, the same twinkle in that eye. 'Sir,' said I, knowing him to be an old friend whom I had met in unknown regions, 'sir,' I said, 'may I offer you a glass of brandy-and-water?' 'Bedad, ye may,' says he, 'and I'll sing ye a song tu.' (*RP* 'De Finibus')

The incident made such an impression on the novelist that when he began to write *The Newcomes* in 1853, the Captain was recalled to life for a last brief appearance in the famous opening scene, in which the Colonel and Clive visit The Cave of Harmony (in real life, Evans' Coffee House in Covent Garden):

> 'He's a great character . . . was a Captain in the army. We call him the General. Captain Costigan, will you take something to drink?'
> 'Bedad I will,' says the Captain, 'and I'll sing ye a song tu.' (*N* I ch. 1)

In fact, the song is a ribald one, and the Colonel escorts his son Clive from the tavern in disgust.

Thackeray represents a general Southern Irish, or Eire, dialect, with the following typical features of pronunciation – many of these are still characteristic of the Irish dialects of English:[1]

1 A retention of the open vowel [ɛ:], perhaps modified to the diphthong [ei], in words which since the seventeenth century have been raised to [i:] in standard English. Often these vowels are spelt *ea* in English, an indication that they formerly had unraised vowels in England also (*Henry*, p. 110):

> 'pines as common as *pays* in the *sayson* . . . and . . . magnolias as big as *taykettles*' (*VF* p. 267); *thayatres* (*P* II ch. 4); *aisy* (*P* II ch. 37); 'as rich as *Crazes*' (*P* I ch. 12).

2 Occasionally, something like the converse of this occurs: the diphthong [ei] is pronounced with an approximation to the long vowel [i:]:

> 'Our *greeps* weighs six pounds every bunch' (*VF* p. 267); 'high-stepping *bee* horses' (*P* II ch. 14); '*Meejor* O'Dowd' (*VF* p. 256); *champeane* (*P* II ch. 4).

3 The first part of the diphthong [ai] is pronounced with a sound approaching [ɔi]; rendered in spelling by *oi* or *oy*:

1 See P. L. Henry, 'A Linguistic Survey of Ireland: Preliminary Report', in *Lochlann: A Review of Celtic Studies* I, 1958, pp. 53–208. Hereinafter referred to as *Henry*.

'Sure, I've made a pie,' Emily said . . . She pronounced it '*poy*' (*P* I ch. 5); 'a black *oi*' (*VF* p. 258); 'the *hoight* of *poloit* societee' (*P* II ch. 4); 'the *proproietor*' (*P* II ch. 8).

4 Probably a more front vowel, [y:], as in French *lune* is indicated by the spelling *u* in Costigan's 'I'll sing ye a song *tu*' (*N* I ch. 1) and Mrs O'Dowd's 'whatever ye *du*' (*VF* p. 257).

5 A more rounded vowel for standard English [ʌ], rendered in spelling as *o*:

Doblin (*VF* p. 256); 'horse . . . that won the *cop* at the Curragh' (*VF* p. 267); 'he must have *pomped* all the blood out of um' (*VF* p. 267).

6 The vowel [ɔ] is lengthened in the following:

prawpertee (*P* I ch. 12); 'I *forgawt* me purse' (*P* II ch. 8).

7 [e] raised to [i] (*Henry*, p. 111):

'no *ind* to the proide and ar'gance' (*P* II ch. 14); *divvle* (*VF* p. 257); *siminary, expince* (*VF* p. 258); *stipt* (*VF* p. 263).

8 [i] lowered to [ʌ]:

'weak-*spurted*' (*VF* p. 419); *guggling* (*VF* p. 267).

Some such vowel, probably lower than the neutral [ə], is very common with unaccented syllables, as the frequent substitution of *u* in spelling such syllables indicates:

'I've known *um* since childhood' (*P* II ch. 8); *horrud* (*VF* p. 258); *tickut* (*P* II ch. 8).

9 A lower medial unstressed vowel is still frequent in some Irish dialects (*Henry*, p. 141, with examples like [beləband] for *belly-band*):

'me most *intemate* friend' (*P* II ch. 8); *sonunlaw* (*P* II ch. 17).

10 When followed by [r], there is much colouring of vowels, as the following spellings indicate:

'his *dorling* Emilie, when she acted the *pawrt* of Cora' (*P* II ch. 37); 'Muryan *Squeer*'; *coorted* (*VF* p. 256); 'that *Garge* should be a brother of my own' (*VF* p. 257); 'no expince *speared*' (*VF* p. 288); 'his "*bird*" . . . had not been shaved' (*P* II ch. 13);

'Was your Leedyship in the *Pork?*'; 'Sir *Chorlus*'; 'his daughther's *choriot*' (*P* II ch. 4); 'Good *marning*' (*VF* p. 302); 'How *dar* he ask ye' (*P* I ch. 12).

11 The word *gold* has retained a long [uː], characteristic of an earlier English pronunciation of the word [see p. 169n.);

'a *goold* medal' (*VF* p. 264).

12 The postdental plosives [t] and [d] often become the fricatives [θ] and [ð], especially before the vibrant [r]:

'The Meeting of the *Watthers*'; 'The *Minsthrel* Boy' (*VF* p. 425); 'a *dthrop* of *dthrink*' (*P* II ch. 17); *sthratagem* (*P* II ch. 37).

13 Or, conversely:

'He's brought the poor girl well *troo* her *faver*' (*P* II ch. 14); 'to tell you the secred *trut*' (*C* ch. 5); '*wid* a Marchioness to teach us the true Parisian pronunciation' (*VF* p. 257).

14 A strong tendency to palatalization of [t], [d] and [ð] is found (*Henry*, pp. 112–18):

ingratitchewd (*P* II ch. 17); *opporchunitee* (*P* II ch. 11); 'How well the *Juke* looked' (*VF* p. 270); *introjuice* (*VF* p. 258); 'fighting a *jewel*' (*P* II ch. 17); 'a nice good-natured way *widg* you' (*VF* p. 257).

15 The development of an on-glide with initial velars [k] and [g] is also common:

'me *cyard*' (*P* II ch. 4); 'a litherary *cyarkter*' (*P* II ch. 11); 'a devilish foine *gyurll*' (*P* II ch. 27).

16 A glide vowel between two consonants is frequent:

'*arrum* in *arrum*' (*P* II ch. 8); *perfawrumance* (*P* II ch. 11); 'He has *overwhellumed* me' (*P* I ch. 12); 'I *scrawrun* any interfayrance' (*P* II ch. 8).

17 The converse of this, a syncopation or telescoping of unstressed syllables, is also found. There is an amusing reference to this characteristic of Irish speech in one of Thackeray's letters, in which he writes of one Father Tom Maguire, who was famous for keeping greyhounds: 'I give them names of one Syllable, Father

Tom said, aisy to be called after them, such as Port and *Clart* and them names' (*L* II p. 362). Similarly:

> *Fitzjurld* (*VF* p. 115); 'be *quite*' (quiet) (*VF* p. 256); *bar'ck*; *brothernlaw* (*VF* p. 258); *weak-spur'ted* (*VF* p. 419); 'as she stipt into the *car'ge* after her *mar'ge*' (*VF* p. 263); *quar'l* (*P* II ch. 8); 'verses and *pomes*' (*P* I ch. 12).

Here we should also include the contraction of the present participial suffix:

> 'It is his nose *bleedn*?' (*VF* p. 267); 'he's *goan* to sing' (*P* II ch. 8).

18 A highly-aspirated initial [ʌ] occurs in words beginning *wh*:

> '*Hwhat's* that gawky guggling about?' (*VF* p. 257).

19 A tendency to accentuate the last, normally unaccented, syllable of a polysyllabic word; it is represented by *ee* in spelling, instead of final *-y*:

> 'He was quitting a city celebrated for its *antiquitee*, its *hospitalitee*, the *beautee* of its women, the manly *fidelitee*, *generositee* and *jovialitee* of its men' (*P* I ch. 16); 'clar't and *burgundee*' (*P* II ch. 4).

In regard to accidence and syntax, the following are noteworthy features:

1 With personal pronouns, *ye* occurs for *you*, *me(e)* for *my*, and *um* for *him*:

> '*Ye* don't mean to say ye saw '*um* and didn't give ''um the letter'; 'that boy whom I loved as the boy of *mee* bosom is only a scoundthrel. . . . I tell *ye* he's no better than an impostor'; 'I want to shoot that man that has trajuiced *me* honour, or *meself* dthrop a victim on the sod' (*P* I ch. 12).

2 *Them* regularly occurs as a demonstrative adjective:

> 'All *them* children write verses' (*P* I ch. 12); '*Them* boys are mostly talk' (*P* I ch. 6).

3 Irregularity of case and concord is a characteristic of Irish as of other dialects, and too frequent to need much illustration, except in one particular: the use of a singular inflection with a

plural subject is notably characteristic of the English of Ireland (*Henry*, p. 130):

> 'Mrs Captain Magenis and me *has* made up' (*VF* p. 257); 'Them filberts *is* beautiful' (*P* I ch. 12).

4 The infinitive without *to* after the verb *to thank* is twice recorded in the dialogue:

> 'I'll *thank ye tell* me what they mean' (*VF* p. 264); 'I'll *thank ye hand* me the salt' (*P* I ch. 12).

5 *Sure* as a sentence adverb has long been a well-known Hibernian characteristic:

> '*Sure* if he's no money, there's no use marrying him' (*P* I ch. 12).

6 Also characteristic is a mild asseveration followed by *and* or *then* to introduce a remark:

> '*Faith, and* she always is then' (*VF* p. 258); '*Deed and* she will' (*VF* p. 257); '*Deed then* they are' (*VF* p. 267); '*Faith then,* he took six' (*P* I ch. 5).

7 A redundant and anticipatory collocation *it's* is typical of Irish English, and as such has been noted also by Trollope in his Irish dialogue (Clark, p. 112):

> 'If a reformed rake makes a good husband, sure *it's she* will have the fine chance with Garge' (*VF* p. 259); 'Sure every one of my frocks must be taken in – *it's* such a skeleton I'm growing' (*VF* p. 425); '*It's* not you are the only woman that are in the hands of God this day' (*VF* p. 299).

8 An additional *ever a*, meaning 'any' but with intensive force is still characteristic of Irish dialects (see *The English Dialect Dictionary* s.v. *ever a*)

> 'She'd never walk behind *ever a* beggarly civilian' (*VF* p. 418).

9 A definite article can occur where an indefinite one is normal English:

> 'She will have *the* fine chance with Garge' (*VF* p. 259); '*the* lying scounthrel this fellow is' (*C* ch. 5).

ANGLO-INDIAN

One other element of importance in the language of Thackeray is the Anglo-Indian. He himself was born at Calcutta on 18 July 1811, and his father and grandfather were Indian civil servants; *civilians*, as they were called, like Jos Sedley (*VF* p. 656). His mother was left a widow in 1816, and was soon re-married to a Major Carmichael Smith, an Indian military man, the model for Colonel Newcome. Thackeray was not six years old when he returned to England. He was sent home, in the company of another small boy, to stay with relatives. The departure was a scene he recalled towards the end of his life in a *Roundabout Paper*, 'On Letts's Diary':

> A *ghaut* or river-stair, at Calcutta; and a day when, down those steps, to a boat which was waiting, came two children, whose mothers remained on the shore.

A *ghaut* (Hindi *ghāt*) is a passage or flight of steps leading to a riverside. The novelist's memories of the subcontinent were necessarily limited; and in later life when composing *Vanity Fair* he wrote to a Major Compton, commander of the thirty-eighth Native Infantry in India, for information: 'I have a chapter about Madras in VF, and don't want to make any blunder' (*L* II p. 327). Jos Sedley gives Becky a full account of 'the manner in which they kept themselves cool in hot weather, with *punkahs*, *tatties* and other contrivances' (*VF* p. 38). *Punkah* is from Hindi *pankhā*, 'fan', originally a hand-fan, later one suspended from the ceiling and worked mechanically. A *tatty* (Hindi *tattī*) was a screen filling up the opening of a door or window, and kept wet to cool and freshen the air in the room. Jos wishes that he could have Becky to sing for him in India after *Cutcherry* (Hindi *kachahrī*), the court-house, where Jos would preside (*VF* p. 41). To be precise, Jos had been a *Collector* (*VF* p. 42), a chief administrative official whose special duty was the collection of revenues, but who also had magisterial powers. Jos was a creature of set habits, who liked his comforts: he drank *brandy-pawnee* (*VF* p. 555), a hybrid word meaning brandy and water (Hindi *pānī*, 'water'). 'He would not think . . . of travelling until he could do so with his *chillum*' (*VF* p. 558), his hookah (Hindi *chilam*). *Tiffin* is also mentioned, a word specialized in Anglo-Indian use for a light mid-day meal (*VF* p. 42); the word nevertheless is not Indian, but originates probably from the English colloquial or slang verb *to tiff*, 'to take a little drink or sip'. Thackeray uses the word *shampoo* (Hindi *čāmpo*) in its earlier and now obsolete sense of 'to massage' – normally applied to a person in a Turkish bath, but by the novelist figuratively to a mattress being pommelled. At the Sedleys' sale old women are described 'pinching the bed-curtains, poking into the feathers, *shampooing* the mattresses' (*VF* p. 159). We now confine the word to washing or rubbing the scalp.

Lady Clavering, in *Pendennis*, had a large fortune from her disreputable father, Samuel Snell of Calcutta, and consequently was known as the *Begum* – a reference to the source of her wealth (*P* II ch. 37). *Begum* is from Urdu, adapted from Eastern Turkish *bigún*, a princess. It was the word for a lady of high rank in Hindustan. Predictably, after his career in the Indian army, Colonel Newcome has some terms from Hindi, calling grooms *saices*, for example (*N* II ch. 28). This is an Arabic loan into Hindi, from *sūs*, 'to tend a horse', and meant a groom, or sometimes an attendant who followed a mounted horseman on foot. He was also proficient at Indian dishes: 'great at making hash muttons, hot-pot, curry and *pillau*' (*N* I ch. 16), originally a Persian word for a dish of boiled rice and meat, coming into English through Urdu. He sends his devoted sister-in-law Martha Honeyman, Cashmere shawls, a brooch and bracelets, which she was proud to wear. Of the bracelets, she used to say: 'I am to understand they are called *bangles* . . . by the natives' (*N* I ch. 15) (Hindi *bangrī*, originally a coloured glass ring worn by women on the wrist). The word was perhaps less naturalized into English in the 1840s than it now is, though Miss Honeyman is rather unsophisticated. Another Indian word of interest is *purdah*, which at this date perhaps has its original meaning of 'curtain' (Urdu *pardah*); more specifically the curtain dividing womenfolk from men and strangers: 'I would like to go into an Indian Brahmin's house and see the punkahs and the *purdahs* and the tattys, and the pretty brown maidens' (*N* I ch. 28).

As a young man, the Colonel's favourite reading had been Orme's History: 'He was for ever telling of India, and the famous deeds of Clive and Lawrence. His favourite book was a history of India – the "History" of Orme' (*N* II ch. 38). Hence of course, his son's Christian name of Clive. To quote *The Oxford Dictionary of English Christian Names*:

> Clive (m.): the surname of Robert Clive (1725–74), the great servant of the East India Company. The name is chiefly given as a christian name by those who have connexions in India, and was perhaps first used in this way by Thackeray in *The Newcomes* (1853–5).

Not everyone liked Clive's father. A widow who set her cap at him in vain described him as 'selfish, pompous, Quixotic, and a *Bahawder*' (N I ch. 5). This last word, from Hindi *bahādur*, 'hero, champion', was affixed to the name of a man of high rank, but it had connotations, when applied to whites at least, of Oriental imperiousness (see *OED Supp.* s.v. *Bahadur*).

CHAPTER 7

The Language of *Henry Esmond*

🙚🙚🙚🙚🙚🙚

DID the imitation of early eighteenth-century language in *Henry Esmond* come naturally to Thackeray? The question is asked by Virginia Woolf in *A Room of One's Own*. In that essay she recalls walking past a 'famous' Cambridge college library (Trinity, in fact, Thackeray's own college), where the manuscript of *Esmond* is preserved:

> The critics often say that *Esmond* is Thackeray's most perfect novel. But the affectation of the style, with its imitation of the eighteenth century, hampers one, so far as I can remember; unless indeed the eighteenth-century style was natural to Thackeray – a fact that one might prove by looking at the manuscript and seeing whether the alterations were for the benefit of the style or of the sense.[1]

In fact, on examining the manuscript (part of which is in Thackeray's hand, part in his daughter's and part in that of his amanuensis, Eyre Crowe), one discovers that there are virtually no archaizing alterations – indeed, there are very few alterations at all.[2] Eyre Crowe, in his book *With Thackeray in America* (London, 1893, p. 3), later recalled that the novel had been written 'with scarcely any interpolations or marginal *repentirs*'. One leaves the manuscript with renewed admiration for the novelist's skill in pastiche.

It is true that it was a comparatively easy matter for a writer of Thackeray's expertise to make a brief use of strongly marked

---

1 Virginia Woolf is perhaps being unduly modest. The manuscript was given to Trinity by her father, Leslie, later Sir Leslie, Stephen, whose first wife was Harriet ('Minny') Thackeray, the novelist's younger daughter.

2 Curiously, the majority of revisions are of proper names. Thus, as J. A. Sutherland pointed out, there is a felicitous revision of Viscountess Castlewood's Christian name from Dolly to Rachel, with its 'faint biblical allusion to the long deferred marriage of Jacob'. See J. A. Sutherland, *Thackeray at Work*, p. 62.

archaism for humorous purposes. A good example of this occurs in *Philip*, when the narrator, Pendennis, visiting Philip's ancestral home with him, addresses the keeper of the lodge-gates with such 'gadzookery' as this:

> Marry, good dame . . . this goodly gentleman hath a right of entrance to yonder castle, which, I trow, ye wot not of. Heard ye never tell of one Philip Ringwood, slain at Busaco's glorious fi—. (*Ph* II ch. 23)

But in *Esmond* something more subtle, more serious and much more sustained than this is intended and achieved. To quote J. Y. T. Grieg in *Thackeray, A Reconsideration* (p. 158):

> As the book purported to be the memoirs of a man born in the late seventeenth century, and living as the familiar of the Augustan wits, a man who drank with Steele, discoursed of state business with Swift, and wrote a *Spectator* paper for the great Addison, it was necessary that his style should correspond. But to say that Thackeray imitated or affected the style of the Augustans is to suggest that the style of *Esmond* is unnatural, – a collection of antiques out of Wardour Street. It is not. The marvel of it is that it always reads like Thackeray, and yet, simultaneously, like someone who had died a century before him – not Steele or Addison or Swift or Pope or Bolingbroke, but someone unidentified who might have been a close friend and admirer of all of them.

As far as detailed matters of technique are concerned, there has been, so far as I know, only one strongly dissentient voice in an otherwise general chorus of eulogy for this linguistic *tour de force*. Fitzedward Hall, sometime Professor of Sanskrit at King's College, London, was no admirer of Thackeray ('From Mr Thackeray, as a novelist, there are . . . lessons to be learnt which are highly valued nowadays . . ., and these are, with others of a similar cast, to disbelieve utterly in human goodness, and to believe every one who is not of your set to be, most likely, a "cad", and to be treated accordingly'); but he brought to his close criticism of the language of *Esmond* such accurate and indeed in those pre-*OED* days such remarkable knowledge, that he cannot be ignored. A book he wrote (in 1873) some twenty years after *Esmond* appeared, entitled *Modern English*, has four pages (pp. 274–7) of detailed and weighty criticism of the pastiche language. He takes to task an enthusiastic admirer of *Esmond* who had written in the *Saturday Review* that 'no man, woman or child, in *Esmond*, ever says anything that he or she might not have said in the reign of Queen Anne'. 'To expose the profound ignorance of this,' Hall writes, 'is sufficiently easy'; and he proceeds with evident relish:

Who, in Queen Anne's time, ever heard of such English as *'was being battered down'*? Or of the verbs *cede, olden, philander*? Or of *aggressive, civilization, transatlantic, unpleasantry, upset* (as a noun). Of *directly, immediately,* and *instantly,* for 'as soon as'? Of *all the same* for 'nevertheless'? Of expressions like *quite a young lad* and *in the interest of justice*; or of *a young person* for 'a young woman'? Who was then so careless as to write *different to* habitually? Or so curious as to have disinterred, and so eccentric as to use, the verb *advocate*, the participle *humiliated*, the adjective *influential*, and the preposition *on to*? It was all very well for Mr Thackeray to call an inn *accustomed*; here and there to introduce phrases like *a-birding, a dish of chocolate, a pretty many, sceptic doubts*; to misuse *imperial* for 'imperious'; and to call a pretty maid-servant *an ancillary beauty*; but in these, and perhaps half a dozen more obsoletisms – the whole of which can be got together in two hours' reading – is comprised everything, in his novel, at all savouring, as to language, of any days but our own. In brief, instead of being 'a miracle of imitative art', the work at which I have glanced lacks no one attribute of a complete failure.

This paragraph is both enviably knowledgeable and grossly unfair. Nearly all these detailed objections are valid, as we can now verify by checking with the *OED*. Perhaps it is only with the phrase *different to*, about which he is so crustily proscriptive, and which is found, according to the *OED*, in writers of all ages, that Hall cannot be justified. All the same (to use what he rightly diagnoses as one of Thackeray's anachronisms), the fire is very concentrated at this point. Spread over the three volumes of *Esmond*, these anachronisms do not amount to much; and they must be set against the many authentic and seemingly authentic idioms that are certainly more than the product of two hours' reading!

The answer to Hall's strictures is best given by T. C. and W. Snow in the Introduction to their edition of *Esmond* (*The History of Henry Esmond*, p. xxvii):

> Partly by natural affinity with the age of Anne, and partly by a skilful use of its forms of speech at selected points, he created an illusion as if it was present throughout, while in fact he was allowing himself abundant material derived from the nineteenth century. Such an illusion does not impose on us when we test the language by analysis, but that is exactly what we are not meant to do, and what the ordinary human reader would not think of doing while he is enjoying the book. If anybody, after the first reading is over, and when he begins to study, enjoys *Esmond* less for discovering that its language could not all have come straight out of the *Tatler* or *Gulliver's Travels*, such a person was not meant by nature to read it at all.

What emerges from close study of the language of *Esmond*, if one is more sympathetic to Thackeray's fiction than Hall, is admiration for precisely this skill as a linguistic illusionist. A clue may be found in one of Hall's instances, *an ancillary beauty*, as a term for a beautiful serving-maid – Esmond is relieved when the Old Pretender flirts, not with Beatrix, but with 'an ancillary beauty' (*E* III ch. 9). This obvious Latinism, from *ancilla*, 'a maid-servant', is said by the *OED* to be 'rare and affected', and it is first illustrated in the Dictionary by this quotation. Yet it does sound appropriate to the Augustan age. Another, differently derived, archaism is *weapon* in the special sense of 'one skilled in the use of a weapon' (*weapon* 1f). The following is the sole *OED* instance, and the word 'quasi-archaism', preceded by a question-mark, is their term:

> Blandford knows which of us two is the best *weapon*. At small-sword, or back-sword . . . I can beat him. (*E* II ch. 8)

A particularly good example of what one might call an informed quasi-archaism is the use of *merchant* in the sense of 'banker':

> There was the house and furniture, plate and pictures at Chelsea, and a sum of money lying at her *merchant's*, Sir Joshua Child, which altogether would realise a sum of near three hundred pounds per annum. (*E* III ch. 1)

To which the Snows have the following note:

> Thackeray must have meant Sir Francis Child (1642–1713), the
> first London banker who dropped the goldsmith's trade en-
> tirely and devoted himself to banking alone. Sir Joshua Child
> was an eminent merchant and writer on economics, chairman
> and despotic ruler of the East India Company, but he was not a
> banker.

Thackeray is here showing his great knowledge of the social
history of the period; yet *merchant* does not occur in the *OED*
specifically in the sense of 'banker'.

As with individual words, so with idiom. A good instance
occurs with one of the words that Hall quotes: *an accustomed inn*,
with *accustomed* in the sense of 'frequented as a customer'. In fact
this is not exactly how Thackeray uses the word. His use is more
predicative than attributive; unlike, it seems, that of previous
English writers. Consequently this quotation rates a section to
itself in the *OED* (s.v. *accustomed* 1b, cf. *accustomed* 2):

> The 'Trumpet' in the Cockpit, Whitehall, an house used by the
> military in his time as a young man, and *accustomed* by his lord-
> ship ever since. (*E* I ch. 14)

Again, an expression like 'The Duchess ... *banged* such a *box of
the ear* both at Trix and Blandford' (*E* II ch. 8), may occur earlier,
and certainly sounds convincingly of the period; but there is
nothing parallel to this combination of the two words in the *OED*
under either *bang* v. or *box* n³. What the novelist may have tried
for, it seems to me, was a turn of phrase sufficiently different from
normal Victorian idiom to be assumed by all his readers who
were less knowledgeable in this field than Hall (in other words,
practically everybody) to be authentically of Queen Anne's time.
To put such a trick across demands great skill in language, since
a constant danger is that the slight eccentricity may become too
manifest, and the illusion be shattered. I append some other
instances of marked words and idioms, tentatively suggesting
that these too should perhaps be included in this category of
quasi-archaic:

> She ... swept a low curtsey, coming up *to the recover* with the
> prettiest little foot in the world pointed out. (*E* III ch. 2)

They raised a great laugh at him when he was *set on* to read Latin. (*E* I ch. 10)[1]

I was glad when you went away, and *engaged with* my Lord Ashburton that I might hear no more of you. (*E* III ch. 4)[2]

(Some women) are *exuberant of* kindness, as it were, and must impart it to some one. (*E* I ch. 9)

She . . . bade him remember that she *kept* two nights in the week, and that she longed to see him. (*E* III ch. 3)[3]

He is here *on a great end*, from which no folly should divert him. (*E* III ch. 10)

Would not Miss Beatrix *hold him company* at a game of cards? (*E* III ch. 11)[4]

The wood being, in fact, a better shelter and *easier of guard* than any village. (*E* II ch. 9)

We see in the last three sentences here a typical variation from the norm: 'on a great undertaking', 'keep him company' and 'easier to guard'. To similar effect, Thackeray exploited fully one of the most variable points in English syntax, whether to use an infinitive or an *-ing* form after a verb or noun governing the item in question. He sensed that by choosing whichever was the more unusual alternative in each case an effect of difference would be achieved which the reader would feel, rightly or wrongly, was the idiom of an earlier age. Thus normal Victorian usage, doubtless, like our own, would favour, 'We took the liberty of breaking the seal'; but in *Esmond* we find 'We took the *freedom to break* it' (III 13). So in the following:

Harry had the satisfaction *to find* that she adopted the counsel. (*E* I ch. 13)

Dick . . . had all the Guards *to laugh* at him for his pains. (*E* I ch. 14)

His mistress never tired *to listen* or *to read*. (*E* I ch. 9)

1 First *OED* example s.v. *set* v. 148f.
2 There is no other instance precisely like this in the *OED* (*engage* 4b, 6c), though the intransitive use (6c) quoted there is perhaps comparable. See also *JAE*, pp. 74–6.
3 Presumably meaning 'was "at home"'.
4 cf. Shakespeare, *Much Ado About Nothing*, I i 91: 'I will *hold friends* with you lady.'

To ask a fond mother's blessing for that step which he was *about taking.* (*E* III ch. 2)

Reverting to Hall's list of anachronisms, and going through them in detail, we note that he has immediately seized on the occurrence of the passive expanded tense, 'was being battered down'. Here, of course, he is quite correct; even Professor Visser's tireless researches[1] cannot unearth any earlier example of the construction than the first *OED* instance from Southey (1795). Yet Thackeray has it more than once:

One of the daughters . . . *was being bred* up with no religion at all. (*E* II ch. 13)

His splendid palace at Woodstock, which *was now being built.* (*E* II ch. 14)

Cede as a transitive verb ('He would . . . *cede* his right to the living' *E* I ch. 10) in fact first occurs in the *OED* in 1754,[2] so that Thackeray is not far wrong in this instance; but the verb *olden*, which occurs both intransitively and transitively ('She had *oldened*' *E* I ch. 9; 'Reading and thought . . . had *oldened* him' *E* I ch. 11) is of the nineteenth century, first illustrated in its transitive use in the *OED* from *Pendennis*. ('This rather rare verb is a favourite of Thackeray's, and no fewer than four of the seven *OED* instances are from him!) The verbal noun *philandering* does occur in the time when Esmond is supposed to be writing,[3] though the verb otherwise, it seems, does not. *Aggressive* (*E* III ch. 1) is first illustrated in the *OED* from Sydney Smith (1824); so that Hall is right to add a footnote: 'This adjective, at least for any notable currency, belongs to our century'. *Civilization* (*E* III ch. 1) in its modern, non-legal sense, was not recognized by Dr Johnson,

1 *An Historical Syntax of the English Language*, III ii 2429. Also *OED* s.v. *be* 15c. The earlier form, active in construction but passive in meaning, also occurs, as, at that purported date, it should: 'In expectation of the stroke that *was now preparing*' (*E* III 10). But this pattern, of course, never died out, and has yielded such idioms as 'There *is* one pound *owing*; there *is* nothing *doing*'.

2 On this verb, see Susie Tucker, *Protean Shape*, p. 115: 'Mrs Piozzi thought that Dr Johnson would not have thought well of using *cede* as a transitive verb – his dictionary recognises no such verb, transitive or otherwise. Yet the evidence of *OED* shows that it was in general use by the mid-century'.

3 The date of the narrative (later by nearly thirty years than the last of the events described) can be more or less fixed by Esmond's incidental remark (*E* III ch. 3) that Swift was still alive, but had lost his intellect. Swift was insane for the last five of his seventy-seven years, dying in 1745.

as the first *OED* instance of the word from Boswell indicates:

> On Monday, March 23rd (1772) I found him busy, preparing a
> fourth edition of his folio Dictionary. . . . He would not admit
> *civilization* but only *civility*. With great deference to him, I
> thought *civilization*, from to *civilize*, better in the sense opposed
> to *barbarity*, than *civility*.

The word was clearly in process of being accepted in Johnson's
day. *Transatlantick* (*E* III ch. 13) appears first in the *OED* in
the correspondence of John Wilkes (1779). '*Upsets*, under that
name,' Hall points out in a footnote, 'were very rare before 1800.'
The *OED* corroborates this; to be less anachronistic, Thackeray
could have used the noun *overset*, which had some currency from
the early eighteenth century. The *OED* also confirms that the
use of *directly* (*E* III ch. 2), *immediately* (*E* II ch. 5), and *instantly*
(*E* I ch. 1) as quasi-conjunctions is not found earlier than the turn
of the eighteenth and nineteenth centuries; so that a construction
like 'He ran across the grass *instantly* he perceived his mother' is
anachronistic.

As to idioms, *all the same* (*E* II ch. 11) meaning 'nevertheless' is
of the nineteenth century, as Hall says. Expressions such as *quite
a puny lad* (*E* III ch. 5) and *quite a child* (*E* I ch. 8) are found from
1756, according to the *OED* (*quite* 4b) so that here Thackeray is
not so far wrong. In objecting to the phrase *in the interest of
justice* (*E* I ch. 5) as not of Queen Anne's time, Hall may at first
seem to be incorrect, since the phrase *in the interest of* occurs in
Addison (*OED interest* 2c). But comparison of the earlier and
later *OED* quotations for this phrase indicates a radical difference
in the meaning of *interest*, from the more concrete and tangible
political sense of 'influence' ('in the *interest* of the present government') to something more abstract, verging on the nature of a
cliché; as the following quotation, dated 1858, shows. This is
clearly a Victorian innovation:

> 'In the interest' (to use a slang phrase just now coming into
> currency) of enlightened patriotism.

The phrase *young person* meaning 'young woman' (*E* I ch. 8), for
which the *locus classicus* might well be said to be in the script of
W. S. Gilbert's *Mikado*,[1] is earlier than Hall realized, the first *OED*

1 See *The Mikado*, Act I: 'It is very painful to me to have to say "How de do, little
  girls, how de do" to *young persons*.'

instance (*person* 2e) being of 1759. Dickens, too, makes much play with this phrase on the lips of the humbug, Podsnap (*Our Mutual Friend* ch. 11). In an irascible footnote, Hall describes *young person* as 'nauseous slang' and 'entirely modern'; but the phrase is in fact a clear instance of something we have already noted – the tendency for respectable eighteenth-century phrases to become vulgar in Victorian times.

A prominent feature of both the syntax and style of *Esmond* is the use of long sentences with such Latinate devices as continuative relatives to join what in the novels set in Thackeray's own period would have been written as separate sentences. We are so used today to a Hemingway-like staccato to convey violent action in narrative, that it is surprising to see how well a master of prose can convey such action in a less jerky way with lengthy sentences, yet losing little of the excitement:

> A very few months after my lord's coming to Castlewood, in the winter-time – the little boy, being a child in a petticoat, trotting about – it happened that little Frank was with his father after dinner, who fell asleep over his wine, heedless of the child, who crawled to the fire; and as good fortune would have it, Esmond was sent by his mistress for the boy just as the poor little screaming urchin's coat was set on fire by a log; when Esmond, rushing forward, tore the dress off the infant, so that his own hands were burned more than the child's, who was frightened rather than hurt by this accident. (*E* I ch. 11)

It will be seen here that not only relative pronouns like *who*, but relative adverbs like *when* (and, in other contexts, *where*) have a continuative function; and such continuatives are much more frequent in *Esmond* than in *Vanity Fair* or *Pendennis*.

Where the long periodic sentence comes into its own, of course, is in discussing character and motive. In the following sentence, made long in this instance by participial devices rather than relatives, the motivation and process of the young Esmond's gradual conversion from Catholicism to Anglicanism are weighed and analysed almost as much by rhythm and structure as by content:

> For a while Harry Esmond kept apart from these mysteries, but Doctor Tusher showing him that the prayers read were those of the Church of all ages, and the boy's own inclination prompting him to be always as near as he might be to his

mistress, and to think all things she did right, from listening to the prayers in the ante-chamber, he came presently to kneel down with the rest of the household in the parlour, and before a couple of years my lady had made a thorough convert. (*E* I ch. 7)

There were also humorous possibilities in the lengthy involved sentence. A superb parodist, Thackeray here matches the contortions of Doctor Tusher's sophistry as he justifies his not attending, as a clergyman, the sick-bed of a parishioner dying of an infectious disease, with a suitably labyrinthine style:

> We are not in a popish country; and a sick man doth not absolutely need absolution and confession. . . . 'Tis true they are a comfort and a help to him when attainable, and to be administered with hope of good. But in a case where the life of a parish priest *in the midst of his flock* is highly valuable to them, he is not called upon to risk it (and therewith the lives, future prospects, and temporal, *even spiritual*, welfare of his own family) for the sake of a single person, who is not very likely in a condition even to understand the religious message whereof the priest is the bringer – *being uneducated*, and likewise stupefied or delirious by disease. (*E* I ch. 8)

I have italicized some of the phrases in which the casuist, with the nicety and inclusiveness of ramification which he would doubtless have learnt in University polemics, succeeds in adding piquancy to the irony.

This lengthiness of sentence lends a dignified formality to the book. Yet, if the story is set in a rather formal age, the elderly Esmond, on the banks of the Potomac, is recounting a relaxed and unbuttoned narrative. It is this paradoxical blend of the formal and the informal that was pointed out by the Snows, in the Introduction to their edition of *Esmond* (p. xxix) as perhaps the most characteristic, or at least the most definable element in the elusive quality of the writing. This style, they admit, is ultimately 'indefinable, but perhaps one secret of it may be found in the use of homely language in the detail of the phrase, combined with a rather precise and formal structure of the sentence'. They illustrate with the following passage, with its Latinate participial constructions on the one hand, and collocations like *flung up* and *pretty prosperous* on the other:

Having paid his court, and *being admitted* to the intimacy of the house, he suddenly *flung up* his suit, when it seemed to be *pretty prosperous*, without giving a pretext for his behaviour. (*E* I ch. 2)

Indeed, there were examples of the informal as well as the formal in the sentence-structure of Thackeray's models. Professor Ian Gordon notes that much of the prose of the period from 1660 to 1760 was speech-based and 'almost undisguised talk'.[1] Like those of the writers on whom his style is based, Esmond's sentences when long are not taut and periodic. Often they are of a straggling kind which could easily be curtailed without damage to the total syntax. Their structure is often loose, florid and tending to asymmetry; and this was true, also, of much of the prose of Queen Anne's day. It was left to the grammarians of the later half of the eighteenth century to do the pruning and tidying up. In the words of Gordon: 'The grammatical doctrine of the 1760's . . . drove a wedge between spoken and written prose'.[2] There had been a much greater likelihood, for instance, of the casually illogical or asymmetrical joining of sentence-elements in Addison's day than in Thackeray's; and Thackeray, one suspects, enjoyed the licence that his archaic *persona* gave him to form sentences which schoolmasters of his own day and later (he had a Shakespearean hatred of schoolmasters) would have frowned upon. He often joins in one sentence what Fowler was later to call 'unequal yokefellows' (a), or deploys unattached participles (b). Nevertheless, the carelessness is often more apparent than real; there is a studied casualness which is not slipshod:

(a) Dr Montague . . . seeing *his familiarity* with these great folks, and *that my Lord Castlewood laughed* and walked with his hand on Harry's shoulder, relented to Mr Esmond. (*E* I ch. 13)

One of the gentlemen was singing a song *to a tune that Mr* Farquhar and Mr Gay both had used in their admirable comedies, and *very popular* in the army of that day. (*E* II ch. 12)

---

1 *The Movement of English Prose*, p. 137.
2 *Ibid.*, p. 142. Gordon points out that at least one grammarian re-wrote loose sentences from the *Spectator* and the *Guardian*, citing Cicero and Quintilian in support of 'suspending the sense till the close of the period'.

Before Mr Esmond left England in the month of August, and *being then at Portsmouth* . . . he heard that a pension . . . had been got for his late beloved mistress. (*E* II ch. 3)

Esmond's General, who was known as *a grumbler*, and *to have a hearty mistrust of the great Duke*. (*E* II ch. 14)

(b) *Riding into the neighbouring town* on the step of my lady's coach, his lordship and she, and Father Holt, being inside, *a great mob of people* came hooting and jeering round the coach. (*E* I ch. 4)

The awe exhibited by the little boy perhaps pleased the lady to whom the artless flattery was bestowed; for *having gone down on his knee* [as Father Holt had directed him and the mode then was) and *performed his obeisance, she said*, 'Page Esmond, my groom of the chamber will inform you what your duties are'. (*E* I ch. 3)

A further method of relaxing formality in the narrative that is appropriate to the period, yet also perhaps intended to be something of an idiosyncrasy of Esmond's speaking voice, is the frequent insertion, not necessarily indicated by punctuation, of small gobbets of direct speech in the writing:

They were ready to cry out *miracle* at first. (*E* I ch. 2)

'Twas in the height of the *No Popery* cry. (*E* I ch. 2)

Here it was her ladyship's turn to shriek, for the Captain, with his fist shaking the pillows and bolsters, at last came to *'burn'* as they say in the play of forfeits. (*E* I ch. 6)

It was, *'Lord, Mr Henry!'* and, *'How do you do, Nancy?'* many and many a time in the week. (*E* I ch. 8)

And now you see what she is – *hands off, highty-tighty*, high and mighty, an empress couldn't be grander. (*E* I ch. 9)

The village people had *good-bye* to say to him too. (*E* I ch. 9)

He dismissed her with a *'pish'*. (*E* I ch. 12)

A tendency towards the abstract is a marked characteristic of eighteenth-century prose, and Esmond has his share of these abstractions in his narrative; abstractions that in Victorian times as well as today would probably have been replaced by a more or less generalized, if not a more concrete, equivalent:

> But for the swords and books Harry might almost think the Father was an *imagination* of his mind. (*E* I ch. 9)

> It was this lady's disposition to think *kindnesses,* and devise silent bounties and to scheme *benevolence.* (*E* I ch. 9)

> Did you ever see such a frigid *insolence* as it is, Harry? That's the way she treats me. (*E* I ch. 12)

> Mr Congreve, who knew a part of *the sex* pretty well. (*E* I ch. 14)

> *Interest* was made that they should not mix with the vulgar convicts. (*E* II ch. 1)

The question of how far an age finds its expression in the abstract or the concrete, however, is not a simple one; nor one that has been as yet much investigated in the study of our language. As some of the quotations above will show, it is connected with the possibility of having abstract nouns in the plural, and with the use of definite, indefinite and zero articles; as well as the tendency to refer to a person by a neuter pronoun, somewhat commoner in earlier periods than today. Nor is this simply a one-way process, from the abstract to the concrete, or *vice versa.* Alongside the above examples, we find others contributing equally to the 'period' narrative, which nevertheless show a preference for the concrete rather than the abstract:

> Of these tales . . . Mr Esmond believed as much as he chose. His kinswoman's greater faith had *swallow* for them all. (*E* II ch. 3)

> In the scholars' boyish disputes at the University, where *parties* ran very high. (*E* II ch. 3)

> You go to Duke Street and see Mr Betterton. You love *the play,* I know. (*E* I ch. 14)[1]

---

1 But this idiom seems not to have been quite dead in the novelist's day. An incident, revealing to both the philologist and the Thackerayan, is quoted by Ray (*Uses* p. 151): 'Like all good and unspoiled souls,' Herman Merivale relates, 'he loved "the play". Asking a listless friend one day if he liked it, he got the usual answer, "Ye-es – I like a good play." "Oh! get out," said Thackeray, "I said *the* play; you don't even understand what I mean".'

Esmond's man was ordered to keep *sentry* in the gallery. (*E* III ch. 9)

The easiest kind of archaic vocabulary for a historical novelist to import into his story is the names of articles no longer found outside museums, but often recalling fairly precisely the period of time he wishes to evoke:

'Why, Harry, how fine we look in our scarlet and silver, and our black perriwig!' cries my lord. 'Mother, I am tired of my own hair. When shall I have a peruke? Where did you get your *steenkirk*, Harry?'
'It's some of my Lady Dowager's lace,' said Harry. (*E* II ch. 7)

We notice that Thackeray, like his great predecessor in the writing of historical novels, Sir Walter Scott, gives a broad hint as to what a *steenkirk* is for the indolent, who will not consult a dictionary. Those who do will find that this 'neckcloth with long laced ends hanging down or twisted together and passed through a loop or ring' is named from the victory of Steenkerke in Belgium, gained by the French over the English and their allies in 1692. Similarly, when the heroine of Esmond, Beatrix, wishes she were a man with the words: 'Had I worn a sword and perriwig instead of this mantle and *commode*' (*E* III ch. 3), the meaning of 'a tall head-dress consisting of a wire framework variously covered with silk or lace' conveys to the informed the most characteristic aspect of female dress of the period. This is the earliest meaning of *commode* in English; quite different from its later connotations of eighteenth-century cabinet-makers and Victorian sick-room sanitation. A word of similar import is *tour*, meaning a high-piled 'tower' of false hair: 'My lady of Chelsea in her highest *tour*' (*E* II ch. 15), indicating another way by which a lady of fashion might, in the language of the time, 'dress her head' (*E* I ch. 7).

Sometimes a rare word would be recalled for an object which, though perhaps not quite obsolete, would serve the purpose in reminding the well-read of the *Esmond* period: the use of *standish* for a stand containing writing-materials, spelt in an old-fashioned way that may (or may not – see *OED*) reveal its etymology, would suggest Pope's poem of just this period: 'On Receiving from the Right Hon. the Lady Frances Shirley a *Standish* and Two Pens':

Pouring out his flame and his passion . . . twisting and breaking
into bits the wax out of the *stand-dish*. (*E* II ch. 10)

Other archaic items are *a paper of oranges* eaten at the theatre (*E* I
ch. 14); *a dish of chocolate* (*E* III ch. 3); *a pair of organs* (*E* III ch. 7),
with *pair* in the sense of 'set', as in the old-fashioned *a pair of
stairs*; and a *mob of coaches* (*E* II ch. 15), with *mob* used of a hetero-
geneous crowd of things instead of people, as in Pope's 'She sees
a mob of metaphors advance'; usage now obsolete, except in
Australia. Various other phrases evoke the earlier time, such as
'Let us *have chairs* and go to Leicester Field' (*E* I ch. 14); 'Light
the candle, you *drawer*' (*E* I ch. 14); 'They *took water* on the river'
(*E* I ch. 3) and 'I treated her to the fiddles' (*E* III ch. 3), with
chairs, of course, in the sense of 'sedan chairs', *drawer* in the
Shakespearean sense of 'waiter', *took water* in the 'chiefly seventeenth and eighteenth century' sense (*OED water* 8b) of 'to take a
boat on the Thames', and the last phrase meaning 'I paid the band
to serenade her'.

There is much talk in *Esmond* of names for dead institutions
and customs: of *ordinaries*,[1] for example, meaning eating houses –
often probably gambling houses as well; and references to *Alsatia*,
a sanctuary for debtors and an asylum for criminals in London.
Shadwell's play *The Squire of Alsatia* had appeared in 1688:

He . . . was no better than a hanger-on of *ordinaries*, and a
brawler about Alsatia and the Friars. (*E* I ch. 2)

The word *toyshop* occurs several times with the meaning of 'a shop
for the sale of trinkets, knick-knacks, or small ornamental
articles'. When Thackeray writes of his very un-Victorian
heroine: 'Her chariot had been rolling the street from mercer to
toyshop, from goldsmith to laceman' (*E* III ch. 6), he may well
have had in mind some such passage from the *Spectator* as this:

1 In the rather different sense of 'a public meal regularly provided at a fixed point
in an eating-house or tavern' (*OED* s.v. *ordinary* 14, as against 14b), the word
survives, as we have seen (p. 125), down to Thackeray's time, especially in the
collocation *farmer's ordinary*; but the advent, from France, of *restaurant* (1827) and
café (1816) has gradually ousted the earlier expression.
   There is, incidentally, a brilliantly witty revival of this word in its historical
sense that Thackeray would have appreciated, in Angus Wilson's *Anglo-Saxon
Attitudes* (ch. 1), where the eccentric historian, Dr Rose Lorimer, shows a typical
blend of scholarship and naive unworldliness by referring to 'her usual "*ordinary*"
Lyons or A.B.C.'

'If they [women] make an Excursion to a Mercer's or a *Toyshop*' (Addison, *Spectator*, no. 10).

Frank Esmond uses (albeit mis-spelt) the early eighteenth-century slang word for money, *rhino*: 'Press the people for their rents and send me the *ryno* anyhow' (*E* III ch. 2); and the word *jade*, a colloquial and contemptuous term for a woman and characteristic of the period (it is twice illustrated in the *OED* from the *Spectator*), is frequent; especially from the lips of the boorish Lord Castlewood: 'Since I have had anything to do with the *jades*, they have given me nothing but disgust' (*E* I ch. 9). The slang word *put*, meaning 'a stupid fellow': 'This old *Put*, my father-in-law' (*E* II ch. 13), and *Teague*, a contemptuous sobriquet for an Irishman (*E* III ch. 2) go back to the seventeenth century, though they last until the novelist's day. Two expressions characteristic of the earlier bibulous age are *fuddling* and *to knock under*. *Fuddling*, meaning 'given to drinking bouts', is illustrated in the *OED* mainly from the *Esmond* period; *fuddled*, the past participle, being now more usual:

> There came *fuddling* squires from the country round, who bawled their songs under her windows, and drank themselves tipsy. (*E* I ch. 11)

To knock under in the meaning of 'to submit' is short for *to knock under the table* as a gesture of submission in a drinking bout. The *OED* quotes the *Gentleman's Journal* for 1691–2:

> He that flinches his glass
> And to drink is not able,
> Let him quarrel no more,
> But *knock under the table*.

The phrase in the more generalized sense is fairly frequent:

> Colonel Esmond *knocked under* to his fate, and resolved to surrender his sword. (*E* III ch. 1)

The collocation *pretty fellow* meaning, to quote Gay (*OED pretty* 3), 'a fine dressed man with little sense and a great deal of assurance', is common in *Esmond*, and also in *Barry Lyndon*. Thackeray might well have met it in the pages of the *Tatler* (nos. 21 and 28). We can compare the nursery rhyme 'Robin and Richard were two *pretty men*':

There were hundreds of men, wits, and *pretty fellows* frequenting the theatres and coffee-houses of that day. (*E* III ch. 5)

The Hebrew name *Abigail*, generalized in the sense of 'a lady's waiting-maid', comes to have this meaning from Beaumont and Fletcher's comedy *The Scornful Lady* (1616), in which Abigail is the name of one of the characters. It normally occurs in Thackeray with no capital, suggesting that the process of 'name into word' is complete (*E* I ch. 12). But when he writes, 'And now the time was come, the Queen's *Abigail* said' (*E* III ch. 10), *Abigail* carries the extra significance of being the Christian name of Anne's powerful favourite, Mrs (later Lady) Abigail Masham. E. G. Withycombe repeats Charlotte M. Yonge's suggestion that *Abigail* went out of fashion through being the name of this unpopular woman.[1]

Sometimes the elderly narrator recalls a word from his youth that he feels is already out of date and requires the apology of inverted commas or italics:

Miss Beatrix at first was quite *bit* (as the phrase of that day was), and did not 'smoke' the authorship of the story. (*E* III ch 3)

The first *OED* instance of *bit* in this sense (*bite* v. 15) of 'to deceive', and also of *a bite* meaning 'an imposition, a deception' (*bite* n. 9) are both from Steele, the writer who figures so prominently in the narrative of *Esmond*. In a phrase like 'the biter bit' this is probably the meaning of *bite* that was formerly intended. *Smoke* in the sense of 'to suspect a plot' survived later; being 'in common use c. 1600–1850' (*OED smoke* v. 8). Again, words like *wits* and *toasts* are already presumed to be used by the narrator to his grandchildren in conscious recollection of a bygone age:

Of the famous *wits* of that age, who have rendered Queen Anne's reign illustrious, and whose works will be in all Englishmen's hands in ages yet to come, Mr Esmond saw many. (*E* III ch. 5)

The young fellows of his society were making merry at the tavern, and calling *toasts* (as the fashion of that day was). (*E* II ch. 5)

1 See Eric Partridge, *Name into Word*, and *The Oxford Dictionary of English Christian Names*, s.v. *Abigail*.

This sense of 'a lady who is named as the person to whom a company is requested to drink; often one who is the reigning belle of the season' is first quoted by the *OED* (*toast* n² 1) from Congreve in 1700. The word is also discussed in detail in two numbers of the *Tatler* (nos. 24 and 31) by Steele. As we might expect, therefore, it occurs several times in *Esmond*. The young Frank Esmond, we are told, 'had been taught to admire his beauty by his mother, and esteemed it as highly as any reigning *toast* valued hers' (*E* I ch. 9). In 1709 Steele had written in the *Tatler* 'The Insignificancy of my Manners . . . makes the Laughers call me a *Quid Nunc*'. This is the first recorded importation of the Latin collocation for 'What now?' as an English word, developing the sense of 'an inquisitive person, a gossip'. We also find the word, predictably, in *Esmond*:

> There were plenty of men in our lines, *quidnuncs*, to whom Mr Webb listened only too willingly, who would specify the exact sums the Duke got. (*E* II ch. 14)

Besides obsolete and uncommon words, Thackeray employs certain words still in regular use, but in obsolete senses. Here, however, it is necessary to be cautious, because we cannot always be sure that meanings which seem old-fashioned to us were old-fashioned to Thackeray. The use of the verb *practise* meaning 'to lay schemes or plans . . . for an evil purpose' (*OED practise* 9), as in 'Is it to *practise* upon the simple heart of a virtuous lady?' (*E* I ch. 13), suggests the Restoration rather than the Victorian period; nevertheless the word does occur with this earlier meaning in *The Book of Snobs*: 'The Right Honourable was the son of a nobleman, and *practised* on an old lady' (*BS* ch. 39). More unequivocally archaic is the word *accident* without its present unfavourable connotations, in the neutral sense which the word *happening* has (or had, until very recently):

> But the campaign, if not very glorious, was very pleasant. . . . The many *accidents*, and the routine of shipboard . . . served to cheer and occupy his mind. (*E* II ch. 5)

Equally of the eighteenth century, though it is usage which survives to Jane Austen, is the use of *admire* mainly in the sense of 'to wonder', but with no suggestion of esteem or approbation. (See also p. 45.) When Henry Esmond in at least two places in the novel admires his relatives, namely Lord Castlewood and Lord Castlewood's son and heir, Frank, it is rather in the sense of marvelling at their weakness or effrontery than wishing to emulate them:

> Harry Esmond *admired* as he listened to him, and thought how the poor preacher of this self-sacrifice had fled from the small-pox, which the lady had borne so cheerfully (*E* I ch. 12)

> What Harry *admired* and submitted to in the pretty lad, his kinsman, was . . . the calmness of patronage which my young lord assumed. (*E* II ch. 8)

Presently, which now normally has the blunted meaning of 'in a little while', still quite commonly occurs in *Esmond* with its more etymological meaning of 'immediately':

> Other gentlemen in power were liberal at least of compliments and promises to Colonel Esmond . . . a seat in Parliament should be at his disposal *presently*. (*E* III ch. 5)

Perhaps intended to be still more archaic is the use of *presently* meaning 'at the present moment'; but this meaning, as Charles Barber points out in his book *Early Modern English* (p. 158), was always retained in Scotland, whence it recently seems to be returning to standard English:

> Doth any young gentleman of my progeny . . . chance to be *presently* suffering under the passion of Love? (*E* III ch. 3)

It is always dangerous to say that a word, or the meaning of a word, is obsolete; and still more dangerous, clearly, to state that a meaning was out of date or even obsolescent over a hundred years ago. But one may with fair confidence predicate obsolescence in many if not all the following; as used by Thackeray they seem to represent conscious archaism:

1 *to illustrate* in the sense of 'to set in a good light':

> Some of the most brilliant feats of valour . . . that ever *illustrated* any war. (*E* II ch. 15)

2 *to dissipate* in the sense of 'to disperse (a crowd)':

> The master came out of his lodge at midnight, and *dissipated* the riotous assembly. (*E* II ch. 10)

3 *approved* in the sense of 'tested by experience':

The young Electoral Prince . . . conducted himself with the spirit and courage of an *approved* soldier. (*E* II ch. 14)

4 *dislike* in the sense of 'displeasure':

A creature of Lord Marlborough, put in much to the *dislike* of the other officers. (*E* II ch. 14)

5 *character* in the sense of 'characteristic':

We might as well demand that a lady should be the tallest woman in the world . . . as that she should be a paragon in any other *character*. (*E* II ch. 15)

6 *web* in the sense of 'woven material' (in effect 'cloth'):

The two ladies insisting on . . . kneeling down at the bedside and kissing the sheets out of respect for the *web* that was to hold the sacred person of a King. (*E* III ch. 9)

7 *genius* in the sense of 'aptitude combined with inclination', but without the modern implication of exalted intellectual power:

Not by the sword very likely. Thousands have a better *genius* for that than I. (*E* II ch. 6)

8 *race* in the narrower sense of 'family':

Establishing the present Royal *race* on the English throne. (*E* III ch. 12)

9 *gazetteer* in the sense not of a geographical index but of one who writes in a gazette, a journalist:

The *Gazetteers* and writers . . . have given accounts sufficient of that bloody battle. (*E* III ch. 1)

10 *imperial* in the sense of 'imperious':

Beatrix . . . ruled over the house with little *imperial* ways. (*E* I ch. 11)

11 *ingenious* in the sense that Aubrey, historian and gossip of the Restoration period, so often uses the word, namely, 'clever, showing talent', but without the modern suggestion of 'manifesting cleverness of invention or construction':

He had not read Monsieur Galland's *ingenious* Arabian tales. (*E* I ch. 9)

12 *prevent* in the sense familiar to Anglicans from various instances in the *Book of Common Prayer* ('*Prevent* us, O Lord, in all our doings' etc.), that is, not 'to stop', but 'to come before with succour':

> Her habit was thus to watch ... those to whom duty or affection bound her, and to *prevent* their designs, or to fulfil them, when she had the power. (*E* I ch. 9)

Here also we might include *great*, meaning 'large in size', with no emotional overtones; *black* 'of dark complexion'; *to love* in the milder sense of 'to like', still possible in positive contexts, but hardly in negative ones; and *High-Dutch*, meaning 'German':

> The sad, lonely little occupant of this gallery busy over his *great* book. (*E* I ch. 1)

> You have got the bel air. You are a *black* man. Our Esmonds are all black. The little prude's son is fair ... fair and stupid. (*E* II ch. 3)

> Take away the books. My lord *does not love* to see them. (*E* I ch. 9)

> A shabby *High-Dutch* duke. (*E* II ch. 13)

We have noted that in attempting to produce a sense of archaism Thackeray tends to favour extraordinary, even slightly eccentric turns of phrase which, while they effectively call up a sense of period, should not perhaps be examined too closely in relation to the language of Queen Anne's day. But there are also, of course, many expressions which have a good pedigree in the earlier language. It is no accident that various idioms which the novelist employs are also quoted in the *OED* from the *Spectator* and the *Tatler*. A *Spectator* essay is fabricated by Esmond purporting to be by Steele: 'for,' the parodist writes, 'as for the other author of the *Spectator*, his prose style, I think, is altogether inimitable' (*E* III ch. 3). Thus *to open oneself*, meaning 'to reveal one's feelings', together with *to break one's mind* (of similar import), and *to open on* (someone), meaning 'to begin a conversation or remonstration' with them, occur more than once, and are very much of the eighteenth century; as are *to draw in* and *draw off*, in contexts of courtship, meaning respectively 'to attract' and 'to withdraw', *to lie* in the sense of 'to sleep, spend the night', and also *in his hand* meaning 'led by the hand' (*OED hand* 29b). Here, too, we might include *crowded*, with the verb *to crowd* in the sense (*OED crowd* 7c) of 'to press upon or beset as a crowd does . . . to incommode by presence of numbers'. Other colloquial idioms of the previous century are *time enough*, used not as it generally now is predicatively, but as an adverb phrase, and *ever* as an intensive to questions, without temporal import:

Addison kept himself to a few friends, and very rarely *opened himself* except in their company. (*E* III ch. 5)

And he cast about how he should *break* a part of *his mind* to his mistress. (*E* I ch. 12)

It was Lady Castlewood that *opened upon* Beatrix. (*E* III ch. 10)

Some rich young gentleman newly arrived in the town, that this incorrigible flirt would set her net and baits to *draw in*. (*E* III ch. 3)

She . . . jilted him for a duke, who, in his turn, had *drawn off*. (*E* II ch. 12)

The great gloomy inn on the road where they *lay*. (*E* I ch. 3)[1]

A portly gentleman, with a little girl of four years old *in his hand*. (*E* I ch. 1)

The three gentlemen in Newgate were almost as much *crowded* as the bishops in the Tower. (*E* II ch. 1)

---

1 See G. W. E. Russell, *Collections and Recollections*, London, 1898, p. 2: 'There was an old Lady Robert Seymour, who lived in Portland Place, and died there in 1855, in her ninety-first year. . . . She carried down to the time of the Crimean War the habits and phraseology of Queen Charlotte's early court. "Goold" of course she said for "gold" and "yaller" for "yellow", and "laylock" for "lilac". She laid the stress on the second syllable of *balcony*. She called her maid her '"ooman"; instead of sleeping in a place she *lay* there, and when she consulted the doctor she spoke of having "used the 'pottecary".' Needless to say, Thackeray was conversant with such vestigial remains of eighteenth-century pronunciation and idiom; indeed he discusses some of them in the *Spectator* pastiche: 'Why should we say *goold* and write *gold* etc.' (*E* III ch. 3).

He will be at Roncq *time enough* to lick my Lord Duke's trenchers at supper. (*E* II ch. 15)

Have you *ever* a hundred guineas to give Cardonnel? (*E* II ch. 15)

The Restoration is probably second only to Chaucer's time as a period of intensive French influence on English. Charles II, chiefly anxious, as he put it, 'not to go on my travels again', nevertheless imported, as did his court, many Gallicisms from their time of exile on the Continent. An embodiment of this influence is a character like the Dowager Viscountess Castlewood, who has lived in France with her husband from 'Worcester fight'[1] till 1660. She speaks a barbarous French *jargon* (*E* II ch. 8) which it was a challenge to Thackeray's virtuosity to reproduce in what purports to be one of her letters (*E* II ch. 2), has a French maid and a habit of speaking French when agitated. She is gratified that her protégé, Harry Esmond, has the *bel air*, but cannot understand what it is about the current Lady Castlewood that makes him and other men so *raffoler* ('dote') on her (*E* II ch. 3). A vain, worldly, and opinionated anachronism from a previous age, in many ways she is the counterpart in *Esmond* of the Major in *Pendennis*, not least in this habit of resorting to French. As a fanatical Jacobite and a devout Catholic, she and her household 'make *meagre* on Fridays always' (*E* II ch. 3). The earlier form of this word for fasting, *maigre*, closer to its French origin, might perhaps have been more appropriate to this date and this speaker (see *OED meagre* 3, and *maigre*), but Thackeray may well have thought that this form better solved the archaist's dilemma of employing attractive obsolete terms while avoiding total incomprehension. (At the end of the seventeenth century, in any case, there would probably be no difference in pronunciation in the two forms.) Another of the Dowager's passions is cards, and it is fitting that her 'curtain line', the last expression Esmond hears from her lips, is 'Tierce to a king' (*E* III ch. 1), meaning a combination of three cards in sequence leading to a king, from the French card game of *piquet*, which she settles down to play as he leaves to 'make the

1 This sense of 'a hostile encounter or engagement between opposing forces' (*OED fight* n. 2a) is 'archaic or rhetorical', according to the *OED*; especially so, one might add, with a proper name attached – the usage of the Civil War. See the *OED* quotation from the *Memorials* of Fairfax, with a reference to *Hornsby Fight*.

campaign'[1] once more. Other French-derived games are mentioned too: *tric-trac*, an old variety of backgammon (*E* I ch. 4), and *billiards*. The young Beatrix told Esmond: 'Papa had gotten a new game from London, a French game, called a *billiard* – that the French king played it very well' (*E* I ch. 11). The French *billard*, from the word for 'cue', is still singular; but already in Elizabethan times this word, known to Spenser, Shakespeare and Ben Jonson (though the game was perhaps very different in Tudor times), had been made plural, perhaps on the analogy of games like *draughts, skittles* and *bowls*, and in the next chapter of *Esmond* the 'new game of *billiards*' takes on its normal English plural form.

Another entry for French terms was through 'the noble science of *escrime*' (*E* I ch. 10). Father Holt, one of the most memorable of Thackeray's characters, first instructs Esmond in the smallsword, and Lord Mohun later rallies the young man on the boldness that 'that infernal *botte de Jesuite*' has given him (*E* I ch. 13); but this *botte*, a thrust or fencing-trick, may have been due to his other fencing-instructor at Cambridge, a French refugee officer and also, it transpires, a Jesuit. Harry boasts, '[Lord Mohun] never could parry that *botte* I brought from Cambridge' (*E* I ch. 14). Another characteristic French-derived word of the period is *billet*, meaning an informal letter or note, confined today to the now jocular *billet-doux*, but illustrated in the *OED* (*billet* n.[1] 2) from Steele, among others: 'Divine Gloriana', the villainous Lord Mohun writes, 'Do you vouchsafe no reply to *billets* that are written with the blood of my heart?' (*E* I ch. 14). A final character in the book much given to French is the disguised Old Pretender, who, however unlike he may be to the Pretender of history, incidentally caused Thackeray to import into the English language the French word for a coach-house, *hangar* (*E* III ch. 13), which was destined for special development in the acronautical technology of a later age.

Henry Esmond had been given a thorough training, not only in fencing but also in Latin, by Father Holt, a character who lards his speech with Latin words (*silentium* for 'silence', *famuli* for 'attendants'). At Cambridge, Esmond's foreign Jesuitical pronunciation of the language had at first caused amusement, but a Latin oration and poems which he composed won respect. It is

1 This archaism is illustrated from 1647 in the *OED* (*campaign* 3, *make* 57b), and the last quotation is from *The Virginians*.

appropriate, therefore, that the narrator of this autobiographical novel should quote the Latin poets, especially Horace, Ovid and Virgil, with some frequency; and Thackeray was able, owing to the purported date of the narrative, to indulge a taste for classical allusion which would be less appropriate in a novel set in his own day. For, in this matter of familiarity with the classics, changes were occurring in his lifetime. It is true that Pitt Crawley, in *Vanity Fair* (set, albeit somewhat insubstantially, in the Regency period), tosses off the occasional line of Horace 'with a House of Commons air' (*VF* p. 333); but when the novelist describes how, in Philip Firmin's college days, a distinguished relative had quoted 'hackneyed old Ovidian lines', he adds in parenthesis, 'some score of years ago a great deal of that old coin was current in conversation' (*Ph.* II ch. 16). Similarly, in *The Virginians*, written a few years before *Philip* in the late 1850s, Thackeray records the changed attitude to classical learning:

> Letters were loved indeed [in the eighteenth century], and authors were actually authorities. Gentlemen appealed to Virgil or Lucan in the Courts or the House of Commons. . . . Their reign is over now, the good old Heathens. . . . The age of economists and calculators has succeeded, and Tooke's Pantheon is deserted and ridiculous. Now and then, perhaps, a Stanley kills a kid, a Gladstone hangs up a wreath, a Lytton burns incense, in honour of the Olympians. But what do they care at Lambeth, Birmingham, the Tower Hamlets, for the ancient rites, divinities, worship? Who the plague are the Muses, and what is the use of all that Greek and Latin rubbish? (*V* II ch. 15)

The reader who understands an allusion is flattered; the one who is continually puzzled may grow annoyed with the book. It was clear that this new readership from the Tower Hamlets and elsewhere, unversed in the classics, must be catered for; and accordingly the novelist tends to choose better-known Latin quotations, to rely a great deal on classical allusion rather than quotation (thus, Baucis and Philemon represent the loving man and wife) and to quote, or make allusions to, Greek much more rarely than Latin.

There was one kind of language, and that particularly appropriate to the Restoration and Queen Anne period, which

Thackeray was debarred by the moral climate of his own age from using; namely, what is sometimes euphemistically called strong language. Oaths, for example, occurred more commonly and in much greater variety in the *Esmond* period than in the novelist's Victorian rendering of that time. It is only occasionally, and usually to signalize a crisis, that extreme oaths appear; and even then a dash may be substituted:

> 'Have you seen him alone?' cries my lord, starting up with an oath; '*by God*, have you seen him alone?'
> '. . . Keep your oaths, my lord, for your wife . . . your Popish wife.'
> 'By —', says my lord, rapping out another oath, 'Clotilda is an angel!' (*E* III ch. 10)

As to the use of explicit language concerning the so-called facts of life, and indeed, the treatment of sex generally, Thackeray seems to vary his position. In two passages in *The Virginians*, as in the more famous Preface to *Pendennis*, he seems to hanker after a freedom which Fielding and other predecessors in novel-writing could take for granted, but which was denied to him and his contemporaries:

> The Comic Muse, now-a-days, does not lift up Molly Seagrim's curtain; she only indicates the presence of some one behind it, and passes on primly, with expressions of horror, and a fan before her eyes. (*V* I ch. 20)

Again:

> In those homely times a joke was none the worse for being a little broad; and a fine lady would laugh at a jolly page of Fielding, and weep over a letter of Clarissa, which would make your present Ladyship's eyes start out of your head with horror. (*V* II ch. 22)

In *Esmond* on the other hand, he mentions, in a kind of euphemistic *occupatio*, the sort of language that Beatrix Esmond would have taken in her stride, but which the novelist earnestly advises the ladies of his own day to avoid:

> Part of her coquetry may have come from her position about the Court . . . where she spoke and listened to much free talk such as one never would have thought the lips or ears of Rachel

Castlewood's daughter would have uttered or heard. . . . If the English country ladies at this time were the most pure and modest of any ladies in the world – the English town and Court ladies permitted themselves words and behaviour that were neither modest nor pure; and claimed, some of them, a freedom which those who love that sex most would never wish to grant them. The gentlemen of my family that follow after me (for I don't encourage the ladies to pursue any such studies) may read in the works of Mr Congreve, and Dr Swift, and others, what was the conversation and what the habits of our time. (*E* III ch. 3)

To render the speech of an outspoken age in the vocabulary of a prudish one is always difficult. Thackeray's most amusing resource is what one might call bowdlerization by aposiopesis: the deliberate breaking into the words of one speaker by another, just when matters are becoming too frank for Victorian comfort. This is a trick that occurs in at least six places, at various points in the dialogue:

'Indeed, Parson Harry,' says he; 'and are you going to take out a diploma, and cure your fellow-students of the —'
'Of the gout,' says Harry, interrupting him, and looking him hard in the face. (*E* I ch. 13)

'I always feel sure that the Captain and his better half have fallen out over night, and that he has been brought home tipsy, or has been found out in —'
'Beatrix!' cries the Lady Castlewood. (*E* III ch. 3)

'I do not chuse that my wife should have for benefactor a —'
'My lord!' says Colonel Esmond. (*E* III ch. 4)

'Give me your honour as a gentleman, for you *are* a gentleman, though you are a —'
'Well, well,' says Harry, a little impatient. (*E* II ch. 8)

The first (1852) edition of *Esmond*, published in three volumes, is set in mock eighteenth-century type complete with long and short 's's' and occasional antiquated spellings, such as *heroick* and *musick* (*E* I ch. 1), *accompt* for *account* (*E* III ch. 2) and *yatches* for *yachts* (*E* II ch. 10). The most interesting spelling, etymologically speaking, is *Cravats* for *Croats* ('He belonged to the Royal

Cravats', *E* III ch. 1), that is, Croatian mercenaries.[1] These troops were distinguished by a linen scarf round their necks, whence the word, and the article of dress, came into vogue in seventeenth-century France. Spellings such as these do not loom large, and most of them were normalized in later editions.

As to the minor syntactic features of the pastiche language of *Henry Esmond*, space will not permit the discussion of the subject here. I enumerate the main points of syntactic difference, however, in an article in *English Studies*, vol. LVII, pp. 19–42.

1 See Eric Partridge, *Name into Word*, s.v. *cravat*.

CHAPTER 8

Proper Names

🙚🙚🙚🙚🙚🙚

THERE is one minor aspect of Thackeray's art in which he excels. This is the selection of wittily apposite proper names for his characters, with appropriate titles, property, and appendages. This is of course how a great many surnames originated. To distinguish two men, both having the Christian name of John, as John White and John Black, might originally reflect an ancestral difference of complexion and hair colouring, however much the accidents of heredity may have obscured the issue. In a more primitive society like eighteenth-century Virginia, such fortuitous nicknames were still in process of acquiring the dignity of proper names, as when a negro slave is named after an American dish:

> The *gumbo* was declared to be perfection (young Mr Harry's black servant was named after this dish, being discovered behind the door with his head in a bowl of this delicious hotch-potch . . . , and grimly christened on the spot). (*V* I ch. 9)

The observation of the Tillotsons in their Introduction to *Vanity Fair* (p. vi) that nearly all the main personages of that novel are named in such a way as to convey moral comment, is true of the other novels, too. They instance the Crawleys, Tom Eaves and Lord Steyne; a glance at that recently re-published book *A Thackeray Dictionary* (I. G. Mudge and M. E. Sears, New York, 1962) will provide many other examples. To take one at random, Blanche Amory in *Pendennis* was christened Betsy by her unpretentious and parvenue mother, Lady Clavering. Doubtless what *The Oxford Dictionary of Christian Names* states of *Betty* is true for *Betsy* also: it was 'fashionable in the eighteenth century until it became too common, was relegated to chambermaids and the like, and gradually died out, to be restored to fashion in the twentieth century.' It was too unfashionable for the refined sensibilities of Lady Clavering's daughter, who took to herself the name *Blanche*. As to her surname, Thackeray hints at its implications in a letter to Jane Brookfield:

> At the train whom do you think I found? Miss Gore, who says she is Blanche Amory, and I think she is Blanche *Amory*, *amiable* (at times), amusing, clever and depraved. (*L* IV p. 425)

His adeptness in the creation of names is well illustrated by those bestowed upon a host of minor characters that populate his world and give it the crowded variety of a Frith canvas. Compared to Thackeray's, Trollope's minor names seem trite and uninventive: a member of the nobility called Lady Auld Reekie, lawyers named Slow and Bidewhile, both in *The Way We Live Now*, merit the condemnation of Henry James in *The Future of the Novel: Essays on the Art of Fiction* (p. 248): 'It would be better to go back to Bunyan at once'. Even the onomastic exercises of Dickens appear by comparison at once too laboured, and too fantastic to be credible, with prominent members of government called Coodle, Foodle, Doodle, ranged in opposition to Duffy, Cuffy, Muffy and so on in the twelfth chapter of *Bleak House*. Thackeray's cleverness consists partly in paying due regard to the likelihood and plausible sound of the name in the first place; so that initially we are often apt to pass on, until the secondary appropriateness of it strikes us. What takes place, in effect, is characterization by shorthand:

> Those Miss *Burrs* . . . how they followed him; how they would meet him in the parks and shrubberies! (*N* II ch. 21)

> The Orthodox Settlement in *Feefawfoo*, the largest and most savage of the Cannibal Islands. (*P* I ch. 22)[1]

> I wish . . . the Colonel would realise even now, like that Mr

---

[1] The reference, of course, is to the nursery story of *Jack the Giant-Killer*, and the giant's cannibal rhyme:

> 'Fee, fi, fo, fum,
> I smell the blood of an Englishman.
> Be he alive, or be he dead,
> I'll grind his bones to make my bread.'

For another nursery allusion, we might compare the unpromising name of Mrs Maria Newcome's housekeeper: 'We have a few friends at dinner, and now I must go in and consult with *Mrs Hubbard*.' (*N* I ch. 7).

Ratray who has just come out of the ship, and brought a hundred thousand pounds with him. (*N* II ch. 27)

The proceedings in the Newcome Divorce Bill filled the usual number of columns in the papers. ... Out of that combat scarce anybody came well, except the two principal champions, *Rowland*, Serjeant, and *Oliver*, Q.C. (*N* II ch. 20)

By adding a suffix (? from *betray*) to a word like *rat*, or otherwise altering the spelling, as with *Roland*, the novelist provides a slight puzzle which it is flattering to the reader to be able to solve. Trollope, secure in a tradition going back to Ben Jonson and beyond, would not have bothered to alter names for the sake of verisimilitude; but Thackeray clearly wished his names to look and sound as authentic as his dialogue. It is quite possible that a mild Wesleyan minister should have been called the *Reverend Luke Waters* (*VF* p. 322); or for a more fiery clergyman to have the name of *the Reverend Lawrence Grills* (*VF* p. 405) – an oblique reference, of course, to the martyrdom of Saint Lawrence on a gridiron. There are other plausibly-named clergymen briefly characterized by their nomenclature: such as *the Reverend Lemuel Whey* 'full of the milk and water of human kindness' (*MW* 'Mr and Mrs Frank Berry'), and *the Reverend Jonas Wales* of *the Armageddon Chapel*, Clifton (*P* I ch. 2). We can trust Thackeray to find the one word (Armageddon) that sounds both apocalyptic and Welsh, even though in fact it is Hebrew!

But names of laymen also manage to be at once plausible and suggestive. *His Excellency Rummun Loll* (*N* I ch. 8) sounds plausibly Hindu; but we are alerted from the start to his being a doubtful character. When, as chief actor in one of Becky Sharp's fashionable charades, '*Young Bedwin Sands*, then an elegant dandy and Eastern traveller' is mentioned (*VF* p. 492), the pun in this plausible name is obvious; but by spelling the Christian name in a way that recalls *the Goodwins*, the novelist suggests that the young dandy is destined to come to grief.

Again, the *Polwheedle and Tredyddlum Copper Mines* (*P* II ch. 4) are contrived to sound authentically Cornish as well as a shaky and doubtful enterprise; and in writing of the *Dumplingbeare* hounds (*P* II ch. 37) Thackeray has not only suggested the Devonshire dumpling connection; he has noticed, long before Ekwall (though not of course in philological detail) the fact that 'in some

SW dialects, especially in Devon, the word *bearu* (OE *bearu* 'grove' normally yielding *beare* or *barrow* as a place-name element) acquired u-stem inflexion and *ea* became ME *ea, e*.[1] Hence actual Devon place-names like *Beer, Rockbeare,* and *Larkbeare,* near Ottery St Mary, which is in fact the Fairoaks of *Pendennis.* The house, if not the grounds, is still much as Thackeray would have known it, and an indispensable place of pilgrimage to those who would fully appreciate that novel. Nearby is the little river, the Otter, re-named by Thackeray so felicitously *the Brawl* (P I ch. 2).

The novelist clearly enjoyed exercising his wit in such *tours de force* of nomenclature. It was also an underscoring of the *vanitas vanitatum* motif that the titles of the grandest nobility should have underlying them such humble domestic agricultural themes as cheese, sheep-rearing and poultry:

Lord *Cheddar* wanted me to go down to Wiltshire. I asked after the family (you know Henry *Churningham* is engaged to Miss *Rennet?* – a doosid good match for the Cheddars). (*N* I ch. 24)

The chief of the *Southdown* family, *Clement* William, fourth Earl of Southdown . . . came into Parliament (as *Lord Wolsey*). (*VF* p. 320)

Sometimes a joke like this is sustained over several pages. Later (*VF* p. 324) we are told of the lozenge on the Southdown family carriage – the 'three lambs trottant argent upon the field vert of the Southdowns'. Or again, in the twenty-eighth chapter of *The Newcomes*, we meet *Lord and Lady Dorking* and their daughter *Lady Clara Pulleyn.* Their estate is at *Chanticlere*, their eldest son is *Viscount Rooster* and other daughters of the family include little *Hennie*, referred to later as *Henrietta*, plausibly enough; and *Biddy*, and *Adelaide.*

Names can also place a family of landed gentry in their historical setting, and even suggest an ancestral fault. In the pedigree of the Crawleys of Queen's Crawley, the roll-call of Christian names of heirs and representatives shows their opportunist, turncoat tendencies. Sir *Pitt* was the son of *Walpole* Crawley, while an-cestors further back include *Charles Stuart* Crawley, afterwards called *Barebones* Crawley [*VF* p. 66). Another ancestor, Sir *Wilmot*

1 E. Ekwall, *The Concise Oxford Dictionary of English Place-names,* Oxford, 1936, s.v. *bearu.*

Crawley, doubtless sycophantically named for John Wilmot, Earl of Rochester, the poet and libertine favourite of Charles II, is seen manifesting the family tendency in a brief reference in *Henry Esmond*:

> My Lord Sark being in the Tower a prisoner, and Sir Wilmot Crawley of Queen's Crawley having gone over to the Prince of Orange's side. (*E* I ch. 3)

The Reverend *Bute* Crawley, Sir *Pitt* Crawley and *Rawdon* Crawley have names which continue the tradition: *Bute* being named after the third Earl of Bute, a prominent minister at the beginning of the reign of George III: 'the great Commoner was in disgrace when the Reverend gentleman was born', Thackeray tells us (*VF* p. 67); and *Rawdon* after Francis Rawdon Hastings, former Marquis of Hastings, sometime friend of the Prince Regent. Other family names may indicate an old Catholic, and formerly recusant stock:

> Sir *Bartholomew Fawkes* will have a fine property when *Lord Campion* dies, unless Lord Campion leaves the money to the convent where his daughter is. (*N* II ch. 8)

Names can be chosen for their onomatopoetic effect: 'Old *Hawkshaw*, whose cough and accompaniments are fit to make any man uncomfortable' (*P* II ch. 29); while even anonymity, paradoxically, can serve in nomenclature:

> If Lord and Lady *Blank*, of *Suchandsuch* Castle, received a distinguished circle (including Lady *Dash*), for Christmas ... you may venture on any wager that Captain *Asterisk* is one of the company. (*N* II ch. 7)

Thackeray's pride in his cosmopolitan outlook (he spent much time at various periods of his life in Paris and Weimar) leads him to choose French, German, Italian or classical Greek names whose appropriateness or ironic inappropriateness may not be instantly apparent: as when he writes of *Zwieback's Conditorey* (*VF* p. 610), *Zwieback* being German for 'a rusk, biscuit' the confectionery being twice baked. Similarly he gives an important London club for distinguished elderly men the likely-sounding name of *The Megatherium Club* (*Ph* I ch. 5), echoing Greek *mega thērion* 'great beast'. The house in Boulogne where Philip Firmin does much of his courting is in *the Rue Roucoule* (*Ph* I ch. 18), *roucouler* meaning 'to coo like a dove'. 'Hush! silence!' Becky Sharp calls out at one point (*VF* p. 488), 'there is *Pasta* beginning to sing'; and the charms of H. E. Madame de *Schnurrbart*, who 'had her night' for receiving visitors at Pumpernickel are somewhat diminished when we remember that *Schnurrbart* is German for 'moustache' (*VF* p. 610). When Becky Sharp claims a dubious descent from a noble family, the *Entrechats* of *Gascony* (*VF* p. 20), her creator would have us remember that to perform an *entrechat* one must have 'jumped up'; and also that the ill-founded boasting of the Gascon has given us a word like *gasconade*, meaning 'extravagant boasting'. Interlinguistic confusion in nomenclature is also a source of humour. The *Hotel des Quatre Saisons* at Rougetnoirburg is so popular with British barristers that it is dubbed the *Hotel of Quarter Sessions* (*CB* 'The Kickleburys on the Rhine', p. 213). *Giglio*, hero of *The Rose and the Ring*, is a name that should be pronounced in the English, not the Italian way, recalling the word *giggle* (see Ray, *Age*, p. 231, and n.); whereas half the fun of the *Poggi* Palace in Florence (*P* I ch. 22) is that it should be given an Italian pronunciation.

The lifelong researches of Geoffrey and Kathleen Tillotson enable us to appreciate Thackeray's onomastic subtleties more than ever before. In their superb edition of *Vanity Fair*, for instance (p. 664n.), they inform us that the names of Becky Sharp's solicitors, Messrs *Burke, Thurtell and Hayes*, who secured for her the payment of Jos Sedley's insurance policy in the dubious business of Jos's death, were also the names of three notorious murderers of Thackeray's day. Did Becky murder Jos? In the manner of Tacitus, Thackeray leaves this sinister hint in the reader's mind, and passes on.

There are several names we cannot fully understand without some knowledge of Victorian slang. When Thackeray writes of 'the great Calcutta House of *Fogle*, Fake and Cracksman', and goes on to mention, in parenthesis, that 'the Fogles have long been out of the firm, and Sir Horace Fogle is about to be raised to the Peerage as *Baron Bandanna*' (*VF* p. 579), we need to know that *fogle* is, according to *Hotten's Dictionary of Slang* of 1859, colloquial Victorian English for 'a silk handkerchief – not a clout, which is of cotton'; and a *bandanna*, of course, is a particularly rich spotted silk handkerchief. Messrs *Stumpy* and *Rowdy* are very suitable names for the bankers of the purse-proud Osborne family (*VF* p. 595); both names are also Victorian slang words for money; both carrying connotations, as slang words for money often do, of filthy lucre. Owing to the comparative evanescence of slang, it is possible to miss much of what such names signify. Thus, while it is clear to all in such a passage as the following that a confidence trick is in progress, the Victorian reader would have learnt more than we do:

> Did *Muff* know where there was a good place for supper? So those two went to supper, and who should come in, of all men in the world, but Major *Macer*? And so *Legg* introduced *Macer*. (*BS* ch. 23)

Thackeray's contemporaries would have recognized *Legg* as a rendering of the aphetic form of *blackleg*, meaning in the forties a turf or gaming swindler, as we have seen (p. 83); and that *macer* was also gaming slang for a swindler. Similarly, any last suggestions of the innocence of 'the Misses Leery' in the following are dispelled when we bear in mind that *leery* was slang for 'wide-awake, knowing, "fly" ':

> Yonder are the Misses *Leery*, who are looking out for the young officers of the Heavies, who are pretty sure to be pacing the cliff. (*VF* p. 208)

Or again, *Herr Spoff*, 'premier pianist to the Hospodar of Wallachia' (how the showman of *Vanity Fair* relished grandiloquent titles, clearly enjoying them quite as much as he pretended to scorn them!), who accompanied 'Madame de Raudon' in a *matinée musicale* (*VF* p. 625), is sketched for us by his name. It sounds superficially Teutonic, but *spoffy* or *spoffish* in nineteenth-century slang meant 'bustling, officious, having the characteristics of a busybody'.

As we have seen, men-about-town are often trend-setters in slang and fittingly they are awarded in the novels either slang names or names indicating a somewhat technical knowledge of their chief preoccupations of cards, dice, billiards and horses. Such are *Captain Raff*, and *Mr Marker* (*P* II ch. 22); *Captain Cannon*, playing billiards with George Osborne (*VF* p. 111); the three 'horsey' men Tom *Cinqbars*, Bob *Martingale* and Jack

Spatterdash, the last two being also names of harness and riding equipment (see also p. 80); a more sinister trio, *Major Loder*, the *Honourable Mr Deuceace*,[1] and *Captain Rook* (*VF* pp. 625, 627); and 'young *Lord Varinas*' (*VF* p. 532), named after a town in Venezuela which gave its name to a kind of tobacco. Various of these gentlemen, like many of the novelist's minor characters, cross the boundaries of more than one book and may even emerge from time to time in essays and occasional pieces. The dupes have also their nomenclature; being represented by names like *Ensign Spooney* (*VF* p. 227), *Mr Frederick Pigeon* (*VF* p. 625), young *Green* of the Rifles, who lost to Colonel Crawley at cards (*VF* p. 353); and, perhaps, despite his name (for this is a field where irony freely operates), young *Downy* of Christchurch, a gentleman commoner who was eliminated from the University (*N* I ch. 9).

Thackeray is also adept at hinting at the disreputable in some of the minor female characters; notably in the naming of those ladies whom Lord Steyne inflicts, along with Becky Sharp, upon his wife's company; *Lady Crackenbury*, *Mrs Chippenham*, and *Madame de la Cruchecassée* (*VF* p. 453). These are the dubious ladies, together with the (presumably) American *Mrs Washington White* (*VF* p. 464) whom Becky was glad to consort with at various stages in her career. Sometimes thus, through a lady's name, the novelist can slip in a sexual innuendo of the kind that he would perhaps have preferred to make more openly if contemporary decorum had allowed it:

> By the way, did you ever see anything like *Lady Godiva Trotter's* dress last night? (*RP* 'On a Hundred Years Hence')

In inventing names of institutions, Thackeray's skill is equally apparent. Regimental names that ring true, yet add a burlesque touch, are the *Queen's Own Piebalds* (*BS* ch. 29) and a Scottish regiment, the *Cuttykilts* (*BS* ch. 37). The choice of the right register for names, whether pretentious or down-to-earth, is infallible. An apothecary's shop in Bradystown, Ireland, is grandiloquently named the *Esculapian Repository* (*BL* ch. 14); while the disreputable James Gann, in *A Shabby Genteel Story*, frequents a public house called the *Bag of Nails* (*SGS* ch. 1). An inveterate punster, Thackeray writes of an undergraduate who runs up a bill for

1 See *OED deuce* 5, 'Two and one . . . hence a poor throw, bad luck, mean estate, the lower class.'

such things as Landseer proofs, named *Dilley Tandy*; and of another of Pen's student friends called *Lord Magnus Charteris*, the *Marquis of Runnymede's* son (*P* I ch. 18). Not surprisingly, perhaps, the latter is a 'truculent republican'. When mention is made, in *A Little Dinner at Timmins's*, of a confectioner's shop 'at the corner of *Parliament Place* and *Alicumpayne Square*', we are to bear in mind that *parliament*, short for *parliament cake*, is a kind of gingerbread, and *alicumpayne* is a sweetmeat containing the herb *elecompane* (cf. *liquorice* and *mint*, which are also names for both plants and sweetmeats).

Certain general characteristics of British nomenclature are pilloried. In *The Book of Snobs*, for instance, the motives behind repetitive personal names are glanced at:

> The first of men naturally are the Buckrams, her own race; then follow in rank the Scrapers. The General was the greatest general; his eldest son, *Scraper Buckram Scraper*, is at present the greatest and best. (*BS* ch. 6)

Double-barrelled names, too, come in for ridicule in due course. Indeed, I believe that Thackeray may well have been the first to apply, or at least to record the application of, the word *double-barrelled* to names. The first *OED* instance of the collocation *double-barrelled name* is from 1889; but the Dictionary also quotes, from *The Book of Snobs*, a nonce-use of *double-barrel* as a verb (italicized) in relation to names some forty years previously:

> He *double-barrelled* his name (as many poor Snobs do), and instead of T. Sniffle, as formerly, came out, in a porcelain card, as Rev. T. D'Arcy Sniffle. (*BS* ch. 12)

As a final specimen of Thackeray's comic nomenclature, as well as of his skill as a parodist, we might take the extract from 'Fluke's Peerage' in the seventh chapter of *The Book of Snobs*, where all history and literature is seen to be ransacked by the snob-motivated genealogist for his purposes. Thus the Muggins family (motto: *Ung Roy, ung Mogyns*) is allotted a largely Welsh and Ancient British family tree (beginning, nevertheless, with Shem); one of the ancestors being *Sir David Gam de Mogyns*, who was distinguished at Agincourt (see *Henry V*, IV viii 109). The whole extract shows the novelist's concentrated satire at its best.

CHAPTER 9

Modes of Address

𝕤𝕤𝕤𝕤𝕤𝕤

As with Jane Austen, modes of address are more formal in the novels of Thackeray than today; and the dispensing with formality too early in a relationship is frowned upon. Gradations in friendship and in courtship can be marked by what George Watson, writing of modes of address in the novels of Trollope, calls 'a glide' – modulating out of the more formal address into a less formal (George Watson, 'Trollope's Forms of Address', *Critical Quarterly*, XV 3, pp. 219–230):

> Pen ... had done nothing but talk to his tutor about *Miss Fotheringay* – *Miss Emily Fotheringay* – *Emily* etc. (*P* I ch. 7)

In this instance the youthful and ingenuous Pen is not even addressing Emily; merely referring to her. He would not have dared to use her Christian name alone when addressing the lady in question, and we may contrast his formality with the informality of Pen's slangy friend Foker. He rushes in where angels fear to tread, addressing 'the Fotheringay' (Thackeray uses the definite article as an ironic tribute to her fame as an actress) with a typical mixture of deference and familiarity as 'Miss Foth', without giving offence: 'She ... gave him a great good-humoured slap. Pen used to tremble as he kissed her hand. Pen would have died of the slap' (*P* I ch. 13).

To return, however, to George Watson's 'glide', we can observe a rather older and more sophisticated Pen, in the company of the affected Blanche Amory, practising upon it as on a sort of sliding scale:

> Say that you have the most beautiful figure and the slimmest waist in the world, *Blanche* – *Miss Amory*, I mean. (*P* II ch. 7)

> I should like never to see that odious city again. Oh, *Arthur* – *that is, Mr* – *well, Arthur*, then – one's good thoughts grow up in these sweet woods. (*P* II ch. 25)

More endearing than this affectation is Clive Newcome's unaffected horror at being addressed too formally by someone to whom he is attracted:

> He had offered to try and take all the young ladies' likenesses. 'You know what a failure the last was, *Rosey*?'
> 'Yes, but Miss Sherrick is so handsome, that you will succeed better with her than with my round face, *Mr Newcome.*'
> '*Mr What*?' cries Clive.
> 'Well, Clive, then,' says Rosey, in a little voice . . .
> 'You know we are like brother and sister, dear Rosey,' he said. (*N* II ch. 6)

As George Watson observes of Trollope's usage: 'A woman has the right to keep the barriers up or even, on occasion, to re-erect them; to man is reserved the right to make the first move towards taking them down':

> 'And do you mean to say, *Bessy*,' I cry . . . 'do you mean to say a fellow like that . . . is a welcome visitor?'
> 'I should be very ungrateful if he were not welcome, *Mr Batchelor*,' says Miss Prior. 'And call me by my surname, please.' (*LW* ch. 4)

It is partly the reversal of these roles that makes Pen's assertion of his social advantage over Fanny Bolton so objectionable:

> 'How beautiful they are, sir!' she cried.
> 'Don't call me sir, Fanny,' Arthur said . . .
> A quick blush rushed up into the girl's face. 'What shall I call you?' she said, in a low voice, sweet and tremulous. 'What would you wish me to say, sir?'
> 'Again, Fanny! Well, I forgot; it is best so, my dear,' Pendennis said, very kindly and gently. 'I may call you Fanny?'
> 'Oh yes!' she said . . .
> 'I may call you *Fanny*, because you are a young girl, and a good girl, *Fanny*, and I am an old gentleman. But you mustn't call me anything but *sir*, or *Mr Pendennis*, if you like; for we live in very different stations, Fanny. (*P* II ch. 8)

Clearly, Thackeray intends us to find this 'pulling rank' on the part of the twenty-five-year-old Pen as insufferable as he does; but the fact that such differentiation is possible suggests the depth of class feeling in early Victorian England.

In matters of friendship, old Osborne, in *Vanity Fair*, ingratiates himself with the wealthy coloured heiress, Miss Swartz, by nicely graded modes of address:

> A warm welcome, my dear *Miss Rhoda* – *Rhoda*, let me say, for my heart warms to you. .... Hicks, champagne to *Miss Swartz*. (*VF* p. 196)

Sir Pitt Crawley, similarly, is mollified by Becky's flattery:

> All these speeches were reported to Sir Pitt ... and increased the favourable impression ... so much so, that ... Sir Pitt Crawley, carving fowls at the head of the table, actually said to Mrs Rawdon, 'Ahem! *Rebecca*, may I give you a wing?' – a speech which made the little woman's eyes sparkle. (*VF* p. 407)

Becky Sharp has come a long way in the Crawley family's regard from the time when, as governess to old Sir Pitt's children, she was patronized and referred to as a servant by her surname alone (*VF* p. 132). But still Lady Jane Crawley, as Thackeray does not fail to note, is less inclined to informality than her husband. On her way to present Becky at court, Lady Jane privately and sorrowfully notes the superior taste of '*Mrs Becky*', and admires out loud her richer lace, but in formal terms: '*My dear Mrs Crawley*, it must have cost a little fortune' (*VF* p. 461). (As R. W. Chapman observes in SPE Tract no. 40 on 'Names, Designations and Appellations', 'At the beginning of a letter "My dear Sir, Smith, John" is more cordial (not necessarily less formal) than "Dear Sir, Smith, John".') The subtlety that was at the novelist's command in such matters is remarkable. These last extracts from *Vanity Fair* introduce two other possible appellatives for a married woman, each right for its context. In an access of family feeling that is not common among the Crawleys, Pitt Crawley thinks of the woman whom he is addressing with such familiar affection as the wife of his brother, namely *Mrs Rawdon*. But when Lady Jane sees her sister-in-law's smarter appearance, devout and charitable though she is, she balances the spoken '*my dear Mrs Crawley*' with, in her own mind, the belittling appellation, *Mrs Becky*.

Among men, surnames were still the rule, with or without the addition of *Mr*, according to familiarity. Too free a use of Christian names by men was deplored in some quarters and considered 'Bohemian':

> Bohemia had no name in Philip's young days. A pleasant land, not fenced with drab stucco, like Tyburnia or Belgravia; not guarded by a huge standing army of footmen ... a land where men call each other by their Christian names. (*Ph* I ch. 5)

The addition of *Mr*, of course, increased formality. Here Philip Firmin, in objecting to his employer's informality, is manifesting what the latter in turn castigates as his 'hawhaw manner':

> 'What right has that person to call me Firmin?' he asked. 'I am *Firmin* to my equals and friends. I am this man's labourer at four guineas a week. I give him his money's worth, and on every Saturday evening we are quits. Call me *Philip* indeed, and strike me in the side! I choke, sir, as I think of the confounded familiarity.' (*Ph* II ch. 15)

Christian names among men were sometimes inherited from school days. When old Osborne after many years had forgiven Dobbin for dissuading George from breaking off his engagement to Amelia, 'he called Dobbin, *William*, just as he used to do when Dobbin and George were boys together' (*VF* p. 589). Such appellatives might also be resorted to in distress, as when Amelia is overwhelmed by her husband George's flirtation with Becky: ' "William," she said, suddenly clinging to Dobbin. ... "Take me home." She did not know she called him by his Christian name, as George was accustomed to do' (*VF* p. 279). The abbreviation of the name added warmth: young Georgy Osborne clearly cannot address Major Dobbin, as his father George does, as *Will* (*VF* p. 206); but he does share with his father the affectionate abbreviation of the surname, *old Dob* (*VF* pp. 279, 648). Two other variants for Dobbin's name, both attesting to Thackeray's skill in this matter of addressives, are *Guilielmo Dobbin* (*VF* p. 51), inscribed in a prize at school, and *Dobbin of Ours*. This last is an originally military use, meaning 'of our regiment'; but, given due prominence as the heading for the fifth chapter of *Vanity Fair*, it also indicates the author's conception of Dobbin as the man who comes nearest to the status of hero in this 'Novel without a Hero'.

One of the best instances of the use of varied titles for fine nuances of feeling occurs when Jack Belsize is told by the woman he had hoped to marry, Lady Clara Pulleyn, that she is engaged to marry someone else. The incident is stage-managed with a nice regard to formality by Lady Clara's mother and father, Lord and Lady Dorking:

> 'We have now to wish you good-bye, *Charles Belsize*,' said my Lord, with some feeling. 'As your relative, and your father's old friend, I wish you well. . . . I request that we may part friends. Good-bye, *Charles*. Clara, shake hands with *Captain Belsize*. My Lady Dorking, you will please to give *Charles* your hand. You have known him since he was a child; and – and – we are sorry to be obliged to part in this way.' In this wise Mr *Jack Belsize's* tooth was finally extracted. (*N* I ch. 32)

We may note here that her father does not allow Lady Clara to address Belsize informally with a Christian name; and that in any case, the Christian name *Charles* is not particularly informal, since Charles is '*Jack*' to his friends.

With military men there was an additional stage between formality and friendship in the use of Christian name along with an indication of rank. Having, as we have seen, addressed Dobbin as William, old Osborne privately recommends him to his daughter as a desirable (albeit unlikely) *parti*, adding the title that is one of his recommendations: 'Them grapes are sour. Ha! ha! *Major William* is a fine fellow' (*VF* p. 589). At Brussels before Waterloo Becky, flirting with General Tufto to the annoyance of Captain George Osborne, enjoys the enmity and embarrassment that such varying usage affords:

> 'My dear Captain George!' cried little Rebecca in an ecstasy. 'How good of you to come. The general and I were moping together. . . . General, this is my Captain George of whom you heard me talk.'
> 'Indeed,' said the General, with a very small bow, 'Of what regiment is Captain George?' . . .
> 'Not *Captain George*, you stupid man; *Captain Osborne*,' Rebecca said. The General all the while was looking savagely from one to the other. (*VF* p. 272)

Military wives reflected the rank of their husbands: 'Before the end of the campaign . . . *Mrs Major O'Dowd* hoped to write herself *Mrs Colonel O'Dowd*, C. B.' (*VF* p. 174).

Normally, only two of the three main stages (Mr Smith, Smith, John) were available to the lady; for her to call a man by the surname alone was a mark of vulgarity:

> Mrs Woolsey is loud. Her h's are by no means where they should be; her knife at dinner is often where it should not be. She calls men aloud by their names, and without any prefix of courtesy. (*Ph* II ch. 15)

In the previous century, this had been more acceptable. Thackeray found a living link with the eighteenth century in Mary and Agnes Berry, born in 1763 and 1764 respectively.[1] Mary Berry never gave up 'the useful and sensible fashion of distinguishing her male friends from her acquaintances by using their surnames' (Ray, *Age*, p. 50). On the other hand, ladies used Christian names to each other much more often than gentlemen, and more freely it seems than they had done in Jane Austen's day; though the novelist is being ironic when, in detailing the rapid intimacy which sprang up between Osborne's daughters and the wealthy Miss Swartz, he writes: 'The girls *Christian-named* each other at once' (*VF* p. 194).

There are still vestigial survivals from an age when modes of address were still more formal. Mr Sedley addresses his wife as *Mrs Sedley* (*VF* p. 27), as Mr Hardcastle had addressed Mrs Hardcastle in *She Stoops to Conquer*; so too with the Reverend and Mrs Bute Crawley; though when the latter lady is being rude to her husband, her usage is different: '*Bute Crawley*, you are a fool,' said the Rector's wife, scornfully (*VF* p. 103). '*Mr George Osborne*, sir, how will you take it?' asks the cashier at the Osbornes' bank, addressing young George in this way to distinguish him from his father, old Mr Osborne (*VF* p. 126); the family servants refer to him as *Mr George* (*VF* p. 120). We may compare the way Mr Frank Churchill is necessarily differentiated from his uncle and guardian in Jane Austen's *Emma*. In the manner of Fanny Burney's Lord Orville, the apothecary Mr Clump counters a tendency to familiarity in his remarks by addressing Mrs Bute in the third person: 'They will restore the roses too to your cheeks,

1 See Lytton Strachey's essay 'Mary Berry' in *Portraits in Miniature*, London, 1931, pp. 108–19.

if I may so speak to *Mrs Bute Crawley*' (*VF* p. 184). This in fact appears to have been an occupational idiosyncrasy of medical men, such as Pen's father: 'He was old compared to – to so blooming a young lady as *Miss Thistlewood* (Pendennis was of the grave old complimentary school of gentlemen and apothecaries)' (*P* I ch. 2).

In letter-writing too, older people could remember when more formality was expected. Colonel Newcome looks back on the punctilious letters he wrote as a boy, and contrasts them with his son Clive's:

> I can't but think that this, the modern and natural style, is a great progress upon the old-fashioned manner of my day, when we used to begin to our fathers, 'Honoured Father', or even 'Honoured Sir' some precisians used to write. (*N* II ch. 1)

One minor formality which remained throughout the century, and is perhaps still not quite dead, is that of referring to, and addressing, the eldest brother or sister in the appellative *Mr* or *Miss*, followed by the surname alone. So, in *Vanity Fair*, *Miss Pinkerton* is distinguished from her younger sister, *Miss Jemima* (although perhaps only a lady as stiff and formidable as the Semiramis of Hammersmith would actually include the title *Miss* when addressing her own sister – *VF* p. 13). As to the usage with men, Becky explains this in a letter to Amelia: 'Then there are Mr Pitt's apartments – *Mr Crawley* he is called – the eldest son, and *Mr Rawdon Crawley*'s room – he is an officer . . . and away with his regiment' (*VF* p. 77).

Some abbreviations were then, and still are, unacceptable. The vulgarian Mrs Sherrick is rebuked by her more refined daughter for addressing Mr Honeyman (in the tradition of Mrs Elton in *Emma*) as '*Mr H*' (*N* II ch. 6). Rawdon Crawley favours inelegant variations in speaking to his wife: 'I'd like to sell him another horse, *Beck*. . . . He'd be what I call useful just now, *Mrs C* – ha! ha!' (*VF* p. 164). The parvenu Mugford's '*Lord R* has come to town, *Mr F*, I perceive' is surpassed in vulgarity only by his major-domo, Rudge, who designates Philip Firmin as '*Mr Heff*' (*Ph* II ch. 2). There is a curious but characteristic blend of the formal and the vulgar when old Osborne draws his attention to young George Osborne with 'Look *Miss O*' (*VF* p. 540).

Details of social usage had a fascination for Thackeray. He

liked to record, for example, that Major Pendennis's valet, Morgan, was known as *Morgan Pendennis*: 'for, by such compound names, gentlemen's gentlemen are called in their private circles' (*P* I ch. 36). Likewise with butlers also:

> ... clubs at the West End, where Lord Todmorden's butler consorted with the confidential butlers of others of the nobility: and I am informed that in those clubs Ridley continued to be called 'Todmorden' long after his connection with that venerable nobleman had ceased. (*Ph* II ch. 2)

Medical men who in Jane Austen's time had been content with *Mr* – she reserved the title *Dr* for Doctors of Divinity – were beginning, especially if they were physicians, and so a cut above surgeons and apothecaries,[1] to call themselves, and to be addressed as *doctor*, with or without surname. Thus Amelia Sedley's medical man, *Mr Pestler*, has an assistant, Mr Linton, for attending to the servant-maids and the small tradesmen. Eventually he rises to become '*Dr Pestler* . . . a most flourishing lady's physician, with . . . a prospect of a speedy knighthood' (*VF* p. 377). Mr Pendennis, Pen's father, began his career as 'a surgeon and apothecary' in Bath (he had his name painted on a board along with a pestle and mortar), but 'he always detested the trade'. In time, he was able to shut up shop, open a genteel surgery, and acquire the title of 'The Doctor'. Eventually, having prospered, he retired to Clavering (Ottery St Mary), as a country gentleman: 'It was now his shame, as it formerly was his pride, to be called *Doctor*, and those who wished to please him always gave him the title of *Squire*' (*P* I ch. 2). This is the kind of territory where Thackeray is so sure-footed; whole social movements being exemplified with great deftness and certainty by individual instances.

Within the family there seems to have been less of a disposition for children of the same parents, when grown up, to address one another as *sister* or *brother* than had been the case earlier in the century among the upper classes. Mrs Bennet, in *Pride and*

---

1 In Pen's illness, Fanny Bolton is ordered by Dr Goodenough to fetch the *surgeon*: 'the *apothecary* . . . came straightway, his lancet in his pocket' (*P* II ch. 14), presumably to let blood. There was clearly much confusion about the function of the various medical men; and it is interesting that near the end of his life Thackeray is one of the first to use the phrase *general practitioner* for a doctor (*LW* ch. 3). The first *OED* quote (*practitioner* 1b) is from Oliver Wendell Holmes, for the same year as *Lovel the Widower* (1860).

Prejudice, had called Mrs Gardiner *sister*, and spoken of *my sister Phillips*;[1] but by Victorian times this seems to have become more the usage of the provinces than of the London and county society that Thackeray was at home in. (Mrs Tulliver and Mrs Pullet, in *The Mill on the Floss*, still favour the appellative; and Mrs Moss refers to Mr Tulliver as *brother*). However, *cousin Clive* occurs (*N* I ch. 29).

Small children of the upper classes regularly address their parents as *papa* and *mamma*. Little Clive Newcome writes a letter to his *dear papa* (*N* I ch. 3); Rawdon Crawley junior writes to his father saying 'I hope *Mamma* is very well' (*VF* p. 409). *Papa* and *mamma* as appellatives had aristocratic sanction and, as the OED says, they were long considered genteel, though they were gradually relegated to the nursery, and are now dead except as facetious archaisms. In his teens Clive Newcome drops *papa*, and addresses the Colonel as *father* (and also, though their relationship is very frank, occasionally as *sir*), and usually refers to him as *my father* (*N* I ch. 21) or occasionally as *the governor* (*N* I ch. 17) or *the dear old father* (*N* I ch. 22). *The old mother* also occurs: 'I needn't be a charge upon *the old mother*', says Pen, asserting his independence (*P* I ch. 31). The feeling for a necessary distinction between address and reference in this respect, as in the Biblical 'I will arise and go to *my father* and will say to him, *Father*, I have sinned,' died hard. The tendency to refer to fathers and mothers without the possessive adjective was not held to be good usage in the nineteenth century.

That arbitress in matters social and linguistic, Mrs General of *Little Dorrit*, advocates *papa* in preference to *father*. She corrects little Dorrit:

1 There are signs, however, that such usage was felt to be bucolic even earlier. In Mrs Cowley's long-forgotten late eighteenth-century comedy *Which is the Man?* there are two rustic characters, Bobby and Sophy Pendragon, aspiring to gentility in fashionable London. The following dialogue ensues:

SOPHY: Brother Bobby, Brother Bobby!

BOBBY: I desire, Miss Pendragon, you won't brother me at this rate; making one look as if one didn't know life. How often shall I tell you that it is the most ungenteel thing in the world for relations to *brother, father,* and *cousin* one another, and all that sort of thing. I did not get the better of my shame for three days, when you bawled out to Mrs Dobson at Launceston concert, 'Aunt, aunt, here's room between brother and I, if cousin Dick will sit closer to father!'

Quoted by J. C. Trewin, *Down to the Lion*, London, 1952, p. 171.

'I think, *father*, I require a little more time.'
'*Papa* is a preferable mode of address,' observed Mrs General.
'Father is rather vulgar my dear. The word Papa, besides, gives
a pretty form to the lips.' (*Little Dorrit* ch. 41)

Thackeray, however, has a strong tendency to regard *papa* and
mamma in adult contexts as an affectation. He tends to employ
them ironically, and to prefer *father* and *mother* for serious effects.
Lord Steyne torments Lady Gaunt with: 'Pray, madam, shall I
tell you some little anecdotes about my Lady Bareacres, your
mamma?' (*VF* p. 470). Barnes Newcome, with condescending
sarcasm, asks Colonel Newcome about his son Clive's interest in
Ethel: 'By the way, Colonel, is our young soupirant aware that
papa is pleading his cause for him?' (*N* II ch. 23). The Osborne
daughters refer to their purse-proud father as *papa*; but when
Amelia quarrels with Mrs Sedley she expostulates with 'O *mother*,
mother!' (*VF* p. 450). The abbreviations *pa* and *ma* were, and
still are, regarded as somewhat vulgar. It is the usage, for example,
of Madame la Princesse de Montcontour, née Higg, of Manchester:
'Lady Clara is a sweet dear thing, and her *pa* and *ma* most affable'
(*N* II ch. 2). Barnes Newcome is not so much vulgar as offensively
familiar when, administering a further blow in the family feud,
he addresses his uncle, Colonel Newcome, as *Nunky* (*N* I ch. 6).
In contrast it is perhaps surprising to find the raucous Foker
addressing his mother formally in the way that Elizabeth Bennet
addressed hers, as *ma'am* (*P* II ch. 1); but Foker, vulgarian though
he is, is not incapable of finer feelings. Moreover, to quote the
OED (s.v. *ma'am*), 'In Thackeray's time every man among equals
of a certain refinement was Sir, and every woman Ma'am.'

Select Bibliography

❦❦❦❦❦❦

A FEW studies in this list are referred to frequently in the text, and for this purpose the abbreviated titles employed are included afterwards, in parentheses.

A STUDIES RELATED TO THE LANGUAGE OF THE NINETEENTH-CENTURY NOVEL

Brook, G. L., *The Language of Dickens*, Deutsch, 1970 (*Brook*).
Clark, John W., *The Language and Style of Anthony Trollope*, Deutsch, 1975 (*Clark*).
Lewis, C. S., *Studies in Words*, Cambridge University Press, 1960.
Phillipps, K. C., *Jane Austen's English*, Deutsch, 1970 (*JAE*).
　'Regency English in the Victorian Period' in *Neuphilologische Mitteilungen* LXXIV (1973), pp. 321–5.
　'Thackeray's Proper Names' in *Neuphilologische Mitteilungen* LXXV (1974), pp. 444–52.
　'The Language of *Henry Esmond*' in *English Studies* LVII (1976), pp. 19–42.
Watson, George, 'Trollope's Forms of Address' in *Critical Quarterly* XV (1973), pp. 219–30.

B BOOKS ON THE ENGLISH LANGUAGE

Adams, Valerie, *An Introduction to Modern English Word-Formation*, Longmans, 1973.
Barber, Charles, *Early Modern English*, Deutsch, 1976.
Chapman, R. W., 'Names, Designations and Appellations', *SPE Tract* XLVII, 1936.
Copley, J., *Shift of Meaning*, Oxford University Press, 1961.
Dobson, E. J., *English Pronunciation 1500–1700*, 2 vols., Oxford University Press, 1957.

Fowler, H. W., *A Dictionary of Modern English Usage* (second edition, revised by Sir Ernest Gowers), Oxford University Press, 1965.

Gordon, Ian A., *The Movement of English Prose*, Longmans, 1966.

Hall, Fitzedward, *Modern English*, Routledge, 1873.

Henry, P. L., 'A Linguistic Survey of Ireland: Preliminary Report' in *Lochlann: A Review of Celtic Studies* I (1958), pp. 53–208 (*Henry*).

Hotten, J. C., *The Slang Dictionary*, London, 1859.

Jespersen, Otto, *Progress in Language, with Special Reference to English*, Macmillan, 1894.

Matthews, William, *Cockney, Past and Present*, Routledge, 1938.

Mossé, F., *Esquisse d'une Histoire de la Langue Anglaise*, Lyons, 1947.

Partridge, Eric, *A Dictionary of Slang and Unconventional English*, Routledge, 1937.
Name into Word, Secker and Warburg, 1949.

Platt, Joan, 'The Development of English Colloquial Idiom during the Eighteenth Century', in *Review of English Studies* II (1926), pp. 70–81, 189–96.

Potter, Simeon, *Changing English*, Deutsch, 1969.

Strang, Barbara, *A History of English*, Methuen, 1970.

Tucker, S. I., *Protean Shape*, Athlone Press, 1967.

Visser, F. Th., *An Historical Syntax of the English Language*, 3 parts in 5 vols., E. J. Brill, Leiden, 1963–73.

Weekley, Ernest, *Adjectives and Other Words*, Murray, 1930.

Withycombe, E. G., *The Oxford Dictionary of English Christian Names*, Oxford University Press, 1945.

Wright, Joseph, *The English Dialect Dictionary*, Oxford University Press, 1898–1905.

Yule, Henry and Burnell, A. C., *Hobson-Jobson: A Glossary of Anglo-Indian Colloquial Words and Phrases*, Routledge, 1968.

C BIOGRAPHICAL AND CRITICAL WORKS

Baker, Joseph, 'Thackeray's Recantation' in *PMLA* LXXVII (1962), pp. 586–94.

Cecil, David, *Early Victorian Novelists*, Constable, 1934.

Crowe, Eyre, *With Thackeray in America*, Cassell, 1893.

Greig, J. Y. T., *Thackeray, A Reconsideration*, Oxford University Press, 1950.

Hannay, James, *Studies on Thackeray*, Routledge, 1869.

Hardy, Barbara, *The Exposure of Luxury: Radical Themes in Thackeray*, Peter Owen, 1972.

James, Henry, *The Future of the Novel: Essays on the Art of Fiction*, ed. Leon Edel, Vintage Books, 1956.

Keating, P. J., *The Working Classes in Victorian Fiction*, Routledge, 1971.

Mudge, I. G. and Sears, M. E., *A Thackeray Dictionary*, Routledge, 1910; Humanities Press, 1962.

McMaster, Juliet, *Thackeray: The Major Novels*, University of Toronto Press, 1971.

Nitchie, Elizabeth, 'Horace and Thackeray' in *Classical Journal* XIII (1918), pp. 393–419.

Page, Norman, *Speech in the English Novel*, Longmans, 1973.

Ray, Gordon, N., *Thackeray: The Uses of Adversity, 1811–46*, Oxford University Press, 1955 (*Uses*).

Thackeray: The Age of Wisdom, 1847–63, Oxford University Press, 1958 (*Age*).

Saintsbury, George, *A Consideration of Thackeray*, Oxford University Press, 1931.

Snow, T. C. and W., eds., *The History of Henry Esmond*, Introduction and Notes, Oxford University Press, 1909; second edition, 1915.

Stevenson, Lionel, *The Showman of Vanity Fair*, Chapman and Hall, 1947.

Sutherland, J. A., *Thackeray at Work*, Athlone Press, 1974.

Tillotson, Geoffrey, *Thackeray the Novelist*, Cambridge University Press, 1954.

Tillotson, Geoffrey and Hawes, Donald, *Thackeray: The Critical Heritage*, Routledge, 1968 (*Heritage*).

Tillotson, Kathleen, *Novels of the Eighteen-Forties*, Oxford University Press, 1954.

Word Index

᠙᠙᠙᠙᠙᠙

Word Index

᭥᭥᭥᭥᭥᭥